WILD COUNTRY

WILD COUNTRY

THE BEST OF
ANDY RUSSELL

Edited by R. Bruce Morrison

M&S

National Library of Canada Cataloguing in Publication

Russell, Andy, 1915–
    Wild country : the best of Andy Russell / Andy Russell ; edited by R. Bruce Morrison.

Includes bibliographical references.
ISBN 0-7710-7887-0

    1. Russell, Andy, 1915–   2. Outdoor life – Alberta.   3. Natural history – Alberta.   4. Ranch life – Alberta.   I. Morrison, R. Bruce   II. Title.

SK17.R88A3 2004   796.5'092   C2004-902340-3

We acknowledge the financial support of the Government of Canada through the Book Publishing Industry Development Program and that of the Government of Ontario through the Ontario Media Development Corporation's Ontario Book Initiative. We further acknowledge the support of the Canada Council for the Arts and the Ontario Arts Council for our publishing program.

Typeset in Bembo by M&S, Toronto
Printed and bound in Canada

This book is printed on acid-free paper that is 100% recycled, ancient-forest friendly (100% post-consumer recycled).

McClelland & Stewart Ltd.
The Canadian Publishers
481 University Avenue
Toronto, Ontario
M5G 2E9
www.mcclelland.com

1 2 3 4 5   08 07 06 05 04

To my children,
Dick, Charlie, John, Gordon, and Anne,
And to my grandchildren,
Anthony, Sarah, and Tim
With love

A.R.

Contents

Foreword

How do you describe Andy Russell without reaching for clichés? He's a unique mix of historian, cowboy, hunter, fisherman, writer, conservationist, filmmaker, and, not unimportantly, "hellraiser." Need some pioneer Alberta history? Andy Russell lived it. Want to know about mountain wildlife? Andy's studied it, hunted it, filmed it. Want to know where civilization has run amuck in the twentieth century? Andy can show you. Few voices today carry the authority his does, whether speaking of the psychology of grizzly bears, the meaning of Native ceremony, or the questionable antics of governments.

Andy Russell is the kind of man they don't seem to make any more. His status as an historian comes not from scholarly study, but from the fact that he was a participant in history. He's a living link with western Canada's past. He was there when Alberta was young and green, and has seen first-hand the homesteading of the southern foothills, and the damming of his beloved Oldman River. Andy is aware of his calling, which, in the words song-writer Ian Tyson used to describe cowboy artist Charlie Russell is to "get 'er all down, before she goes." Andy Russell has been "getting her all down" – on paper, on celluloid, and with his voice – for almost sixty years.

In his fascination with wildlife, Andy brings the perspective of a hunter – a true hunter who feels an intense and at times painful connection to his quarry. It can be argued that the deepest understanding of Mother Nature's tragic and funny idiosyncrasies comes to those who hunt. It can be not just argued, but firmly proven, that the greatest protectors of North American wildlife are organized hunters. Andy Russell makes no apologies for his hunting, and his extraordinary understanding of wildlife demands and receives respect from people of many stripes. When he speaks as a hunter, environmentalists listen. When he speaks as a conservationist, hunters listen. He has embraced the crucial role of convincing society that the two are not opposites.

Perhaps this is simply a manifestation of another Russell gift: his ability to see – and understand – the big picture, even while living in a snapshot with the rest of us. This vision allowed him as a young man to anticipate the effects of development on his guiding-outfitting business and prompted his decision to make wildlife films when nature photography was barely even a category. It showed him as an older man the future consequences of a dam on the Oldman River. Today he still sees beyond the next corner on conservation issues, and perceives the convoluted agendas of various "stakeholders."

It's true that other people observe, photograph, and write about history and wildlife in the west. Some of them do it nearly as well as Andy does. His greatest gift, though, is one that few of the others possess. It's the grand and sacred gift of storytelling, which Andy learned and valued through his lifelong association with early settlers and aboriginal Albertans. Andy Russell is a sneaky storyteller. When you've finished reading a story you might discover that you've not only been entertained, you've also been taught, for embedded in his stories is a great treasure trove of information.

Try, for instance, "Seppi: A Bird Dog" in this collection. If you weren't familiar with the history and background of the German shorthaired pointer before, you are now. This combination of research, experience, and storytelling is uniquely Andy Russell.

My first encounter with Andy Russell was in the library of Victoria Composite High School in Edmonton in 1967. I found and thumbed through a copy of *Grizzly Country* when I was supposed to be studying mathematics. I then borrowed the book, and read it at home when I was supposed to be writing an English essay. Later, when I helped run a fly-fishing store in Calgary, Andy would occasionally come in to get some flies or leaders. Every purchase was accompanied by a wonderful story – of a fish, a horse, or an adventure. When he was through he'd tip that big black hat, smile, and disappear around the corner like something I had only imagined. Though I grew up in the city, I have always felt a far stronger connection to what lay outside the city. Some of this is Andy's doing. It was an honoured occasion many years later when we met at a writer's conference and had our photograph taken together at his home.

For many years Andy presented historical vignettes in a radio series called "Our Alberta Heritage." The title was intended to describe the programs, but it really describes the man who presented them. His cumulative efforts at recording and preserving Alberta's heritage have been acknowledged repeatedly. The plaque honouring him with the Order of Canada hangs without pomp alongside sheep and elk heads on the wall of his log house near Waterton Park.

The cultural roots of Alberta are not found at West Edmonton Mall or the Calgary Tower. They are found in the grass, the hills, the trees, and the sky. Like it or not, what got us here is our connection to these things. Our heritage is rural. Yet it's my sad observation that at best our society tends to forget its rural heritage, and at worst we outright try to distance ourselves from it as though it were a source of embarrassment. Why do we do that? Other parts of North America are proud of their roots, and we should be too. Andy Russell's stories confirm this and provide a fine and strong antidote to our silly preoccupation with our own sophistication.

Pure storytelling is a gift practised by fewer and fewer today. I blame it on the pace of our culture and the speed of our computers. But read these stories. Read them slowly. You'll hear no electronic beeps or burbles. Instead you'll smell coffee and pipe smoke, you'll hear the wind in the trees, and you'll know where your roots lie.

Jim McLennan
Okotoks, Alberta

Introduction

In 1970 Andy Russell brought his film *Grizzly Country* to Edmonton's Jubilee Auditorium. Having just moved to Canada, I had never heard of Andy Russell. I really wanted to learn something about grizzly bears because I planned to trek in the Rockies and the possibility of meeting a grizzly face-to-face filled me with trepidation. I was hoping this film would convince me that I had nothing to worry about.

The foyer was crowded when I arrived. There were too many people between me and the bar to make a move in that direction practical, so I contented myself with people-watching. The first interesting person that caught my eye was a tall man with a weathered face and a beaded buckskin jacket. Being an urbanite, I thought, "What a bizarre outfit to wear to a movie." The man's Stetson was pushed back on his head and a lazy smile animated his face. Whatever he was saying gave him the undivided attention of the small group surrounding him. Suddenly everyone, including the speaker, dissolved in laughter. I started to make my way through the crowd to get a closer view of what was happening when the bell sounded, ushering us into the hall.

After we had taken our seats and the lights dimmed, I was astonished to see the very same figure I had watched in the foyer stroll onto the stage. He stopped in the centre, established eye contact with the audience, and then nonchalantly said, "Hello, I'm Andy Russell, and I'm going to show you a film I made about grizzly bears." The rustlings of the audience immediately died down, the film appeared on the screen behind him, and Andy started to talk. He seemed to be speaking to each one of us personally, just as if we were sharing a campfire with him in some remote mountain camp. Within minutes he managed to weave a spell that kept us, like the group in the foyer, stuck tight to the story, waiting for the next revelation. Andy guided us on an adventurous journey of discovery, his narrative often humorous and always respectful of the animals. We learned that the bears were not the one-dimensional raging caricatures so often portrayed in the tabloids. A close-up shot of a mother grizzly nursing her cubs illustrated the trust the Russells had been able to establish with some of the bears. In a quiet voice, filled with the authority of experience, Andy spoke eloquently of the need to understand bears better. Misunderstandings, he said, usually resulted in either people or bears dying. The magic was broken, and then only reluctantly on our part, when the lights came on signalling the end of his presentation. As I walked out of the auditorium into that dark winter night, I could hear people happily sharing their favourite parts of the show.

Andy Russell has been weaving spells for more than fifty years. As a storyteller, he is a Canadian icon. His tales of wilderness adventure and the wild animals of the Rocky Mountains have entertained and moved us. In recognition of his unique achievements he has been awarded the Order of Canada, three honorary doctorates, and numerous accolades both from environmental groups and from sportsmen's associations. With thirteen successful books and more than fifty magazine articles as well as the popular film *Grizzly Country* to his credit, he is respected by conservationists, sportsmen, wilderness enthusiasts, and the thousands of readers who just enjoy a good yarn.

This volume is a celebration of Andy's rich literary legacy. It includes selections from his best-selling books, and many tales published in outdoor, sporting, and natural-history magazines. It represents a wide spectrum of his writing, including stories about cowboys and ranch life, stirring adventures in pursuit of game, and articles about the need to protect and understand North America's wild heritage. There are also accounts about Andy's adventures as a wildlife photographer.

In the politically correct world of today, Andy Russell is a maverick. He defies easy classification because his vision extends beyond the narrow confines of any single interest group. He is a sportsman, a naturalist, an environmental activist, a wildlife filmmaker, and more. Like the American conservation legend Aldo Leopold, Andy sees no inherent conflict between hunting, fishing, and good environmental management.

When Andy asked me to be his biographer, I turned from being a fan to trying to understand who he is and how he came to be a master storyteller. I soon discovered that his life is as engaging as his stories.

Andy Russell is from pioneering ranching stock. His grandfather came to southern Alberta in 1882, when the area was part of the Northwest Territories. He made his home near Lethbridge at the confluence of Pothole Creek and the St. Mary's River, close to the Blood Indian reserve. The North-West Mounted Police had arrived in the west to quell the whiskey trade with the Indians only nine years before. As an inducement to settlement the government had made treaty with the Blackfoot and other aboriginal groups of southern Alberta. The North-West Rebellion, which frightened Alberta settlers with the threat of widespread violence, would not begin for another three years. It was a time of great opportunity, adventure, as well as hardship for immigrant settlers. Unfortunately, similar opportunities were not extended to the aboriginal inhabitants, who were confined by treaty to reserves.

Andrew (Andy) G.A. Russell was born on his grandfather's ranch in 1915; his brother, John, was born four years later. Although Alberta had been a province since 1905, the region was still sparsely settled. In 1919 Andy's father, Harold, decided it was time to strike out on his own. Mounted on his saddle horse, he rode south and west until he found a place that suited him, on the banks of Drywood Creek. The homestead he bought was on the flank of the Rockies, not far from present-day Waterton Lakes National Park. A year later his wife, Lorenda, and two sons joined him. The family ranch had a formidable effect on young Andy. He grew up on horseback, helping his father and learning the skills of the cowman. He was lucky to have had a first-rate tutor. Andy describes his father as a cowboy's cowboy, a man born to the saddle, someone who could ride and rope with the best.

Horses have played an important part in Andy's life. Not only were they necessary in the daily workings of a ranch, but they were essential to almost every other aspect of everyday living. Andy, like the children from neighbouring ranches, commuted to and from school on his saddle horse. When he visited neighbours or needed to go to town, he rode a horse. Teenagers thought nothing about riding twenty miles each way to attend a local dance. It must have been disconcerting for a young horseman to suddenly find himself afoot when he moved to Lethbridge to attend high school.

There was more to learn on the family ranch than just the techniques of working cattle and horses; there was also western history. As a boy, Andy heard tales about or met many of the colourful characters of the American and Canadian west. Cowboy lore and western history became one of his special loves. Andy is quite proud of *Our Alberta Heritage*, his radio series of historical vignettes that he broadcast for ten years. He speaks with an authentic voice; he can ride the rough string, rope and trail horses through the bush. The stories in Part One of the collection show how he makes personal experience and western history come together seamlessly. They capture the colour, adventure, and hardship of our heritage.

Andy's education was not limited to the classroom or the ranch; he also learned in the wild. Hunting, fishing, and trapping were part of a pioneer ranch boy's life. In fact, Andy, often accompanied by his brother, John, escaped to the wild whenever opportunity presented itself. Just beyond their doorstep, the rugged vastness of the Rockies beckoned. Not infrequently, they got into trouble, as young boys are wont to do. But they survived, with only minor abrasions, some lessons learned, and a wealth of good stories. Their misadventures did nothing to diminish their appetite for wilderness adventure, and Andy's boyhood forays in the bush created a lifelong passion for the wild.

As a young man, Andy found a kindred soul in the person of Bert Riggall, an immigrant sportsman from England. Bert had a spread about ten miles from the Russell Ranch. Although nominally a rancher, his real love was the mountains. Bert had arrived in Calgary in 1904 and by 1909 had established a fishing camp for tourists in Waterton. His first pack trips into the mountains began in 1910. In the mid-1930s Bert hired a young ranch boy named Andrew Russell to help break horses. That signalled the beginning of a relationship that altered Andy's life.

Bert became not only Andy's boss, but also his mentor. They both shared a passion for hunting and exploring the nearby mountains. Bert was a fine hunter, mountain photographer, and gunsmith, as well as an amateur naturalist. His wilderness hunting trips became occasions to investigate local flora and fauna. As they rode mountain trails, Bert often identified local wildflowers, giving them their correct Latin names. He recorded what he found interesting with his cameras, as well as noting his observations in journals and in the margins of his natural-history books. Aided by a photographic memory, Bert, like Andy, was a fine raconteur. After a hard day on the trail, Bert shared his knowledge of the natural world and his adventures in the mountains. He was also a skilled marksman. Under Bert's tutelage, Andy honed his knowledge of firearms and the finer points of shooting. He was to go on to become a champion marksman and shooting coach.

Bert Riggall's outfitting business was in many ways a family business. His wife, Dora, and later his daughters, Kay and Babe, were first-rate camp cooks and managers. Eventually, Andy fell in love with Kay, married her, and bought the business when Bert was ready to retire. One of the selections in Part Two describes Andy and Kay's honeymoon pack trip. They ran the business as a team: Andy handled the horses, the dudes, assistant guides, and wranglers; Kay managed the all-important cooking duties, the complicated logistics of provisioning a wilderness pack trip, the bookkeeping, and the children. Later, as their children grew, they assumed some of the responsibilities that go with running a mountain pack string. The stories in Part Two vividly portray the adventure and rewards of the hunt, as well as the pleasures of camp and trail.

Writing was a natural extension of Andy's love for both storytelling and reading. Before television and radio, storytelling was a valued personal attribute. Men and women told stories as they gathered around the kitchen table or shared a campfire in the mountains. Their tragedies and adventures, woven by a skilful storyteller, entertained, educated, and enlightened. Andy often jokes that when he was a young man he practised his yarns first on his dog, then on his horse, and finally on his parents.

In the mid-1940s, Andy decided to find a wider audience. *Field and Stream* magazine published his first story about grizzlies. From that time until the early 1970s, Andy wrote for a variety of outdoor and natural-history magazines. His stories ran the gamut from hunting and fishing tales to pieces promoting conservation and a better understanding of nature. One of the remarkable things about Andy's stories is that he could successfully weave these themes together in the same article.

Although Andy has written many memorable hunting stories, he has written few fishing tales. This is curious, given the fact that he has been a passionate fisherman all his life. His fishing stories appear most often as parts of larger wilderness narratives; this is the first time they have appeared together in one collection. Andy's well-honed sense of humour appears in many of his stories: one of my favourites is the story about the Judge, which appears in "The Wilderness Fisherman" in Part Three.

A major turning point in Andy's life was his decision to give up guiding in order to become a wildlife photographer. It was a major gamble; wildlife photography in the 1950s was not the popular profession it is today. But Andy was convinced that the outfitting business, as he knew it, was doomed. Industrial development in wilderness regions not only had a detrimental effect on wildlife, it destroyed, through the construction of road networks, the region's remoteness. As an outfitter, he felt he could no longer provide a wilderness experience for his clients.

Taking families on extended pack trips in the mountains was an important part of the family guiding business. Some of Andy's clients enjoyed making home movies of their mountain trips. Andy learned the rudiments of operating a movie camera from watching and talking to his clients. When he decided industrial development was ruining his guiding territory, he turned to movie-making as an alternative career.

With a newly acquired movie camera, Andy launched his career as a filmmaker. It was a bold move, since he had little prior experience. His first film, *Wildlife of the Canadian Rockies*, was shown to appreciative audiences in both Canada and the United States. The success of this modest film encouraged him to take on bigger projects. His next film focused primarily upon bighorn sheep, and the trials and triumphs of making it are vividly described in Part Four, as are the adventures and lessons learned in making his classic *Grizzly Country*. Although the sheep movie was never shown because of disagreements with the film's sponsor, it provided Andy with the experience he needed to tackle the daunting task of photographing grizzly bears at close range. In the course of making the grizzly film, Andy and his sons Dick and Charlie broke new ground in the understanding of grizzly behaviour. The film, and later the book, had an important impact on how we think about grizzly bears today.

Bert Riggall introduced Andy to the literature on natural history. As a naturalist, Bert kept an extensive personal library. He was well read in the genre, his agile mind worked back and forth between what was observed in the field and what was revealed in his books. This process of combining field observation with scholarly inquiry rubbed off on Andy. He had always been an avid reader. Under Bert's tutelage he gained an appreciation for combining what he learned in the field with what he learned from books. Riggall and Russell looked with critical eyes on what they saw in the mountains, talked about it, and tried to understand it. That habit of constant observation, analysis, and wonder at the natural world has stayed with Andy and is reflected in the stories again and again.

At the same time Andy began writing for sporting magazines, he also sent stories to natural-history publications. For most of his life he has been curious about why animals behave the way they do. Because he spent so much time in the wild, in all seasons, he is in a unique position to try to make sense of animal behaviour. Sometimes his observations put him at odds with prevailing wisdom, be it scientific dogma or local lore. The selections in Part Five and elsewhere abound with Andy's take on current thought.

When it comes to defending the environment, Andy enjoys

describing himself as a "hellraiser." He has been an executive board member of numerous environmental and sportsmen's conservation groups. In his writing, in his public lectures, and in the courts, he has challenged local, provincial, and federal government policies. He has also taken on such corporate giants as Shell Oil and Esso, and won. One of the battles closest to his heart was the fight over the Oldman River dam. His book *The Life of a River* is a poignant portrait of the Oldman River and the meaning it has had for generations of people and wildlife living along its banks. Part Six includes a selection from that moving book.

The last piece is an epilogue written by Andy. It is fitting, I think, to conclude with some of Andy's thoughts on his life, and his relationship with the wild country that has been his home for so many years.

At one point in the preparation of this book, I wondered if the subtitle should be "The Best, But Not All of the Best, of Andy Russell." When Andy asked me to assist him in the preparation of the manuscript, I asked him why he didn't simply put together what he thought were his best stories. He said that someone else, someone not as closely associated with the work, might make a more objective selection. When I agreed, I imagined myself sitting in a comfortable chair, puffing on my pipe, and reading the wonderful tales I'd grown to love. It wasn't long before I realized that I was in trouble. There were simply too many good stories to include in one volume. I decided my only recourse was to fit in as many good tales as I could and direct the readers to Andy's original works, where they could enjoy the stories I had, of necessity, omitted. In the bibliography at the end of this volume I've listed his books for all who want to continue the adventure. By the way, you don't have to be a pipe-smoker to enjoy these stories.

Among those who have made important contributions to this book are Valerie Haig-Brown, Dawn Roberts, Doug Jones, John

Russell, Don Bourdon, Don Messerschmidt, and especially Joyce Morrison. We would particularly like to thank M&S editors Elizabeth Kribs and Peter Buck for their excellent editorial advice as well as their encouragement.

R. Bruce Morrison

WILD COUNTRY

PART ONE

COWS AND COWBOYS

The mythic cowboys of the American and Canadian west have deep roots in North American culture. These tales intertwine the rise of the historic cowboy and Andy's own story as he became one of that fabled breed. Andy's tales are larger than life. They depict the danger and the excitement of the real west.

The Last of the Free Range

In 1882, the north end of the free range of Canada was just beginning to be taken up by settlers. It was known as the North-West Territories and encompassed the country reaching from Winnipeg to the Rocky Mountains, a vast sweeping stretch of prairies that was the choicest part of the Great Plains of North America, where the short buffalo grass lay curled as thick as the coats of the animals from which it got its name. Along its western rim, and in the foothill country of the mountains to the north toward the brush country, the buffalo grass gave way to bunch grass that grew stirrup-deep. All of this grass was unique in its propensity to cure on the stem so that it was little affected by frost and retained its food value for grazing animals during the cold months of winter.

Unlike the United States, where the settlers came ahead of established law, in Canada the opening of the west for settlement started with the arrival of the North-West Mounted Police in the late summer of 1874. The first thing the police did was close all the whiskey trading posts, a matter of making up the traders' minds

From *The Canadian Cowboy* (1993)

for them, for the buffalo were getting scarce and there were few beaver and little of any other kind of fur left. Colonel Macleod would have liked to have purchased the well-built Fort Whoop-Up from whiskey-peddling Fred Hamilton and John Healy but they couldn't agree on a price, so he took his force on west up the Oldman River about thirty miles where he camped on an island among the big cottonwoods. There the North-West Mounted Police built their own fort – Fort Macleod, the headquarters of law and order in western Canada. It was from this pinpoint on what was a vast expanse of prairie, foothills, and mountains that the Queen's War Hounds, as the artist Charlie Russell called them, proceeded swiftly to build a very profound and well-earned reputation among both the warlike Blackfoot Indians and the white men. Dressed in their navy blue uniforms from helmet to gleaming boots, with brass buttons shining in the sun, each man was armed with a .455-calibre Webley revolver and a .52-calibre breechloading Snyder rifle, and mounted on a big hunter-type Irish thoroughbred horse; they were impressive. There was not a man among them less than five feet, ten inches tall and most of them were six feet or over. About as physically tough as men could get, they were fearless but also fair, and they treated all men alike in enforcing the law.

When one American cowman drove a small herd of cattle into the valley of the Oldman River above the fort, he left a pair of pants on his wagon seat in camp while out riding with his cattle. An Indian came along and appropriated the pants, whereupon the cowman rode to the fort and stomped into the commanding officer's office to ask permission to shoot the Indian. The policeman pinned him in his tracks with a pair of cold blue eyes and briefly informed him that if he shot the Indian or anybody else he would be arrested and tried for murder, and if found guilty would be hanged by the neck till he was dead. There was no further discussion.

It was this kind of firm, unwavering principle that very quickly established the authority of the North-West Mounted Police. They were few in number, only two hundred men, but big in their attitude. Any cowboy riding into a settlement firing his six-shooter off to get attention generally found himself facing one of the Queen's men, who would calmly appropriate the gun, and if that cowboy ever saw it again, he was lucky indeed.

The first big herd of cattle to come to Canada from the south came into British Columbia in 1860 with John Park from Washington. He drove them up the Okanagan River and on north up the great valley past the lakes, then over the summit into the drainage of the North Thompson River heading for the Caribou gold fields via Williams Lake, where he swung north up the Fraser River to the placer mines. He sold the steers to the gold miners at a good profit. These were for the large part longhorns, with some crosses with British breeds, the kind that the settlers had brought with them by wagon train across the prairies and mountains into Oregon and Washington from the eastern states.

As John Park rode up the Bonaparte River in the country around Cache Creek, he crossed miles of valley country where grass up to his stirrups waved in the wind. He looked it over again on his way back and decided it was a good place to set up a ranch. So he headed south to gather another herd of breeding stock. His ranch on the Bonaparte River a few miles up from Cache Creek was the first in British Columbia. His grandnephew, Gordon Park, still operates it.

Before the North-West Mounted Police arrived, the Blackfoot Indians were still the power to be reckoned with though their numbers had been depleted by smallpox. There were buffalo to hunt and their horse herds were numerous, but their sun had almost set. In 1874, the I.G. Baker Company had shipped a quarter of a million prime buffalo hides by steamboat east to St. Louis from Fort Benton on the Missouri River in Montana. In about six years there were very few buffalo left in any part of the Great Plains. When my grandfather, George Russell, arrived at Fort Macleod in 1882 with a government survey party from Ottawa, they killed an old bull close by the Cypress Hills about a hundred miles east of the fort. I recall him telling of seeing seven or eight buffalo on the south slope of the Porcupine Hills up the Oldman River about thirty-five miles from the police headquarters.

The Indians were starving and there were few cattle in the country to feed them. John and David McDougal had brought a small herd from Fort Edmonton up on the North Saskatchewan River south to Morley on the Bow River in 1871. In 1872 they went south and bought another hundred head in Montana.

By the time the buffalo had disappeared, there was a huge sea of grass with very little of anything to feed on it. When the Treaty of 1877 was signed with the Blackfoot, relegating the Indians to live on reserves, the Canadian government was bound by it to help the Indians, but there was no one in charge in Ottawa that knew how. As various settlers came into the prairie region with cattle, they had a rough time with the Indians, who were very adept at killing their beef and just as quick when it came to eating it. The police were having some worrisome difficulties handling the Queen's adopted children. The pundits in Ottawa proceeded to try to supply cattle to the Indians so that they could go into the cow business and raise their own beef, but the trouble was there was no cattle available in sufficient numbers and the Indians were very much inclined to just eat anything they received rather than herd them. Then they appointed a member of Parliament from central British Columbia by the name of Edgar Dewdney as Indian commissioner as the best man to handle western affairs. When he arrived in early July 1879, people at the fort were just recovering from a very bad winter and an epidemic of typhoid fever brought on by the carcasses of cattle that had died in the harsh weather along the river. The infant cattle business of the western plains had suffered much, and everybody was complaining about Indian depredations among their surviving herds.

Dewdney had seen roaming bands of braves desperately hunting for the vanished buffalo herds on his way west. When he got to the fort there were about five thousand Blackfoot camped around it hungrily and yet trustfully waiting for the government to keep its promises. They couldn't be blamed for sallying forth in small parties to kill a beef. When they did, they had scouts riding with them, and when a cow was shot the scouts kept a lookout for intruders. The dead animal was quickly skinned and cut into pieces. Every Indian grabbed a piece and took off for camp knowing that if they weren't caught with a branded animal on the ground there was no way they could be convicted of stealing.

Even when a charge was laid against them, it was not easy to get a conviction. On one occasion a white man rode up to a group of Indians who were busy butchering an animal. He was literally standing over them before they saw him, and the cow they were butchering was obviously branded. He reported the theft, but when the case was tried in the presence of Commissioner Dewdney with Colonel Macleod presiding as judge, the witnesses for the Indians overwhelmed the cowboy's evidence to the point where the case was dismissed. This caused some heartfelt swearing among the ranchers and no doubt some smiles among the Indians; they were learning fast how to deal with the white man's law.

There were two young Englishmen, Ted Maunsell and his brother George, who had taken up a ranch a few miles upriver from the fort. They purchased a herd of 103 cattle to stock their new ranch and moved them to it with great difficulty due to their inexperience. Finally, after much riding, they arrived late one evening at their corrals. Tired and hungry they went to their cabin to find the door open and the interior in considerable disarray. Obviously the place had been raided by hungry Indians and they were assailed by a feeling of real discouragement. But when one picked up the flour sack it was to find enough flour in the bottom to make a couple of batches of biscuits. When they looked at the nail where a side of bacon had been hung, there was a small piece left – enough for a couple of meals. If ever there were two young ranchers grateful to thieves, it was those two. The Indians had left enough food to keep them alive till they could get more.

The first round-up of cattle ever held in Alberta took place in early August 1879 in the vicinity of the fort, with a rancher by the name of Parker ramrodding the operation and sixteen very green men riding for him. They had a wagon, but the men were poorly mounted, some were riding mares with colts at heel, and they only had one mount apiece. Their supplies were so limited that they sometimes gathered duck eggs from the sloughs and boiled them hard to take care of those containing birds. For the large part these were eastern farmers, inexperienced, and about as green in handling cows as they could get. But they rounded up over five hundred head and branded the new calves, though it was obvious to all of them that there were a great many fewer cattle than the count of the previous fall.

Of the 103 purchased by the Maunsell brothers about thirty days before, there were only fifty-nine left. For the most part the ranchers did not blame the Indians, but they very heartily cursed the negligent government and its Indian agents.

Meanwhile, Commissioner Dewdney had purchased supplies for the Indians from the I.G. Baker Company store at the fort, the only store in the region, which was supplied by bull teams hauling freight from their headquarters at Fort Benton. His purchases were very economical, for Mr. Dewdney was a very careful man with government funds, and while the Blackfoot were grateful, the goods were gone like magic. Dewdney was stingy to the point of bungling and was just as unpopular in his dealings with the white settlers as he was with the Indians. Had he been working in the United States, somebody likely would have shot him, but here he could count himself lucky for the restraint of not only the Indians but the white men as well and their collective regard for the Mounted Police.

The budding cattle-ranching industry on the Canadian prairies was running into many difficulties. The fall of 1880 was a bad one, with prairie fires burning off the range in many places. The worst one in the Macleod district was caused by an old trader, Fred Kanouse, who purchased a good-looking pony from an Indian. It showed some signs of mange, so Fred proceeded to rub some kerosene into its hide by way of treatment. Then he took his newly acquired horse down to the blacksmith shop on the edge of the settlement to brand it. As he pressed the red-hot iron against its hide, there was a sudden flash, and away went the horse burning like a torch across the prairie. Before the poor animal died it had set fire to a half-mile of grass. The fire almost burned out the whole settlement before it was extinguished by the hard work of every man available.

It was considered a very serious offence to start a prairie fire and charges were laid against the erring Fred Kanouse. He was fined twenty dollars.

The Mounted Police had built a post on the Bow River about 105 miles north of Fort Macleod which they called Fort Calgary, the location being in the middle of the present-day city. It was kept in supplies by the I.G. Baker Company, bull teams hauling huge wagons, each one drawn by eight yokes of big oxen, and four wagons making up a train. Each brigade had a foreman and a cook. Oxen are powerful animals but they move very slowly at a plodding though steady walk.

How slow is well illustrated by the experience of Major Walker, a man who had come west with the first detachment of the Mounted Police and, after doing good work in Saskatchewan, had retired from the force. He was headed for Calgary when he rode into Fort Macleod, where he asked for his mail and was told it had left for Calgary two weeks previously by bull train. It had been raining and the low spots on the prairie were boggy, and to the major's surprise, he caught up to the wagons at High River forty miles south of Calgary, crawling along at a snail's pace. The foreman told him that with any luck and some good weather he would be in Calgary in ten days.

Major Walker understandably felt that bull trains were too slow for mail carrying, so he proceeded to organize a mail service. He rounded up a good number of subscriptions at twenty-five dollars apiece, and made a contract for two trips a month with a newly arrived Englishman named "Lord Hugill" at sixty-five dollars a trip.

When my grandfather came to Fort Macleod in 1882 it was the end of a long journey by Red River cart from Brandon, Manitoba. He had trailed with a government survey party as part of their crew from Ottawa. A machinist by trade, he had worked indoors long enough to find out that it disagreed with his health, threatening him with tuberculosis, and his doctor advised him to go west to a drier climate. It was good advice, for by the time he arrived at the end of that journey he was in top physical condition, hard as iron, with all the makings of a real frontiersman. Perhaps it was his interest in working with iron, for about the first thing he did was make his way to the blacksmith shop, where he found the blacksmith at the tag end of a horrendous hangover and very low in his mind. He had what amounted to a monopoly on a considerable business repairing wagons and gear for the I.G. Baker Company's bull trains. Apart from the big wagons, iron parts that wore out, and wheels that needed repairs, there were the chains running from the heavy yokes of each span of oxen back to the wagon. These often broke, so there were always chains to be fitted with new links, which he forged and welded from iron rods of the correct diameter. Besides that, there were shoes to be made and fitted to the oxen as well as to the police horses and work coming from settlers.

Old Smiley, as the blacksmith was known, could not stand prosperity; it worried him to a point where he proceeded periodically to go on a prolonged drunk that ended only when he ran out of money. It was at this kind of low tide in his life that Grandfather found him. Not only was his head aching, but his credit at the store had been suspended till he paid his bill. He was out of food and could not get the needed iron and other material to proceed with his blacksmithing. So when he saw this obviously green young man come into his shop, he naturally hit him up for a loan.

It was perfectly obvious to Grandfather that this was a good business and just as plain to him why the owner needed money. His experience in judging men was limited but he knew good blacksmithing when he saw it, and there was nothing wrong with Old Smiley's work – when he worked. So after some due consideration, he loaned Old Smiley some money and got him to sign a demand note. Grandfather hadn't heard of the western way of sealing deals by a handshake and the blacksmith was in no position to argue about it. So the blacksmith shop was back in business and Grandfather left with the survey crew for the rest of the summer and fall.

When early winter came he resigned from his job with the survey and rode back to the fort, where he looked up Old Smiley to find him recovering from another drunk and in no way able to repay the loan. So he took over the business and hired Old Smiley to work for him, allowing him a part of his wages in cash and crediting the rest to the note. Together they proceeded to forge iron, and the old blacksmith was happy and stayed away from the bottle most of the time.

But he slipped once, with a comical result. One night he went to the local saloon, where he apparently met some cronies and proceeded to get very drunk. In the small hours of the morning he staggered off heading for his cabin, but couldn't find it in the darkness. It was very cold and he finally found his way to the blacksmith shop, where a banked coal fire in the forge generated a little warmth. Crawling up on the bench alongside a pile of bull chains, he fell asleep. After a while he began to get cold and reached for the blanket that wasn't there, but his groping hand found the chains, which he proceeded to pull across his middle. This operation must have been repeated several times, for when Grandfather came to the shop later in the morning it was to find Old Smiley still snoring with about two hundred pounds of chain piled across his body.

He dug him out and sent him home for the day. Old Smiley came back to work the following morning not much the worse for wear.

By spring, after a busy winter, Grandfather had his loan back plus a fair profit, so he tore up the note and turned the shop over to its original owner. Then he saddled up his horse and proceeded to go looking for a suitable place to make himself a ranch. In due course he rode out on the rim of the hills overlooking a lovely valley at the confluence of Pothole Creek and the St. Mary's River, about six or seven miles above the location of abandoned Fort Whoop-Up and eleven miles south of the new village of Lethbridge (now a city of sixty-five thousand people). As he sat on his horse looking at it, the folded hills and draws on both sides of the valley were green with the new sheen of spring grass sprinkled with wildflowers nodding in the breeze. Directly across the river was the Blood Indian reserve. Seventy-odd miles to the west the solid phalanx of the Rockies stood gleaming with snow in a long jagged row of peaks against the faultless blue of the sky. The silvery rope of the river made a long lazy S bend with the creek running into it on the near side at the top of the second curve. It was an ideal location, but somebody was ahead of him, for he could see buildings and a set of corrals beyond the creek at the near end of a long, almost perpendicular, bank about three hundred feet high. He could also see some saddled horses in the corral, so he rode down into the valley for a closer look.

The ranch belonged to a colourful character by the name of Paddy Hassen, a squaw man who had recently buried his wife, a Blood Indian woman. There were some questions as to the cause of her death among her Indian relatives, but nothing was ever uncovered to prove it was anything but natural. Paddy's hospitality was warm and into his house he invited my grandfather, who, in the course of their conversation, offered to buy him out. Paddy was willing to sell, so they arranged the details. Thus Grandfather became the new owner of the ranch.

He knew the railway was getting close and, before he left Fort Macleod, he had ordered a brand-new Buckeye horsedrawn mower with a three-foot cutter bar and a one-horse hay rake from the I.G. Baker Company. Grandfather was aware of a demand for hay to feed the teams employed in building grade. When the new machinery was delivered to Lethbridge, he headed east with it along with a wagon, hay rack, and a team acquired as part of his deal for the ranch. Upon reaching the end of steel, he worked out an arrangement with the contractors to deliver hay at eighteen dollars a load, which was a lot of money in 1883. All he had to do was go out on the prairie, mow the wild hay, rake it up in bunches and then fork it into his hay rack, piling it as high as he could throw it, and pack it down by tramping it. Then he hauled it and stacked it close by the survey line. When the weather was good, he could average a load a day and sometimes more. By fall he had a considerable stake.

Grandfather was on the move. Ever since he had left Ottawa to come west, he had been dreaming about a dark-haired young lady by the name of Isabella Bell whom he had left behind. The youngest of her family, with three tall older brothers, she was a very striking girl with flashing brown eyes, of medium height and stately bearing, well educated and with a keen mind. She could cook, sew, keep a neat house, and had all the other skills girls of that time were expected to learn, plus some other things like rowing a boat and handling a team of driving horses. She had learned about boats when her brothers went fishing on the Ottawa River. Horses were part of life for anyone who owned property in those days.

Grandfather had been corresponding with Isabella and that winter he went east by rail. When he came back early in the spring of 1884, she was his wife.

That summer the railway reached Lethbridge, and she came west to join him on one of the first trains to reach that very new town. She rode the last hundred miles from Medicine Hat sitting on a plank laid between two sawhorses in the caboose of a construction freight train.

For some reason, Grandfather was late to meet the train. Grandmother, nineteen years old, and fresh from the city, walked down the platform in her stylish long dress with the white and black ostrich plumes on her hat waving at every step. Leaving her pile of luggage with the station agent, she crossed the dusty street to the trading store. The place was full of Indians and when they saw her they covered their mouths with their hands in sheer astonishment. Then they crowded around her, so close she was frightened. But the storekeeper came to her aid.

He knew who she was, for he said, "Give me your hat for a minute, Mrs. Russell."

So she unpinned it and handed it to him, whereupon he took it to the other end of the store with every Indian following, their eyes fixed on those wonderful graceful plumes. In their own language, he told them about the feathers, how they came from across the big water from a huge bird as tall as a horse – a bird that did not fly but could run like a deer. They were deeply impressed and looked at Grandmother with awe as she pinned the hat back on when the storekeeper returned it.

"They never saw feathers like that, ma'am," he told her. "They think very highly of feathers and these are big medicine to 'em."

From that day forward, the Bloods called her Bird Woman.

Grandfather came with a team and a buckboard to gather her up along with her luggage and they drove out across the great prairie to the ranch. What her impressions were as they came out on the rim of the valley overlooking the river shining like silver ribbon thrown down between the hills, with the mountains lifting on the horizon beyond against the western sky, she never told me. Maybe she was a little scared as she sat on the wagon seat gazing at this immense lone land, but her back was straight and her head up as she looked. It was her new home. She would never regret that she came.

Bird Woman she was to the Indians and no doubt the moccasin telegraph was busy telling of her arrival as well as of her marvellous feathers. Occasionally some Indians came to visit and would be served tea as well as offered some small gifts that were always on hand for them. They called my grandfather White Shirt, for he always wore one. He made it very plain that when he was not at the ranch they were not to bother my grandmother. For a while the Indians honoured his wishes.

But one day, when she was alone, she took out some colourful braided rag mats and hung them on the rail fence in front of the house. There was a camp of several teepees across the river and no doubt the Indians saw the rugs. She was sewing by the front windows when a party of braves rode up. A big brave, likely a sub-chief, got off his horse and proceeded to lift one of the rugs off the pole and throw it over his horse's back. She came out the front door with her broom in her hand and ordered him to put it back. He just ignored her and stood looking at her, his face a mask of imperious indifference. She told him again and, when he refused to move, she whacked him soundly over the rump and pointed at the fence. No doubt he had never been struck by a woman before and, given the moment and the experience, he probably would have liked to have killed her for this insult. But her eyes were flashing and she showed no fear. Besides, he knew that if he laid a hand on White Shirt's woman there would be big trouble. After all, even among his people, she of the big feathers was well known and her medicine was strong. So he put the rug back in its place and mounted his horse. Among his braves there was some sign of smiles, while the people watching from the camp across the river must have been amused as the whole party followed him away and left her alone. It was a year or more later before any of the Bloods bothered her again.

My grandmother's mother came out from the east to visit her at the ranch, and being a city woman she was no doubt appalled at the great sweep of country and its remoteness, to say nothing of the sight of wild Indians riding their ponies across the river flats. One fine summer morning they were by themselves at the ranch when a small party of young braves crossed the river on their horses and rode into the yard. They wanted to talk to White Shirt, they said, which was likely not true, for they must have seen him ride away. Grandmother told them he was not home. Great-grandmother was terrified at the sight of these half-naked "savages" and wanted to hide in the cellar, which Grandmother refused to do. She chose to ignore them and they proceeded to hang around the yard, squatting on their heels and talking. This went on for several hours. Along about four o'clock in the evening, Grand-mother decided it was time to do something about them, for not only were she and her mother getting hungry for supper, but the cheeky teenagers made her a bit angry.

The horses were standing patiently with their bridle reins tucked under a driftwood log down by the river. She went out and began picking up bits of wood as though in preparation of lighting her fire, putting them in a fold of her long apron. Back and forth she went, while the Indians watched her. Finally she worked her way close to the horses and then she gave her apron a quick toss, scattering woodchips all over them. Naturally, the horses pulled the reins loose and stampeded out of there heading for camp across the river, with the Indians *ki-yi*-ing along behind trying to catch up to them.

That was the last time any of the Bloods ever bothered her. Bird Woman and White Shirt were always friendly but firm and enjoyed the respect of the red men and women.

As far as I know, my grandparents never locked the door of their house in their lives. Their quiet hospitality became well known, for it was enjoyed by all who visited the ranch. My father was born in a little stone cottage in the town of Lethbridge in February 1886, the first of six sons and a daughter. Most of them entered the world at the home ranch; some of them without even the help of a midwife.

I remember my father telling of one birth when he was about nine years old. The baby came sooner than expected, and was alive and well, but Grandmother was slowly hemorrhaging to death. Grandfather was unable to do anything for her and he sent my father on horseback in the dark of night to a ranch about six or seven miles away to get help. It was a lonesome ride but he finally saw a light shining in a window. The rancher hitched up a team and drove his wife as fast as possible to the ranch, where she was able to stop the bleeding in time.

My grandmother was a tough lady but the paramount quality in her character was dignity. She had a retentive mind with a marvellous memory for things she read as well as for times, places, and figures. She kept the books for the growing business and did it with her usual attention to detail. As a boy I recall her getting into an argument over some figures with her lawyer, which she won without any fuss, in a quiet way that was very final and left him red-faced. I always remember her as a very beautiful woman whom

I adored. My only regret is that I never got around to telling her how much I loved her, but somehow I am sure she knew. Indians and white people alike all respected her, even the rascals.

Two of the neighbours, one Dave Acres, the other Tom Purcell, who had taken an early retirement from whiskey trading when the North-West Mounted Police came west, went into partnership on a ranch but got into a quarrel and split up. Dave Acres took up a homestead on Pothole Coulee several miles up the creek from the Russell ranch.

My grandmother was making breakfast early one morning, while Grandfather was out at the barn feeding the horses, when a knock came at the door. When she opened it, there was the tall, buckskin-clad figure of Dave Acres.

"Good mornin', missus," he said. "I just shot Tom Purcell. Where's George? I want to give myself up."

"You what?" my grandmother asked in amazement. "Did you kill him?"

"Christ, yes, missus," Dave replied matter-of-factly. "Deader 'n hell!"

When Grandfather came, he told Dave to put his horse in the corral, and they had breakfast. Then he drove the confessed killer into Lethbridge, where he gave himself up to the police.

If the two hard cases had not been bragging so much about how they were going to kill each other at the first opportunity, Dave would likely have got off on a plea of self-defence. He had been saddling his horse in the corral that morning when Tom Purcell suddenly rode in, obviously somewhat drunk, and attacked him with a heavy elk-horn quirt. Dave had been scared of Tom for some time and had a rifle cached behind one of the corral posts. Backing toward it, while he parried the blows at his head, he swung it clear, pointed it, and shot all in the same motion, wiping his assailant out of his saddle very dead indeed. As it was, he got three years for manslaughter, the sentence being served at Fort Macleod.

There was a rather amusing sequel to this story. While in jail Dave was put to work repairing, cleaning, and oiling police harnesses. Being a squaw man, married to a Blood woman, he had lots of in-law relatives who often came to visit him. Whenever the chance arose, he would slip them a piece of harness through the bars, which was then hidden under their blankets. Then he would make another piece to take its place. When he was finally released, he had a fine four-horse set of harnesses waiting for him, a caper which of course delighted the Indians.

My grandfather did not believe that fortune comes to those who just stand and wait. They were building a cattle herd and had acquired some horses. Every second year or so they added another son to the family, all healthy potential cowboys. The range was open to anyone with the livestock to feed on it. It was not all roses in the prairie garden, however; they both were concerned about the lack of school to educate their family. They solved this problem in due course by hiring as governess a lady who had recently arrived from the east with her family. She lived with them and taught the Russell youngsters reading, writing, and arithmetic – the three Rs as they were popularly known.

Grandfather looked at his horses, for the most part small, wiry Indian cayuses, about as tough as horses can get pound for pound, but too light for harness. He sent east for an imported hackney stallion and introduced him to his cayuse mares. The hybrid colts that ultimately arrived soon outgrew their mothers: big handsome horses that made great saddle and light driving animals with all the toughness of the native breed.

Every settler in the country mined his own coal from seams that were exposed along the banks of the river by the action of the water. It would burn, but was somewhat oxidized by the exposure to weather and water which made it smoky and filthy. Having done some prospecting up on the slopes of the valley away from the river, Grandfather sunk a shaft straight down in a likely spot in search of a minable coal seam with the help of an immigrant coal miner from England. They found a seam of good clean coal. With some careful measuring and rough surveying of the angle of the slope, they dug another horizontal shaft into the slope below until they reached the seam. It was shored up with timber and fitted with some mining cars running on tracks out to a timber chute where wagons could be loaded. Thus coal mining was added to the ranch business.

As the country opened up, there was a big demand for heavy draft horses for the hauling of freight and for farm work. So Grandfather contacted a Clydesdale horse breeder in the east and eventually received a stallion and several mares of this big handsome breed. Most of them bays, though some were black, they had white stockings with much feathery hair around their feet, were up to seventeen hands tall, and, fully grown, weighed close to two thousand pounds. A well-matched team of Clydes fitted with adequate harness looked mighty handsome hitched to a big wagon with red wheels and a green double box. They were longer in the leg than the Belgian or Percheron breeds and active as cats.

I remember Dad telling me the hackney stud hated the big Clyde with a burning passion and was always trying to get at him, so much so that they kept him shut in the corrals. But one day when everybody was at the dinner table, the hackney wound himself up and jumped the fence. The next thing they knew all hell broke loose out on the big flat in front of the buildings as both stallions squared off squealing like banshees.

There are few things in the world more fierce and final than a pair of fighting studs. Unless they are evenly matched, the death of one is almost inevitable. In this case the hackney was a David attacking a Goliath with almost half a ton difference in weight. If the big horse got hold of him with his teeth the fight would be short.

The Clyde was fast for such a big animal and had enormous strength, but the hackney was as quick as lightning. The big stud tried to strike but the little one gave him no chance to get close as they reared and struck at each other. When the Clyde tried to reach him with his teeth, the hackney whirled and kicked him hard on his front legs knocking him off balance. Whirling and squealing, they clashed and broke fast, the bigger horse always a little late in his lunges to bring those powerful jaws into action. Once, the big horse got his teeth into the hackney's rump, but the hackney kicked him hard on the shins so that all his opponent got was some hair in his mouth. Before the fight could proceed two riders came in from opposite directions, two lariats shot out, and the horses were separated with no real injury to either one.

By the time my father was sixteen, he was riding on the round-ups tallying the cattle wearing the 2G brand on their left hips as they were gathered and branded. He was very young for such responsibility, but he had been doing a man's work for some time and his age was no handicap among such a crew. He could rope and ride, had a good eye for cattle, and was no stranger to the prairie country, for he was part of it. He was a real cowboy in a crew of such men, for the Canadian cowboy had acquired all the skills of those from south of the border because quite a number of Americans had come north with their skills. Young Canadian men, along with those from Britain, who were moving into the west looking for opportunities and adventure, were not long in adopting the colourful dress and expertise of working cowboys. Naturally some were better at it than others. A round-up camp could find college graduates rubbing elbows with Texans, born and raised with cattle and horses, who couldn't write their own names. There were half-breed Indians, scions of eastern North American society, and maybe a Mexican or two thrown in for good measure, but they all worked at the same kind of jobs, largely spoke the same language, dressed more or less alike, and generally blended into the cowboy culture. If some of them were green, they did not stay that way very long; learning was a matter of sheer survival. The best of them were found in the round-up camp.

There were two kinds of round-ups: the spring round-up where the cattle were gathered every day in a chosen region and new calves were branded the same as the mother; and the fall beef round-ups which were for gathering mature steers and dry cows for shipping by rail to market. Each round-up crew, made up of riders from various ranches, was commanded by a captain, chosen by the ranchers, who was in charge and also arbitrated any disputes that might arise regarding ownership of an animal. There could be twenty or thirty riders, each with eight to ten horses, a chuckwagon with a cook, and a horse wrangler whose job it was to keep the saddle horses together and to drive them into the rope corral every morning at daylight.

One or two of the best ropers roped out the horses the men wanted. When these were saddled up, there were always some that bucked the kinks out of themselves and their riders, action usually accompanied by some cheering or raillery depending on the cowboy's ability to stay in the saddle.

Then the round-up captain took the crew up onto the nearest high ground and sent them off in pairs in various directions to comb the country for cattle. Meanwhile, the cook packed his wagon, hitched up his four-horse team, and headed out for a designated spot, and he was usually followed by the horse wrangler herding the cavvy. When they got there, a fire was built and the noon meal was prepared in time to feed the riders bringing the cattle. If the weather was hot, the men might take time off to have a nap, mend equipment, or do whatever else came up till mid-afternoon. Then the branding began, with a couple of chosen ropers heeling the calves and dragging them to the branding fire, where teams of wrestlers threw them, and held them down to be branded, castrated, and earmarked. As the ropers brought the calves in they called the brand of the cow that was its mother's and thus each ranch was able to tally their cattle. It was up to the various reps to see that their home ranch got fair treatment.

It was hot, sweaty, dusty work where a young cowboy received no favours for his youthfulness nor did such a youngster expect to be treated otherwise. He worked like a man, was paid a man's wage, and demanded to be treated like one as long as he did his job.

I recall a story Dad told me of meeting a youngster only fourteen years old by the name of Elderidge, a tough, hard-riding, cheeky kid, who could sit a bucking horse or handle his rope as well as or better than most grown men. There was nothing retiring about him, for the chip on his shoulder was bigger than most and he would give some lip to anybody at the slightest excuse. The round-up captain ran out of patience one day. He and one of the riders tied the kid down to the wagon tongue and gave him a sound spanking with a pair of chaps – a punishment that stung his pride more than his bottom – and it did nothing but make him smoulder. The outfit was gathering beef and, coming in off his turn at night herding, young Elderidge sneaked into camp to slip his rope gently around the boss's feet as he lay in bed dead to the world. Before he knew what was happening, that worthy gentlemen was bouncing out across the prairie behind a running horse. The kid refused to turn him loose till he promised there would be no retribution. The boss didn't have much choice. He walked barefoot back to camp under a high moon gathering up various personal belongings on the way, while no doubt fervently contemplating murder. History leaves no record of the kid dying violently, so it can be assumed that he learned the virtue of keeping his mouth shut before somebody wiped him out.

The most important man in the crew was the cook. Most of them could put together a good meal cooked in Dutch ovens over an open fire. Some of them were artists who could bring forth fluffy biscuits that would melt in the mouth of a hungry man. Occasionally one would even find a way to make doughnuts, cooked in hot lard and rolled in sugar while hot and served as dessert for the evening meal along with stewed prunes. "Bear sign" they sometimes called them, and most cowboys would ride miles out of their way for the chance to have a feed of them. Every chuckwagon had a small crock of sour dough for making pancakes, biscuits, and bread. It was a kind of frontier yeast culture put together with tender loving care by somebody with the knowledge and then kept warm and alive for years. There are records of the same batch of sour dough being used for over half a century. Every time it was used some was kept in the bottom of the crock and before it was put away more batter of flour and water was added and mixed to be ready for the next day. It gave a distinctive though not unpleasant sour-yeast smell to people who ate it regularly and didn't take a bath every day, which was just about everyone, there being no indoor plumbing in the country, much less in a round-up cow camp.

A routine day on the trail drive began when the cook rolled out well before sunrise to start his fire and put together a breakfast of cornmeal mush, steak or maybe salt pork, fresh biscuits, and coffee. Lunch was usually a biscuit or two stuffed in a saddle pocket at breakfast time, along with a handful of dried jerky. Supper was more steak or stew, sometimes alternated with Dutch-oven beans, corn pone, or occasionally roots or greens picked up along the trail by the cook during the day. In season, the meal might be topped off with fresh wild berries and, of course, more coffee. A good cook could turn out tasty food even though the larder was limited. Meat was the main item, sometimes antelope, more often venison, but rarely beef. Killing a cow was something of a waste unless it was a yearling, for there was no way to keep it fresh for long in hot weather.

For some reason or other camp cooks can be very cranky and sometimes eccentric. If they were good at what they did, and most of them were, they were treated like fine china – very carefully, for nobody ever rawhided a good cook. Good food and lots of it was something every cowboy appreciated and one of the few real pleasures they encountered out there on the open prairie. It didn't have to be fancy – just tasty and plentiful.

Though noted for being crotchety and temperamental, these cooks were not entirely without a sense of humour. There is a story of one who was working in a remote camp one spring. The weather was very wet, and then got even wetter when a three-day storm blew in, and it rained till small creeks turned into rivers impossible to cross and even the coulees were swimming deep. Supplies were running low and about all he had left to feed the crew was beans. A hungry stranger showed up unexpectedly and asked if he could have something to eat. "Sure thing," said the cook. "We got thousands of things to eat – all of 'em beans!" Then he proceeded to ladle out a plateful from a big pot simmering on the stove.

While at family ranches the lady of the house usually oversaw and participated in the preparing and serving of meals, on larger ranches where a bigger crew was employed the year round, the cook was a part of it and almost always a man – sometimes an immigrant Chinese but more often a retired cowboy who through infirmities caused by accident or age could not hold down a rider's job any more. They had developed a culinary skill by way of following the only life they knew and retained a place on the payroll. It was a lot easier than working cattle while riding snorty horses in all kinds of weather. Most of them did a good job or else they didn't last very long, and some were superlative. All of those able to hold down such a job were treated with great deference even if they were as cranky as bears or as temperamental as opera singers. Nobody on a crew ever gave the cook a bad time intentionally, though sometimes when a horse blew up on a cold morning and bucked through the breakfast fire on a round-up, scattering pots and pans all over the place, everyone present was treated to some plain and classical profanity from the "kingpin" of the chuckwagon. It was a time when those that had been served breakfast ate it in silence and those that hadn't probably went without.

A top cook was usually famous far and wide, for the crew of his outfit never missed a chance to brag him up or give glowing accounts of his skill as a teamster. As has been said, it was always the cook's job to move the chuckwagon on from one camp to the next on a trail drive or a round-up.

My father told the story of how the foreman took the crew up onto the top of a butte at daylight one morning to line them out for the day's gather of cattle on a spring round-up.

Down on the flat below, the cook was up on the wagon just starting out for the next day camp, when all of a sudden the four-horse team hit the ground flat-out in a runaway. Swearing, the boss dispatched some riders to help get the team back in control before they piled the chuckwagon up in a coulee or washout. Their efforts to catch up were not aided and abetted much by the cook, who was popping his long-lashed whip on each side of the lead team. By dint of some hard riding the cowboys rode in on each of the team to find the cook had somehow lost his reins, but they grabbed them up near the bridles and stopped the wagon.

They were sorting things out when the boss rode up to ask the cook what the hell he was trying to do, wreck the outfit? The cook sat on his seat rolling a smoke as he let the silence sink in and then said, "About the time I started, a cross line broke at the lead team. I knowed that if I hung on to those lines, I was sure as hell goin' to do something wrong. So I throwed 'em all away and took down my whip to keep those boogers runnin' straight."

Apart from some bedrolls that got bounced off the prairie no damage was done, but the cook's reputation as a real "skinner" didn't suffer any either. That story went all over the country fast and it is still going.

As a boy I heard another story about a round-up cook who had the reputation for being about as ornery as a cook can get. He was a very good cook, but he had certain set hours when meals were served and anybody missing them just went hungry. They were gathering beef on a fall round-up and one day, about an hour after lunch, a cow buyer showed up to take a look at the herd. The boss showed him around and then he asked if he could ride to the wagon for something to eat. Upon being assured he was welcome, he headed to where the wagon was parked and the boss went back to work. The cook saw him coming when he was still some distance away and when the visitor got there he found the gnarled, hairy old cook dressed in nothing but his battered hat and beat-up boots stirring a big pot of stew with the long barrel of a .45 Colt Peacemaker as he eyed the late-arriving visitor with all the promising malevolence of a cornered cougar. Not a word was spoken. The cow buyer just rode on past headed for town.

It was wild country, big and limitless in its expanses, with its share of eccentric characters. It was a place where boys grew into men in an inordinately short period of time and my father, Harold, along with his brothers, Frank, Andrew, Ernest, and Fred, were not exceptions. Grandfather and Grandmother imbued them from birth with a strong sense of responsibility, fairness, and honesty, and the country taught them fearlessness but also a measure of caution, however small that measure might be. So they were part of the life of that big land, getting a portion of their education from it as they grew through the experience of doing many things, much of it hard work but all of it challenging and sometimes thrilling adventure. It was a way of life nobody could encounter now, for the prairies, foothills, and mountains have changed. In those days there was not a barbed-wire fence from the North Pole to some-where away to the south. It was wild then and it was wonderful.

Life in Cow Country

It was a huge land covered by an ocean of grass, where people worked with horses, either riding them or hitching them to wagons or buggies to get from one place to another. The wagons moved freight or livestock feed, and the buggies, which had springs and were generally drawn by light horses, and could be fancy and stylish with tufted leather upholstery, were used for quick travel across country to visit neighbours or to go to town.

It was in Lethbridge, Alberta, in Canada, that I was born in 1915. By that time the great ocean of grass that made up the Great Plains was divided up by barbed-wire fences. The buffalo were long gone and so were the longhorns, but my father, Harold George Russell, who was the first white boy born there in 1885, had seen the prairie when it was still wide open, and had helped gather the last of the longhorns at the round-ups with men who had ridden with the trail drivers from the south. He was the first real cowboy I ever met.

It was his stories of the old days on the range that had more than a little to do with my abiding fascination with cowboy

From *The Canadian Cowboy* (1993)

culture and history. Raised on a cow and horse ranch at the foot of the Rockies, about eighty miles west of the old ranch taken up by my grandfather in 1883, with the smell of corral dust, saddles, cows, and horses in my nose, my memories of those days are keen.

I recall my mother's buggy, given to her by my father as a wedding present. It was silver-mounted and well-sprung with hard rubber tires on the wheels. The harness was light with silver-plated buckles and snaps. It was a beautiful outfit, and with it a fast-stepping team could trot at about six miles per hour all day, which, as wheels went in those days, was fast – much faster than a wagon drawn by heavy horses with no springs and iron tires on the wheels.

Because we lived with horses and worked with them every day, we had a great respect for them, looking after them and keeping them well-fed. A man who abused his horses or didn't care for them properly was held in very low esteem.

The land was wild, many of the horses were half-wild as the spirit moved them, and the early ranchers were sometimes inclined to kick the lid off of boredom with a great bang of energy and let the pieces fall where they may. Dignified they could be, but most of them enjoyed handling high-spirited horses. Most of them enjoyed a joke, even on themselves.

The Maunsell brothers, who established a ranch a few miles up the river from Fort Macleod, were an enterprising pair of Englishmen. Ted Maunsell, the elder, was the better businessman of the two. Though both were good riders and not afraid of hard work, it was he who accumulated the land. He never did learn to tell one cow from another and totally depended on his foreman to take care of such details. His brother, George, eventually drifted away by himself, but Ted proceeded to put together one of the biggest ranches in the Fort Macleod country. As a sideline business, he set up a butcher shop near town.

One of his neighbours was an American by the name of "Hippo" Johnson, who had drifted north from the States driving a herd of longhorns. He was suspected of being very handy with his rope when it came to putting his brand on mavericks, but nobody caught him at it. He branded his cattle with a big O around a hip joint, hence his nickname. Hippo never missed a chance to badger Ted Maunsell with tricks that the Englishman always ignored with a certain dignity.

One morning Hippo was riding to town when he spotted a big calico-coloured steer wearing Maunsell's brand. He proceeded to drive it to Ted's butcher shop, where he put it in the pen at the back. The owner was presiding over the place alone while waiting for his foreman.

"Good morning, Ted," Hippo greeted him. "Come on outside. I just drove in a damn fine steer you might like."

When Maunsell went out with him to the pen Hippo conveniently manoeuvred the animal so its brand was out of sight against the fence.

"What's he worth?" Hippo asked.

"A prime animal," Maunsell observed. "Forty dollars is the going price. I could use him right now." Whereupon he led the way back into the shop and wrote Hippo a cheque. Hippo thanked him, pocketed the cheque, and rode away into town.

Later in the day, the foreman showed up and was surprised to see the fresh hide hung across the top rail of the corral fence and even more so when he took a closer look at it, for he usually picked the animals for butchering. He went into the shop and confronted his boss.

"How did you come by that steer?" he asked.

"Hippo Johnson drove it in," came the reply. "I needed a beef, so I bought it."

"You what?" the foreman roared. "You bought your own steer!" If there were times when the man weighed quitting against the comfort of a good job, this could easily have been one of them.

He rode into town at a gallop looking for Johnson with much violence preying on his mind.

Upon finding that worthy at the bar, he somehow smothered an inclination to kill him on the spot. He labelled him for a thief with some additional smoky adjectives thrown in, which Hippo heard with an expression of injured innocence.

"I come across that steer a mile or so out of town and just drove him in. Ted admired him plenty and handed me a cheque. It ain't every day I get offered forty dollars for just showing a man one of his own steers, so I took it. But seein' as how you're so damn sore about it, I'll give it back."

He duly gave the cheque to the irate foreman and the pregnant hush in the place was broken by a laugh and then the whole saloon was rocking with mirth. It was another of Hippo's jokes on Maunsell and the foreman had no choice but to join in.

As a slave on a Texas ranch, John Ware grew up working with horses from the time he was old enough to ride. In his mid-teens he suddenly found himself free, able to go where he pleased whenever the notion took him. Tall for his age, very active and extremely strong, he was a superb rider who knew cattle, so it was natural for him to take to the life of a roving cowboy. Finding work was easy, but getting paid what he was worth was something else in a country just emerging from slavery. But he had a sunny smile and a quick mind and was always willing to take on any job. He was scrupulously honest and able to take responsibility. Life was still hard for a black man, but he survived. Fascinated with seeing what was over the next hill, he drifted from one job to another, gradually working his way north. Eventually he found himself in Idaho, flat broke and hungry, with only the clothes he stood up in, when he had the good luck to run into the Bar U crew.

Tom Lynch, foreman of the Bar U ranch west of High River, Alberta, was at Lost River, Idaho, in the spring of 1883 buying cattle. He was short of men to move several thousand head of cattle home, when a big black man showed up dressed in rags and a cheerful grin asking for a job. At first Lynch was skeptical, but when John Ware proceeded to ride a snaky cayuse to a standstill, he got a job. When the new man proved adept at handling cattle besides being very good at getting along with men, he was promoted to trail boss of one of the herds for the drive. Thus John Ware came to Alberta to stay and become a part of history in that last expanse of open-range country in the west.

Ware found Canada to his liking, for the country had never known slavery and among cowboys a black man was judged by what he could do rather than by the colour of his skin. For John Ware, life was a round-the-clock celebration of freedom. Here was a man who had never known anything but hard work; it was his play. Laughter was always close to the surface in his make-up. Kindhearted, generous, and happy, he was just as likely to laugh at a joke on himself as on anybody else who was handy. There wasn't a mean bone in his body, but he loved to play a joke on others.

One day on round-up in the spring of 1883, he rode into camp to get a fresh horse, when he noticed the horse wrangler asleep in the bed tent. It was this man who night-herded the cavvy – the string of saddle horses used by the crew – and brought them in at dawn every morning when the cowboys caught their mounts for the day's work. John saw his chance to play a joke. He stretched his rope across the front of the bed tent from a stake to the wheel of the chuckwagon. Then he began vigorously slapping the roof of the tent with his hands and yelling at the top of his voice for all and sundry to watch out for the stampede. The wrangler woke up from a deep sleep with a start, leapt to his feet, ran out of the tent, tripped on the rope, and came down with a crash flat on his face. All he saw was John and the cook doubled up with laughter. Of course, everybody in the crew had a great laugh about it and thought it was a huge joke.

But the joker, however entertaining he might be, puts himself in a vulnerable position, for there is always someone in a crew of men who waits and watches for a chance to play a joke on him. John Ware was not an easy man to catch off guard. He was a keen observer, a great rider, and absolutely tireless, but he had one weakness. He was deathly afraid of snakes, and one way or another somebody in the crew was aware of it. It was a fear that probably stemmed from when, as a boy, he had been whipped with a snake by his boss back in Texas. One morning when he left his saddle horse untended for a few minutes, somebody wrapped a small dead garter snake around his saddle horn. When John took hold of the horn to mount the horse, he barely suppressed a scream of terror. Fun is fun, but he saw nothing funny about a snake – even a little dead one.

Fred Stimson was round-up boss that year and he and his friend George Emerson were sharing a small tent. The weather was good, so the rest of the crew just made their beds out on the prairie under the sky. A cowboy's bed is made up of blankets covered with a rectangular piece of canvas long enough to be folded over and under it. John Ware rolled his bed out not far from the tent, then joined the rest of the crew around the campfire. In the dusk of evening George Emerson sneaked the coiled end of his lariat under John's blanket and took the free end into the tent.

When John went to bed, he was almost asleep when something moved under him. He froze and then the thing moved again.

"Snake," he howled as he came up on his feet running. His toe caught the rope stretched between his bed and the tent, and, scared as he was, he knew he was the butt of another joke. Fright turned to anger. With one sweep of his hand he flattened the tent and with another he snatched the covers off the two men, loomed over them like a mad bear, and grated out between his teeth, "Somebody goin' to get a beatin' fo' this!"

Fred Stimson came up on his feet with a gun in his hand.

"What in hell is the matter with you? Nobody hurt you. Go back to bed before this gun goes off!"

"Nobody done hurt me, only scared me half to death! An' Ah think it was yo, boss. Ain't dat so?"

By that time every cowboy in camp was on his feet. One of John's closest friends took him by the arm and said, "Go easy, John. It was only a joke. Go back to bed and I'll put the boss's tent back up."

John did as he was told, but he didn't sleep. He was ashamed of himself and regretted his anger, but he was uncomfortable working for Fred Stimson after that. And somehow he was never quite as carefree again.

His adventures and experiences were many, but perhaps the most astonishing and significant of them happened one hot July day when he was riding for the Bar U. His horse was tired and thirsty when he came to a slough and rode into it to give the horse a drink. But the horse refused and began to paw at the water. Somewhat puzzled, John noticed a scum showing on the surface. Riding back to shore, he got down and looked closer. The scum was oily and smelled a bit like kerosene. He struck a match and held it close to the water, when suddenly the whole surface of the pond burst into flames. It was light crude oil that had seeped up into the slough from underground.

Some years later, in 1914, a well drilled not far from this spot struck a real gusher, the first oil well in what was to prove to be the first big oil field in Alberta.

John Ware homesteaded on what is now Ware Creek, a few miles northwest of the present town of Turner Valley, where he and his bride, Mildred Lewis, a black girl from Edmonton, proceeded with raising a family. He eventually sold his homestead and bought a small ranch near the town of Brooks, about a hundred miles east of Calgary on the main line of the Canadian Pacific

Railway. It was there he died when his horse stepped in a badger hole and fell on him.

His funeral was held in Calgary and was attended by people from all over the country. One of these, a well-to-do rancher by the name of Sam Howe, intended to go to the funeral but his good intentions got sidetracked.

To Sam, whiskey was the juice to celebrate a happy event and to wash away the tears of a sad one. Sam was feeling bad when he bought his ticket to take the train to Calgary at Brooks. He sat down at the bar to wait for the train, but his private wake got a bit out of hand and his sense of direction twisted. He was sleeping on the train when the conductor shook his shoulder. "Sam! Wake up! Where are you goin'?"

"Where do you think I'm goin'? I'm goin' to John Ware's funeral in Calgary," answered Sam.

"Hell, Sam! This is the eastbound train. John was buried two days ago and we'll be in Medicine Hat pretty quick!"

That little piece of humour would have made John Ware roar with laughter had he been able to hear it.

Cowboy humour runs from the sublime to the utterly ridiculous, and more than one joke intended to die with a chuckle has proliferated and even boomeranged. A story is told about Seven U Brown, who was ramrodding a round-up near High River in the 1880s, when the green kid of the outfit asked one of the cowpunchers who the boss was.

With a perfectly serious expression on his face, the cowboy informed the kid. "That's Old Seven U Brown, you'd better watch out for him – he shot his wife."

The boy was flabbergasted and, after some considerable thinking about this dramatic revelation, he wanted to find out more, so he finally sidled up to Brown and asked, "Did you really shoot your wife?"

"Who told you that?" asked Seven U, whereupon the cowboy pointed him out.

Next morning, when Brown was lining out the crew for the day's gather, he left out this particular rider who had enough good sense to stick with the boss and say nothing till he was directed to otherwise. Seven U, riding a magnificent horse that day, made a tremendous ride without even noticing his companion. Arriving back at camp that evening, he turned to the cowboy sitting on his weary mount beside him and asked, "Are you hungry?"

"Plumb starved!" admitted the cowboy.

"Are you tired?"

"Dead beat!" came the reply.

"Good!" said Seven U. "That'll damn well teach you not to go around telling people I shot my wife."

When the great Matador ranch sold out its vast holdings on the Texas-Mexico border in the early 1890s to a Scottish investor, the deal was for all the land and cattle. But either some of the cattle were hidden in the brush or the original owners bought five thousand head, for it wasn't very long before the Matador was trailing north one of the very last herds of longhorns heading for the open range in the Northwest Territories of Canada. My father remembered this big herd when it came into Alberta – an undulating, seemingly endless line of cattle with their horns glinting in the sun. They didn't find suitable range that was not already being used in Alberta, so they turned east into Saskatchewan and set up a ranch in the huge sweep of prairie northeast of what is now the town of Maple Creek.

It was getting near impossible to drive cattle across country from Texas, for the country was being rapidly fenced and the fees levied by the farmers for damage to fields of grain was a constant and expensive irritation to the stockmen owning trailing herds. When the Wilkinson–McCord ranch in west Texas sold out, they loaded their cattle, horses, and equipment on eight big trains heading north to unload at Billings, Montana. There they began a trek north, across the border and on for about five hundred miles to Sounding Lake, Alberta, arriving late in the summer of 1902. It was long-grass country, where their longhorns thrived on the bunch grass that stood up to their bellies, and for a while the herds flourished and multiplied on range that was ideal.

But in the late fall of 1906 a blizzard struck with driving snow and temperatures dropped to fifty degrees below zero. There was no break in the weather; one storm followed another and the cattle drifted, starving and freezing, and there was nothing that could be done to stem the tide of one of the hardest winters in the history of the cattle industry.

The buffalo, nature's wild cattle, now long gone, could survive such weather, for they turned their big woolly heads into the storm and worked their muzzles deep enough into the snow to get to the grass. But cattle just turn their heads south, maybe hoping to get closer to the sun, and nothing can be done to stop them. Even if they come to a sheltered spot or an obstruction of some kind, they just pile up and perish. The weather has always been the great unknown to ranchers, and when conditions like those of the winter of 1906-07 hit the range country the only survivors were a few small ranchers who had put up hay in stacks fenced like barricades, and even then these owners lost cattle that joined the drifting herds.

Many years ago I talked to one old cowboy who grew up in the Sounding Lake country and remembered that winter of death. He told me of seeing one steep-sided twisting draw almost full of snow and dead cattle. One drifting herd after another got trapped in it to freeze solid in three separate layers. He said that for years afterward it was hard to ride across it through the piled-up bones and horns.

When the spring broke and the snow melted in 1907, the whole range was wide open again. Nearly all the big ranchers were broke, including the Wilkinson-McCord outfit and the Matador. Stories were common of men lost in winter storms and never found, until the spring thaws revealed their remains.

Many feats of endurance were recorded. None could be more outstanding than one involving Bill Greathouse, a neighbouring horse rancher. By February, the whole crew of the Wilkinson-McCord ranch was down to just surviving, for they were powerless to do anything for their cattle with temperatures at fifty below zero and snow lying two feet deep on the level and much deeper in the low places. The ranch cook, a Mrs. Ellis, became dangerously ill. She was not only a fine cook but very well liked by all who knew her. Determined to help her, if he could, Bill Greathouse saddled a big grain-fed horse and headed for Stettler and a doctor, a hundred miles away.

The records do not tell what he was wearing, but he was likely outfitted with long woollen underwear, a wool shirt and pants, two or three pairs of wool socks, Indian-tanned moccasins inside overshoes, Angora woolskin chaps, a buffalo-skin or sheepskin coat, buckskin mitts with wool liners, and a fur cap.

Hitting a steady pace and keeping as much as possible to high ground where the snow wasn't so deep, he headed for the nearest ranch in line with Stettler. Upon reaching the place, he quickly told the people there of his needs and hurriedly changed his saddle to a fresh horse, the best they had. So he rode, changing horses four times on the way. Upon arriving in Stettler, he immediately saw the doctor, and while the physician was putting together a packet of medicine with instructions for its use, Bill took his horse to the livery stable, fed it well, and proceeded to take on a big meal for himself. Without stopping to rest, he then stepped back into his saddle and headed for home.

On the way back, he reversed the procedure, changing horses at each ranch till he came back to his own mount at the beginning of the last lap. He delivered the medicine in time, for Mrs. Ellis recovered. He made the round trip of two hundred miles in an astonishing thirty-six hours, through a vast, cold, snow-blanketed country, under conditions where landmarks were often invisible in the whiteout, and without hurting one of his mounts. It was an epic of sheer guts and endurance. Of such men the north-western frontier cattle country was made. Bill Greathouse was big and tall as men go, but when heart and determination counted, he was a giant.

Not all of the cattle died that winter, for here and there a few big four-year-old steers and dry cows survived.

My father told of cattle that drifted south in such storms clear to the Missouri River from the Canadian ranges. Some of them then drifted as far southeast as the North Dakota badlands. By the time they were found they were getting fat again and they were rounded up and shipped on east to Chicago.

The Mexico ranch arrived at about the same time as the Wilkinson–McCord outfit, and by the same means. Wilkinson and McCord went north as far as the Red Deer River and established a headquarters east of where the Dinosaur Provincial Park is now located. It was owned by a British aristocrat, son of the Marchioness of Waterford, a family that could trace its lineage back to William the Conqueror. He was one of five brothers and, being an adventurous type, headed for North America, where he set up two ranches in Mexico. He was known to all as Lord Beresford and, although he was labelled a remittance man, he was good at business, but had very little use for convention. His love partner was a black woman by the name of Flora Wolfe. Beautiful, loyal, affectionate, and shrewd, she did much to help build his fortune. Neither one of them made any bones about not being officially married.

Shortly after Beresford's two thousand cattle and six hundred horses arrived by rail, a Texas cowboy by the name of Hansel Gordon Jackson, better known as "Happy Jack" Jackson, came into the country with a shipment of cattle for Gordon, Ironside, and Faires, a big ranching company. Jackson was an Irishman born in South Carolina or Georgia who grew up with cattle. He drifted onto the Mexico ranch in 1903, where Beresford hired him as foreman.

Tough and gruff, he ruled his cowboy crew with an iron hand, though he was fair and worked harder than any of them. Though buried deep behind his stern countenance, his sense of humour was strong, and he had a penchant for going on periodic drunks of enormous proportions and was adept at scaring the hell out of everybody by shooting flies indoors with his Colt .45 revolver. He must have had very specially constructed ears, for history makes no mention of his being deaf. Shooting inside a building is ordinarily a first-class way for anyone to damage his hearing.

Lord Beresford obviously appreciated Happy Jack's ability to get things done, as well as his eccentricities, for they were together for three years before Beresford got wiped out in a train accident while journeying between his farflung ranches. After several years of litigation by Flora Wolfe to lay claim to a fair portion of the Beresford property, she received an out-of-court settlement of modest proportions. She moved south to more familiar surroundings and the Mexico ranch was no more.

With all the cattle, horses, and cowboys gone, Happy Jack had nobody to swear at but the government, for when he filed for a homestead on the site of the headquarters, he was required to pay $125 for the "improvements." "I built the goddamn thing in the first place," he swore, as is recorded by Ed Gould in his book *Ranching*.

Michael Klassen, another chronicler of Happy Jack's life story, by way of a motion picture titled *Hell Ain't a Mile Off*, wrote an article prior to the movie script which tells at considerable length of a diary kept sporadically by Happy Jack from 1908 to 1942, when he was found dead in his cabin at the age of eighty.

Lois Valli, a neighbour, wrote: "It was very well known that Happy Jack drank a great deal at times, and who could blame him? He lived like a coyote, or worse. Though I think he did it because he chose to. Happy Jack was there on his own quite a bit you know. I think he drank from pure loneliness."

In a page of his diary written in his usual cryptic, humorous, though somewhat bitter way on the blank pages of *Dr. Chase's Almanac*, he left a record of his years in that big, lonely, semi-desert land, which is salutary and very rare in western history, where the old-time cowboys played such a big part. He complained, poked fun at himself, directed pointed barbs at the politicians of his time, and damned the heat and cold and drought that beset him and his livestock there in the Deadlodge Canyon Badlands.

For instance, he wrote:

1909. Aug. 17 crossed cattle (over the river)
Aug. 18 Buck & The Kid Was Here
Aug. 23 Hot as hell every day
Sep. 5 Still Mosquitoes Plenty
Oct. 14 Blue Heifer Had a Calf
15 Worked Cattle Branded Calves
19 Cowboys shipped
20 Cowboys Quit
Nov. 1 Branded Horses 13 Head
Nov. 15 8 Below Turned Horses Out
Dec. 1 Mosquitoes is Played Out

Another excerpt says:

1913. Apr. 20 Drunk
21 Drunk
22 Drunk
23 Drunk

24 Red Had a Calf 8 Days over

25 Still Drunk

26 Sick

27 Dam Sick

28 Worse

29 Very Feeble

30 Long Live Booze. Hurrah for Hell

The building of a railway into the area, the installation of a ferry crossing the river close by Happy Jack's cabin, and a flood of homesteaders all contributed toward taking away the prairie wilderness. The United Farmers of Alberta (UFA) government, the temperance movement, and suffragettes such as Nellie McClung, were all held responsible for his unnecessary discomfort. The vote for women was won and Prohibition took the bottle away from all, much to Happy Jack's disgust. He wrote:

1916. Mar. 31 No Booze this Month. Sounds like Prohibition.

1916. Jul. 1 Prohibition Starts. Hurrah for Hell

2 Damn Drunk for Several Days

31 Damn Prohibition

Aug. 3 One Bottle Thank the Lord

12 One More Bottle

27 Damn Prohibition

Sep. 30 Good old Prohibition Still in Force

    My Title for a Jug

Oct. 26 Pretty Drunk cost $8.00

28 Drunk as Hell

30 Hurrah for Prohibition

People couldn't make a living farming in that country, as Happy Jack told them at every opportunity, and one by one they left until he had the country pretty much to himself again.

The latter years of the 1920s were tough and lonesome for him, but only a portion of what was to come during the Hungry Thirties when the Great Depression took hold. The hot winds blew up the dust in clouds hiding the sun at many times and buried the abandoned homesteaders' cabins to their windows in great drifts.

Happy Jack's journal notes:

1931. Apr. 7 Cyclone all Day

9 Wind Wind Damn the Wind

17 Worst Wind Storm yet

27 The Ground the Bottles and all is Damn Dry

30 Good old Prohibition Days Wind Wind Every Day

1933. Jan. 31 Depression Still Here

Feb. 28 Hurrah for Depression Long May She Wave

Mar. 31 Long Live Depression Gets Worse

June 23 Hot & Dry God Damn the World by sections

Happy Jack was not the only one looking for a way to improve things, and when William Aberhart came along with promises of better times via the path of Social Credit and a monthly stipend to all, he likely looked on with some hope. But when the Social Credit party swept the election, he was no longer so optimistic. In fact he rejected Social Credit. In an October 1935 newspaper interview, the old cowboy simply stated, "I don't believe 'em. This country isn't ready for fanatics to run its affairs." Premier Aberhart's wild promise of a monthly payment of twenty-five dollars in credit per month to every citizen of the province to cover their basic necessities never came to anyone. Where he once wrote, "My kingdom for a bottle," he now wrote, "My kingdom for a basic dividend." In his journal he waxed satirical and sarcastic.

He was getting old, and when he sold his cows on June 23, 1938, he was truly alone except for a few horses he didn't bother ever to round up. In his last few years, his neighbours looked after him. Warren Fulton and his family, his closest neighbours, made sure that he had enough to eat and helped him all they could. When he died alone in his cabin after thirty-five years on the Mexico ranch, he left a legacy of a tough, unbending, lonely record of his life there – and his loaded Colt .45 was near at hand.

His passing is a milepost marking the end of an era; he may not have done anything great but he survived in about as tough a place to make a living as there is in all the cow country of Alberta, where the winters are freezing cold and the summers are burning hot. Nobody lives on the Mexico ranch today and there is little left to mark its location except the weathered old cabin and some other buildings that show bullet holes where Happy Jack shot flies, and perhaps an empty whiskey bottle or two hidden in the weeds.

By the River

I t is a part of the tributary system of the mighty Saskatchewan River, which sprawls across the plains of western Canada like a great fallen tree with its branches and twigs caught among the crags and spires of the Rockies. It is one of the smaller rivers that hungrily collect the waters from melting snowfields and glaciers and in turn feed them to the main stream. It has roared and rumbled and murmured sleepily in moods revolving with the seasons for many thousands of years, while countless hordes of living things drank of its life-giving wetness, waded and swam in it, and sometimes drowned in its flood. It has been there since the huge masses of the Ice Age began to retreat and the Great Plains begin to green up after millennia of frozen silence.

The first drops oozed from the melting ice gathering in pools, and when these pools could hold no more, little rills spilled out to play and join on lower ground to form creeks, which in turn gathered and gambolled noisily with more creeks to mingle in an even bigger stream. So the river was born, predestined by the sun to flow down across the low places in the land, carving the country

From *Trails of a Wilderness Wanderer* (1978)

into hills and valleys to fit its need for running space, and influencing every creeping, walking, running, and flying thing living within its drainage.

Unlike a river, a man is born holding his luck in his two hands, good or bad, instinctively squalling in his helplessness. Regardless of the influence of the sun on his destiny, he has no control in choosing his sire or his dam, and nothing whatever to say about the general geography of his birthplace. His childhood – the beginning rills of his life – can be bank-full with joy and love, or maybe drowned in creeks of tears and misery. He may die before he has the chance to taste of living or any part of the independence of choosing his own trail; but regardless of what happens to him, he will owe his life to water, and unless fate decrees that it be melted from a polar ice cap, that water will come from a river. So the lives of men and rivers are tied inexorably and inseparably together, and nothing can change that relationship.

I was born luckier than most – close to this beautiful river in southwest Alberta, first of a second generation born in the same place. The river is called the St. Mary's, and, needless to say, the name is much younger than the stream.

My grandfather came here from the east across the oceans of grass with an early survey party. He came most of the way by Red River cart, before there was any railroad, part of a group of government surveyors preceding the flood of settlers to follow. The year was 1882.

He travelled by boat and rail from Ottawa to Winnipeg, which was then a young city, taking root around the old Hudson's Bay Company trading site of Fort Garry. There he bought a saddle, a .22-calibre single-shot rifle, and a .45-calibre Business Sharps, a somewhat lighter version of the Big Fifty Sharps, the favourite rifle of the buffalo hunters. He already had a 12-bore muzzle-loading shotgun, so his arsenal was complete, and along with an axe and a few other necessities, he had the basic tools of the frontiersman.

The head of the railroad at that time was Brandon, a few miles across the prairies west of Winnipeg, and it was here that the party outfitted itself with horses and Red River carts to take it the rest of the way, to the foot of the Rocky Mountains.

The Red River cart was an ingenious and practical contrivance, if not very beautiful, which was invented by the Métis, the French half-breeds of the Red River Valley. It was a two-wheeled contraption made of tough cottonwood or aspen tied and lashed together with rawhide, sometimes without a nail or a bit of iron in its entire make-up. It was a sort of compromise between an Indian travois and the heavy American freight wagons drawn by bull teams. The wheels were held together and shod with rawhide, which shrinks and grows iron-hard with drying. The rawhide carry-all, slung in a stake basket over the single axle, held the load. It could be drawn by one horse working between shafts or two pulling on each side of a tongue.

No blacksmith or wheelwright was needed when a Red River cart broke down. Grandfather once told me that the only things required to make repairs were a sharp axe, a good knife, a rifle, and some native craftsmanship. The axe and the knife were used to carve the replacement piece from the first suitable tree encountered. The rifle was employed to shoot a buffalo, from which the necessary rawhide binding was obtained. When buffalo grew scarce, other kinds of hide were used. Most of the time the axles ran dry, for grease collected sand. They ran wood on wood, creaking, howling, and groaning across the prairies with such a din that a string of carts could be heard long before they were sighted. Wet weather was not good for Red River carts, for prolonged soaking made the rawhide go slack and then the vehicles tended to fall apart. They were good for fording streams, however, for they floated like corks and were light enough to be manageable behind swimming horses.

By the time the railroad reached the country just east of the Rockies, my grandfather had taken up a ranch on the bank of the St. Mary's River at the fork by its confluence with Pothole Creek just across from the Blood Indian reserve. The country was still a wilderness then, without a wire fence between the North Pole and Texas. But changes were in the wind, for no longer did the rifles of the buffalo hunters boom. The buffalo were mostly gone except for a few scattered and bewildered stragglers and a herd of wood bison in the north. It was cow and horse country, where the old-time cowboy was king.

It was a time of swift transition, for although only a few short years had passed since the first white man had settled here, by the time I was born the plains were mostly cut up by wire fences. Farmers were turning over the deep prairie sod – ploughing under the rich buffalo grass, and the square bulk of grain elevators lifting against the blue of the big sky spoke of the fertility of the soil and sealed the end of the kingdom of the cowboy.

Only the river still swept eastward, unchanged and free. I have an early memory of taking a walk one afternoon with a great-aunt when I was still a very small boy. We went out across the flats and climbed up onto the rim of the plains overlooking the valley. We went quietly, without much talk, for my aunt was very deaf, so that it required a shout to make her hear. She was content to say only enough to keep me from falling in a washout or getting into trouble with a prickly-pear cactus. Our relationship was placid, wherein we communicated by looks and touch of hands, and were content with it.

We climbed up a long hogback ridge to the edge of the prairie above to stand looking back down at the ranch buildings crouched in a scattering of cottonwoods and willows. Under the afternoon sun the river looked like a long silver lariat thrown out in careless curves along the floor of the valley. It came sweeping around a bend at the foot of a high bank a mile above the buildings, slid down a long rapid to a bend at the forks, and then went glinting and dancing along to finally lose itself behind a jutting whaleback ridge away down-valley.

As far as we could see up and down the river, cattle and horses dotted the slopes and flats. Most of them wore my grandfather's brand.

The far rim beyond the valley was flat and on the same level as the spot where we stood. Beyond it, far off, the mountains lifted tall and deep purple in the afternoon sun, somehow mysterious; big and wonderful in a country that was so flat.

Dominant, standing out by itself from the ranks of peaks, was a mountain looking like a great square block. My mother had told me it was called Old Chief, and now I stood gazing at it, wondering as usual why it looked so little like an Indian. My reverie was broken by the sound of Grandfather's big touring car coming along the trail from town. He brought it to a stop in a swirl of yellow dust to pick us up for a ride back to the buildings. For me, riding in that car was a transport to heaven, tremendously exciting, full of strange smells, noises, speed, and great surges of power. I can still see Grandfather sitting with the steering wheel clasped in his powerful hands, his inevitable bent-stem pipe gripped in his teeth and his hat sitting on the back of his head. His craggy face glowed with good nature and enjoyment and his eyes gleamed with humour. Being a trained machinist, he was mechanically inclined and owned one of the first cars in the country.

Grandfather fitted into this big country, and when he came he planned to stay. The ranch buildings were standing proof of his intentions. They were constructed of solid concrete and stone with walls and gables a good foot thick. The concrete had been manufactured on the ranch in a kiln he constructed, which had been fired with coal dug close to the site. His method was simple. He dug a chimney-like hole about eighteen feet deep close to the edge of a perpendicular cutbank, which he lined with fieldstone.

Digging into this hole from the bottom of the bank, he installed a burning chamber and heavy grates made of railroad iron. The kiln was filled with chunks of almost pure limestone picked up in the immediate area. A supply of coal was dug from a five-foot seam exposed by the river about ten steps from the fire-hole. So he burned lime and manufactured the basic ingredients of concrete from what lay around him on the land. All of the buildings – even the chicken house – were built like fortresses, strong and weatherproof. Some of these buildings still stand in use, proof of the character of the man who built them.

My father built his cottage the same way. It stood about two hundred yards across a coulee from my grandparents' house, and it was here that my brother John and I started out on our respective life trails. Although I did not know it then, mine was destined to follow the river to its headwaters away up among the high crags of the Rockies, and then to wander all over the length and breadth of the wilderness country stretching between the water-carved canyons of Idaho's Salmon River country to vast northern tundra prairies of the Alaska and Yukon Arctic.

Those first steps on the old ranch were a prelude to adventure – not altogether a unique thing, for life is an adventure for all of us. It matters not where we start it, for it is still an adventure. Whether or not we enjoy it depends on some luck, but perhaps more on one's desire to understand and enjoy even the pesky things with which we become inevitably entangled. It is then that the ordinary ceases to be ordinary and the dull takes on a shine, for all things have a story to tell if uncovered and understood.

If someone were to ask me what was the most valuable thing I have inherited from my forebears, I would certainly not list property, but rather an ingrown curiosity about living things and a built-in desire to respect and enjoy the adventure of living. My luck in having an environment in which to fully grasp the fun of being alive made itself manifest early in the game. The everyday happenings at the beginning showed me this before I had walked very far, leaving impressions that still stand paramount.

There was the time I stood on the perimeter of the yard in front of the house, a small figure on the edge of a vast rolling sea of grass, watching in fascination the flickering, ribbon-like gambolling of a weasel. No other animal moves quite like a weasel, for it never walks but always runs, and the running is with a silken poetry of motion – a cadence of muscle and gleaming fur in search of prey.

The weasel was all around me, prying and sniffing into every hole and tuft of grass, paying me not the slightest attention beyond a sharp-eyed stare or two, although it came several times within inches of my bare toes. I did not realize at first that the weasel was hungry and hunting for a meal. All of a sudden it must have run into a mouth-watering scent coming downwind from a chicken coop between me and the house, for it paused with uplifted head and then streaked straight for it.

A fat old hen was living there with a clutch of newly hatched chicks, all placid and self-satisfied until hell arrived and the feathers began to fly. I ran to the coop to kneel and stare spellbound through its slatted front as the weasel began to massacre chicks with all the dispatch of a master killer.

My enchantment with this scene of murder and mayhem was suddenly interrupted by the indignant arrival of my mother carrying a broom. With an angry shriek she opened the coop, turned the survivors loose, and in the same motion took a swipe at the weasel. The little animal dodged the blow with neatness and promptly ran down a gopher hole nearby. The vigour of the blow broke the broom handle, but when the weasel stuck its head up out of the hole to shriek at Mother in return, she attacked it with what remained of the handle.

Now her weapon was much less unwieldy and her blows quick and accurate, but the weasel moved like flickering light, dodging every swing. The battle was resolved in a stalemate. In no way ready to give up, Mother gave me the club with instructions to keep the murdering little beast in the hole while she went for a bucket of water out of the rain barrel. Her strategy was to drown the weasel out into the open.

It took a lot of water before the hole filled up, leaving the weasel almost totally immersed except for its head and neck, but the little animal did not make the expected break for the open. It just stood eyeing us sharply and then opened its mouth to squall in defiance. Mother took a swift chop at him with her club. But as usual the weasel ducked like a flash, and the blow spent itself harmlessly. The animal's head came up again with a battle cry.

My father was out riding for stock that morning, so my mother was more or less left to her own devices to eliminate this raider of chicken coops. There is no telling which way the battle would have gone had not the hired man chosen this moment to unexpectedly appear.

It was his day off, and he was dressed in his Sunday best, complete with white shirt, blue serge suit, and polished boots – all ready for his visit to town. Taking in the situation at a glance, he volunteered his services.

"Just hold on a moment, ma'am," he said. "I'll get the boss's gun."

He went into the house and shortly reappeared, fumbling a fat red cartridge into the breech of the shotgun. Whatever his abilities as a hired man, they did not penetrate very far into the dynamics of ballistics and hydraulics, for without undue preamble, he walked right up to the hole. As Mother stepped quickly to one side, taking me with her, he deliberately aimed at the weasel at a range of perhaps three feet and blazed away.

It might be truthfully said that he fired into the hole and the next split second the hole fired at him; for what happens when an ounce and a quarter of closely bunched birdshot goes into a gopher tunnel full of water at that range is most impressive, to say the very least. The hired man was transformed into a blinded, dripping mess of mud and water mixed with fragments of weasel. He stood in shock, pawing at his face. A piece of bloody skin to which was attached the bedraggled tail of the weasel hung over one ear. He was a total wreck from head to foot.

My mother and I stood paralyzed, staring at him in wide-eyed astonishment. Then, as he began to partially recover, Mother suddenly covered her mouth with a corner of her apron and ran swiftly for the house. Meanwhile, he had opened the gun and ejected the spent shell. I saw it lying in the grass and picked it up to curiously examine it. It had an acrid smell of freshly burned powder – a somehow attractive odour that I sniffed with enjoyment as the hired man headed morosely for his quarters.

Ever since that day, when I see some uneducated pilgrim carelessly waving a gun around with no regard for himself or the innocent bystanders, I long to arrange for him to shoot at something in a gopher hole full of water. Nothing could possibly leave anyone with a more lasting impression of the destructive power of a loaded gun.

For some reason I sometimes still find myself sniffing absent-mindedly at the open end of a fired shell with unexplainable enjoyment along with a vivid memory of the weasel that took shelter in a hole.

Early life along the bank of the river was full of first-time things one remembers best. Someone once said that the three greatest adventures of life are being born, becoming married, and dying. Nobody has as yet commented on the comparative quality of the last from first-hand experience; but there are a lot of unlisted chapters in between worthy of mention. Certainly time and geography were kind to my brother and me, for just being born on the edge of the frontier when it was changing so rapidly was in itself something to see, and the seeing was greatly enhanced by being part of a family that had so much a part in it. Like all people, we had our share of disappointments, frustrations, hardships, and tragedy; but it was not a family characteristic to spend undue time dwelling in self-pity or indulging in the luxury of prolonged attempts to lay the blame for our misfortunes on others.

The river was an influence in its interminable journey downstream – always ready to provide us with water when we needed it, a boundary marker for the ranch on its western side, always moving, except in winter – a sound reminding us day and night of the inevitable journey of life. In summer the sound was like a lifting and falling lyric, sweeping down from between the hills. In winter the stream snapped and boomed in its shackles of ice, contracting and expanding in the changing temperatures. At break-up time in spring it put on a show to leave one shaken with the power of it; for as the warming sun rotted the ice and melting snow swelled the side streams running into it, there was a building up of pressure to a point of sudden bursting. At some hour of the day or night there would be a sudden cannonade of breaking ice that echoed off the banks, and like magic the whole surface of the river would be on the move with legions of ice blocks of every size, shape, and form, heaving, grinding, and gouging as they swept away downstream. Sometimes the blocks would jam, forming temporary dams that would back the water up, flooding bars and flats. Then the pressure would smash its way through and just as rapidly the waters would recede, leaving acres of stranded ice blocks high and dry – incongruous-looking baby icebergs lost from their element, crying sadly in the sun.

The river was a constant provider for men and stock, but it took its toll on the unwary, the young, and the inexperienced. Almost every year somewhere along its length there came a story of tragedy. The survivors were strong and fearless swimmers with a built-in brand of courage no longer so evident among prairie dwellers.

My father tells of an experience encountered at an age when most modern youth have never had to make a vital decision and take their exercise riding a machine.

In 1907 he and a cousin, Joe Bell, were coming back from a spring round-up in the Little Bow country. They were driving a gather of cattle wearing my grandfather's brand, as well as their *remuda* of eighteen or twenty saddle horses, one of which was packed with their warbags and bedrolls, when they ran into a flood. The rivers were out over their banks where they came to cross at the forks of the Waterton and the Belly, swimming deep from bank to bank with some flooded cottonwood timber in between. Waiting for the water to go down was out of the question, for the men's grub was running low and they were anxious to get home. So they took off their chaps and boots and tied them behind their saddles and made ready for a big swim.

First they drove the loose horses into the water and then the cattle. As they rode in behind the tail of their herd their saddle horses were at swimming depth in two steps. Both riders were ready, their cinches loosened as always before hitting deep water, for a tightly cinched saddle horse will sink. If their horses got into trouble, they could slip off and take the mount by the tail, for a horse can swim better this way and he can still be steered. Furthermore, when shore was reached the rider would be with his horse. Most drownings occurred when a man panicked and quit his horse or was not properly prepared for swimming water. But there was no trouble in this instance, and in no time they were across the raging flood. But they still had one more river to cross before they could sleep under a roof.

It was midnight when they drove their stock down off the hills to the edge of the St. Mary's, and it was in full flood. They had a choice of sleeping out in a steady drizzle in bedrolls soaked from the first crossing or heading into the river. Sopping bedrolls held small promise of comfort and it was too wet to build a fire and cook some supper, so again they drove the horses and cattle into the river and headed across. My father comments: "There is no more lonesome place in the world than swimming a flooded river at midnight, but we made it. We had good horses that had been swimming rivers since they were suckers." They had been swimming rivers since not long past being suckers themselves, which no doubt contributed to two successful crossings in one day; for indecision or fear could be fatal in such places, especially swimming in the dark of midnight.

When I was four years old and my brother John was still a babe in arms, my father moved us to a new ranch away up on a tributary called Drywood Creek at the foot of the Rockies. Here we came to know the mountains, and here the stream was small enough to wade most of the time, as well as being so icy cold that it gave us small chance to learn to swim. But we came back in summer to visit our grandparents and there we learned to swim in the river.

I remember standing on a ledge one day, just off the edge of deep water, fishing for whatever would take a minnow on a hook. Suddenly there was an explosion at the end of my line – a smashing jerk that almost tore the willow pole from my hands. Before I knew what was happening, I was thrown off balance and yanked bodily into the river over my head. I came up spluttering and spitting out river water, more surprised than scared, with the current sweeping me downstream along the foot of an almost perpendicular rocky bank. There was no place to grab hold and climb out for some distance and no choice but to swim. Up to that point all the swimming I had done was dog-paddling across quiet places where I could touch bottom with my toes. This was for keeps. I kicked and aimed for a point jutting out into the river downstream. It seemed like no time till I had a solid hold and was pulling myself out on the bank mighty glad to be free of the river.

My rod had disappeared and I never did find out what kind of monster had grabbed my hook.

When I came into the house a bit later wet to the top of my head, dripping water all over the floor, my grandmother eyed me sharply and asked what had happened. If it had been my mother I might have lied a bit to save her some worry and fuss, but it was no use lying to my grandmother. She had a second sight – a kind of magic vision that allowed her to see right through people, especially boys, with whom she had accumulated an uncommon amount of experience.

So I told her. "A big fish grabbed my hook and pulled me in the river."

"Hmm," said my grandmother. "How did you get out?"

"I swam out," I told her proudly.

She looked at me keenly and silently for a moment before saying, "You must practise swimming until you can swim anywhere. It would be very difficult for me to explain to your mother if one of you drowned."

There were no warnings, no fuss. Just plain common-sense advice from a woman who knew what it meant to survive on the frontier.

I was ten that summer and my brother was six. Being four years younger he learned to do everything just about four years sooner than I. Following Grandmother's advice we practised swimming till we were worked down to rope-thin, sun-browned little savages. Then one day we tackled the river all alone.

I will never forget that swim.

It was a blazing hot day when we came to the edge of a big sandbar between a strip of willows and the water. We stood looking at the water slipping past, cool and inviting in lazy swirls. Across the river at the foot of a three-hundred-foot-high bank, deep, cool shade beckoned where a sandy cove cut a bay into the bank. Without any talk we slipped out of our clothes to plunge into the current and began to swim across.

At this point the river was about seventy-five yards wide with a fairly easy current. We were halfway across before we began to feel the effort, but it didn't bother us at first. My brother was swimming a bit upstream and just ahead of me, with his feet stirring the water about even with my shoulder.

Another few yards brought the far bank closer but then we hit faster current and the distance began to tell. My arms felt heavy and hard to pull through the water. For a long moment I wondered if we were going to make it and for a second I faltered in what could have built into big trouble. The difference between being obliterated and surviving the first real test of danger is the ability to recognize it, dodge, and keep going. John was still ahead of me, his stroke still steady but slower. The current had swung him past me so that he was drifting downstream with it. I turned to follow, picking up my stroke. Almost magically the going was much easier and then I felt sand under my knees. We were across.

There was an unforgettable feeling of relief and triumph all mixed up. We didn't have much to say to each other for want of the wind to say it. We knew that we had been flirting with disaster. We sat naked on the sand, shivering a bit, hugging our knees and soberly contemplating the way back. It was one thing to swim the river, but now we were on the far side without our clothes and no place to go. It never occurred to us to just stay there and wait till someone came looking for us. That would be an unforgivable concession to fear. We didn't even contemplate the possibility that we might be in a very real predicament. We just sat and looked at the river going by, wondering how it was going to be on the way back.

But the river had taught us something valuable, for when we were rested and ready for the return, we walked upstream a ways to a little gravel bar jutting out into the current, and from its point we began to swim side by side on a long slant downstream. Coming back was so easy we hardly took a deep breath. As we put on our clothes, enjoying the heat of the sun, we both knew we could swim. What was more important, perhaps, was that we had learned to go with the river and not fight it.

Learning in the Horse Corral

After I quit school, not all of my experience dealt with wandering in the mountains, fishing, hunting, and trapping. Dad always had a bunch of horses, which ran free in the mountains — mostly brood mares and colts, including those younger horses that weren't gentled or trained for any kind of work. There is nothing that will match the sight of a bunch of wild, free-roaming horses running, their eyes flashing and nostrils flaring, their tails and manes streaming in the wind, and the drumroll of their hoofs stirring up a cloud of dust. I did a lot of work with them, both in and out of the horse corral.

My brother and I were practically on horseback before we could walk, sitting in the saddle in front of Dad as he rode a gentle horse doing ranch chores. We grew up with the smell of leather, dust, and sweat in our noses. During the summers we just about lived on horseback. There wasn't a kid in the country that didn't have one or two horses for his or her own use. These carried us for miles as we rambled the wilds exploring, fishing, visiting back and forth, and doing ranch chores. Most of us rode

From *Memoirs of a Mountain Man* (1984)

bareback, using saddles only when work required them. It was a wonderful, carefree life, and nothing had a more profound impact on it than horses.

For that matter, no other animal has had such an influence on the cultural and social development of man down through history from the time some enterprising caveman tamed the first one. Certainly no animal contributed more to the opening and developing of western North America than the horse. Those early explorers and trappers rode them, drove them in harness, packed them, and on occasion of dire need for food to keep from starving, even ate them. Those of us who rode when the west was young know that at one time or another we would have been dead without the strength and speed of the horses we rode over rough, wild country.

Like most boys growing up on a ranch, we had aspirations to be cowboys and we had plenty of opportunity to learn. We also had Dad for an example of what a real cowboy could do, for as I have said, he knew how to ride and use a lariat. Like every kid raised on a ranch, we had lariats, and we practised on about everything. I remember one rancher remarking that his boys roped anything that stuck up off the ground and that "even the damn fence posts duck when they ride by." We roped chickens, dogs, geese, cats, calves, and sometimes each other.

Once when I was pretty young my mother got me all dressed up one Sunday to meet some expected guests, and I was wandering around morosely with nothing to do and feeling uncomfortable when Dad's saddle rope caught my eye. He did not like anyone using his rope, but I took it off its peg and began throwing loops at the end of a rail sticking out from the corner of the corral. Then a big steer came to lick salt with the milk cows not far away. With no real intention of catching him, I sneaked up and threw a loop at him, more to spook him than anything else. He threw his head up and caught it beautifully right around his horns.

Whereupon he wheeled and headed for timber, and I hung on for want of something better coming to mind. In two jumps he was going at a dead run, dragging me along like a wet saddle blanket on the end of the rope. The ride didn't last long; I hit something that knocked my wind out and I burned my hands on the rope. When I got to my feet, I was a mixture of cow manure and stinkweed juice from head to foot, and the steer was long gone.

Dad was watching the whole misadventure and gave me a blistering chewing-out, while I stood sadly inspecting my burned hands. Then he saddled up his horse to get his rope, while I headed for the house to collect another scolding and get cleaned up. It was a lesson that fooling around with a lariat was about as smart as playing with a loaded gun; sometimes it was a lot easier to catch something than to turn it loose.

The lessons learned in range work often came unannounced and completely unexpected, and were the kind that lasted for a lifetime. I was still pretty young, maybe ten or twelve, when Dad and I had a run-in with a bull that was the kind of milestone on the road of experience that is never forgotten. One of our bulls had gone visiting a neighbour's herd, where he was making a nuisance of himself, so we rode out to bring him back.

We cut him out of their cattle without any trouble, but the closer we got to home, the more he tried to break back. When we got him to our pasture gate, he suddenly wheeled and charged my horse, which jumped out of his way, and the bull headed for the timber on the dead run. In a flash Dad's rope was down and a loop shot out to snap around the bull's horns when he was about two jumps from the trees. Dad's big saddle horse tucked his rump down and set his feet to stop the rampaging animal, but the offside latigo broke, whereupon Dad and his saddle shot over the horse's ears. Dad hung onto his dallies and still had both feet in the stirrups as he flew out of sight into the aspens.

Then all hell broke loose. Timber began to break, the bull was roaring, and profanity was crackling like red-hot chunks of iron hitting cold water. Then out of the general uproar came shouted orders for me to come and tie up the bull. I was scared and wanted no part of this mix-up, but Dad was in trouble. Besides, by the sound of him it was no time to hesitate, so I sneaked in and sized up the battleground from behind a big tree.

Dad was under his saddle still hanging onto his dallies, and the saddle was jammed into the base of a tree. At the other end of the rope the bull had circled another tree two or three times and was so mad he was fairly howling as he tried to get at us with his horns. It was a new rope strong enough to hold him, which was fortunate. I got hold of the loose end and tied some wraps on another tree. Then Dad slipped his dallies and I took up the slack as he scrambled up and away.

Dad got his horse and fashioned a latigo with one of his bridle reins. Soon he had his rig cinched down solid again, and then he came to take control of the bull. When they came out, the bull promptly charged his horse, but he sidestepped, and away they went on the dead run with the bull in the lead.

Then I saw something I had never seen before – a trick very few people know how to do now. He rode up about even with the bull's hindquarters, threw slack rope over his back on the offside, and then rode off at an angle at top speed. When the bull stepped into the rope and the slack came out of it, the bull's legs were swept from under him; he left the ground completely and took a half-turn in the air to come down like a wagonload of bricks. The wind was knocked clear out of him, so he couldn't get up for a while. When he did scramble back on his feet, all the fight had gone out of him.

It wasn't long after that Dad started me heeling calves for branding. We were a bit short-handed and were just cleaning up the tag end of that year's calf crop. John was old enough to look after the irons and the fire, so I suddenly found myself promoted to roper

— a job that usually goes to the top hand. Since I was too short in the leg to reach Dad's stirrups, I just poked my toes through his stirrup leathers and used his horse.

This kind of roping requires flipping the loop on edge under a calf's belly, so that when he steps ahead, both hind feet go into it. Then the roper snaps the loop shut with a flip of his wrist, takes his dallies around the saddle horn, and heads for the fire. There, two wrestlers grab the calf, one by the front and the other at the tail, throw it, and hold it for branding — and castrating, if it is a bull.

Most of my practising with a rope had been done from the ground, although some of it had been done from a horse on our gentle milk cow's calves, so I missed some. But that big horse knew his business. He helped me every way he could and made me look a lot better than I really was. Feeling about ten feet tall when I dragged in that first calf, I went back for another. When twenty had been branded, my arm was getting mighty tired. By noon it felt as if it was about to fall off, and I was having more trouble making my loop behave.

But Dad was patient and let me finish the job. The last calf was wild and foxy. After a half-dozen misses I got mad and threw the loop over his head. Dad was leaning against the corral sharpening his knife as he coolly surveyed my catch skidding in close to the fire, stiff-legged, with the rope on the wrong end of him. "You better get off and show us how to throw a calf with the rope on his south end," he said.

So I got down and started up the rope for that scrappy animal, feeling as though I had put myself out on a limb and somebody was about to saw it off. The first thing he did was jump on my foot with a sharp hoof and I wanted to kill him. With a short left-handed hold on the rope by his neck, I reached over his back with the other and grabbed his flank. He jumped again, and more out of pure luck than good management I heaved at exactly the right moment. He went down flat on his side with a grunt, with me still hanging on and my knee planted hard on his ribs.

I was feeling mean and raunchy, and without even thinking, I said, "Now if somebody will come flat-ass this sonofabitch, I'll go unsaddle my horse!"

A neighbour who was helping snorted through his nose as he grabbed the calf by the hind leg and sat down behind it. Somebody else took it by the front leg and knelt on its neck. I took my rope off and was about halfway across the corral when, suddenly feeling appalled at being so cheeky, I sneaked a look back past the horse trailing behind me. Dad was standing with his hat tipped back with a half-surprised, half-amused look. But he never said a word. I guess he knew how a kid feels when he is played out and hungry enough to bite a skunk.

Part of our work involved keeping track of those loose horses and rounding them up twice a year for branding and gelding the colts, and cutting out some for gentling. Getting those wild old range mares down out of the peaks was an education of a nature few people ever encounter any more. It called for some wild riding. It also trained us to read tracks, for the horses had to be found in a vast expanse of very rough, heavily timbered country that was rocky and steep. Finding them when there was snow on the ground wasn't very difficult, but the footing was poor then, and it was hard for even the best saddle horses to stay on their feet.

We would scout around until we found some fairly fresh sign, and work out the tracks until we finally spotted the bunch we wanted. Then John and I took the time to contrive some kind of strategy – what amounted to figuring a way to get them home without losing them. They knew the country better than we did and the old lead mare was plenty foxy. If she got the jump on us somewhere, we had to start all over again, and she quite often made fools of us. The trick was to be close enough when we jumped them to keep them in sight and together. If we ever lost track of them, even for a minute, it was usually all over for that day, for they knew how to hide and could run like the wind.

We would jump them off some steep meadow on a mountainside, yelling like a couple of wild Indians to keep them a bit distracted till we got them lined out, and the country they usually chose was no bridle path. We had to figure ahead on what they would do when they reached certain places and be ready to turn them. We took turns, one riding behind and the other taking one side or the other to be in position to head them off if they made a break.

Our saddle horses were grain-fed and hard, so we had some advantage, but that didn't lessen the exertion. Some of the rides we made after that wild bunch had all the action and more than the most reckless rider could expect. How we managed to avoid broken bones is still something of a mystery to me. We rode by balance, and it was some job to stay with our mounts as they plunged and wove down mountainsides, across ravines, and through the timber. We often got skinned up and bruised, even though our horses were good at missing trees and anything else that might gouge our legs.

One day I was riding flat-out to head the bunch down a slope along a fence toward an open gate. There was a clump of willows coming straight at us and I set myself for my horse to jump it as he usually did. But this day it must have looked too high, for when he got to it, he made a quick dodge around it, and I all but left him. With only one boot touching my saddle I went over the willow with my reins in my hand, expecting a hard fall, but my horse ducked back under me and I grabbed a handhold that got me back where I belonged. My horse never missed a stride and we got the bunch through the gate.

Another time when we were running a bunch in snow I came down off a bluff into some timber, going like the wind, when my horse saw the bunch and made a break to cut back toward them.

He turned so fast that his feet skidded. He stayed right side up, but I lost a stirrup and flew out of the saddle at high velocity to land flat on my back in the soft snow. It broke my fall, but when I stood up, I saw two little tree stumps as sharp as needles – one on each side within six inches of where I landed. Just a little bit either way and I would have been skewered.

Back came the horses with John *ki-yi*-ing on their tails and I was too busy to think about it.

John, though four years younger, was a superlative rider capable of sticking like a burr to the saddle in the roughest kind of going, but he had his share of falls. One spring, we were bringing the wild bunch down off Drywood Mountain along the steep-pitched top of a hogback ridge flanking a ravine full of hard snow. The horses ran down to a spot where the draw narrowed to a cut choked with snow. There they slowed down to a walk, stepped gingerly across a strip of hard ice, and went hightailing back up the mountain. John was ahead of me on a fast little mare, and he turned her out across the snow slope to head them off. She stepped on some slushy ice and fell sprawling.

They must have slid a hundred yards before they stopped. At first John was on the low side, but she rolled clear over him. When they finally stopped, he was sitting on the high side gasping for breath, with a shovelful of cold snow inside his shirt. He wasn't even shaken up or scratched, but he sure was wet from head to foot.

Sometimes now I go back into that country for a look at some of the places we rode on the dead run and it makes my hair stand on end. Recalling the wilderness and the excitement of it – two kids flirting with a bone-smashing wreck every jump on those steep slopes – quickens the blood even yet. Those who have never ridden mountain country after wild horses really haven't lived.

When the snaky old sorrel mare that led that bunch of broncos was about sixteen years old, I decided to halter-break her. Cutting her alone into a small circular bronc corral, I rode in with her and threw a loop over her head. She fought like a tiger till she choked herself down. Letting her up, I kept working on her till she got too tired to fight any more – or at least it appeared that way. Slipping off my horse and talking to her all the time, I walked real easy up the rope. All of a sudden she exploded, striking at me with her front teeth and narrowly missing, then whirling to kick. I threw my weight on the rope and checked her, but she was boiling with a killing rage. It took me a long time to get my rope off her. It was no use trying to gentle that one; she had run free too long.

There were lots of tricks in gentling a horse. We needed them, because the horses were four and five years old when we started on them in those days. When we were young and just as green as the colts we worked with, Dad gave us yearlings and two-year-olds, but when we got our growth we worked with all ages. I can still see him sitting on the fence watching us make a first ride on a new colt. "Hang and rattle, kid!" he would yell. "Hang and rattle!"

Like all kinds of work of this nature, there are easy ways and hard ways, and the hard ways are rough on men and horses. More than once I have taken a green unbroken bronc and if he had the character to respond to gentle treatment, I could be riding him around the corral bareback in a fairly short time. But then there was the kind that didn't care about anything but running the ridges. Strangely enough these generally made the best horses, but it sometimes took a fight to subdue them. This is not to say their spirit was broken; they had to learn to conform to the wishes of the rider, but without losing their spirit.

Character is every bit as complex in animals as it is in people. No two individual horses are alike, and for some reason you have to vary the gentling approach to some extent to get the desired response. This is particularly true with saddle horses, because you are always closer to a saddle horse, physically and mentally.

One of the best saddle horses I ever rode was one who did not like to be patted or stroked. He was as thoroughly independent as an individual can get. He was nimble on his feet, smart, and incredibly tough. I once rode him fifty miles in a day over some rough country and he was still going strong. When I unsaddled him I couldn't resist patting him on the neck. He chucked his nose and gave me a look that as much as said, "Cut out the damn nonsense and bring something to eat." But when I first rode him, he would give me a hard session of dirty, crooked bucking almost every time I got on him.

I never used a trip rope or Spanish hobbles, as some bronc riders did. If a horse tried to buck, the rider would yank his front feet away and roll him over. It worked, if the rider didn't get caught under the falling horse. If he did, he could get badly injured.

Others used a four-way hobble with ankle straps on each foot and short chains leading to a central ring. A green bronc was turned loose in the corral with these tied on and of course if it tried to jump, it fell. It was a good way to teach a horse to stand for saddling and mounting if you were up against a whole string of snaky wild ones. But there was always a chance of injury to the horse unless the hobble was rigged properly.

There are very few horses that refuse to respond to kind treatment and patient handling, which was my father's method and also mine. His motto was: Never punish a horse from the ground. If he needs some discipline to show him who is boss, do it from the saddle.

Many people who gentled horses had problems because they failed to relate to the horse. One of the finest horsemen I ever knew said, "If you don't know more than the horse, you ain't going to teach him much." In part, that means understanding and being able to crawl inside his hide and think like him. The craft and skill of being a good horse trainer isn't learned overnight – it

takes years, and even then one runs into problems never encountered before.

I broke my first horse to ride from scratch when I was fifteen,
and I probably learned a good deal more than the bronc in the
process. She was a nervous but responsive and intelligent filly –
not very pretty, but well put together and tough as rawhide. Inside
a week I was working cattle with her. In another week, she was
coming to me to be caught.

A green bronc can learn a bad habit just as quick or quicker
than it can learn a good one. Let a horse get away with something
and it will try it again. I traded for a horse one time – a pretty
dappled grey mare that was gentle and nice to rein, as long as you
were sitting in the middle of her. Getting on her was something
else. Just as soon as your weight came on the stirrup to mount her,
she would make a big jump and then run. I tried hauling her head
around close to me and then slipping into the saddle, which was
some better but a long way from good.

One day I walked her into my lariat loop, passed the rope over
her shoulder just forward of the saddle, stopped her, and then got
off. Getting a good grip on the rope, I booted the stirrup and
when she jumped, I stepped back and laid my weight on it to
throw her. I rolled her tail over tea-kettle, but in the process my
boot heel slipped into a gopher hole and I badly sprained a knee.
The experience did something for the horse but very little for me.
Thirty-five years later that knee still bothers me on occasion,
which is mostly why I remember that horse so well.

Sometimes knowing a trick or two doesn't hurt, and can save
a lot of hard work and rough riding. I bought three horses one
time, and to get them home I had to trail them across some miles
of rough country through timber. They had been used to running
together, so keeping them in a bunch wasn't likely to be much of
a problem, but they knew the mountains, and keeping them in
sight wasn't going to be easy. My chances of losing them were big,

for they weren't halter-broken, and I sat down against a corral post to think about it. The man who had sold them to me didn't have much to offer and was too busy to help.

Then I remembered something an old cowboy had told me. Looking around the ranch shop, I picked up three rusty old nuts about big enough to fit three-quarter-inch bolts. Then I went back to the corral and shook a loop out on my lariat. Roping each horse by the front feet, I threw and tied them down. Then I braided a big iron nut into the long foretop mane of each one. When they got up, they put on quite a show, bounding around and pawing the air when those iron nuts banged them on the forehead. But horses are smart animals and it wasn't very long before they figured out how to travel without hammering themselves.

When I turned them out of the gate, they ran and snorted for a way, but shortly they slowed down so they could control those nuts. It wasn't a very fast trip, but my saddle horse and I had it easy. By the time we got home, those horses were travelling with their noses out like elk, and going real smooth.

PART TWO

WITH PACKHORSE
AND RIFLE

Good hunting stories have a way of kidnapping a reader's imagination. Before you know it, Andy has you stalking big game. To reach a bedded buck, you remove your boots and tiptoe across broken rocks, your heart in your throat, afraid the slightest sound will alert your wary quarry. He doesn't disappoint when it comes to capturing the spine-chilling experience of coming on a grizzly unexpected.

Being an outfitter is more than simply escorting clients into the field. A large part of it is knowing your horses and, as Andy humorously describes, dealing with their sometimes eccentric behaviour.

Pack-Train Personalities

A mos was all alone, and worried. His ears wobbled at half-mast and he nickered unhappily. Threading his way at a fast walk through down logs and big timber, he followed a trail winding down through the Wall Lake basin amidst some of the roughest country in the British Columbia Rockies. The little runnels of sweat that darkened the black coat along his neck and shoulders emphasized his anxiety; actually, the day was cool and the going downhill. His instinct was to gallop, but he went at a walk, his four white stockings flashing. Holding his blazed face low, he sniffed for scent of his friends. Cautiously, he eased the bulky boxes slung on each side of his packsaddle around snags and trees, as though he knew what they contained. Anyone seeing him would have pronounced him lost, but this was not true. The rest of the pack train was lost, and he was looking for it.

Meanwhile, miles ahead, I led the pack train out of the timber onto the open beach of Cameron Lake, on the Alberta side of the Continental Divide. Turning in the saddle, I checked the forty-horse lineup behind me, which I was able to see from end to end

From *Field and Stream* (August 1961)

for the first time since breaking camp that morning. Immediately I missed Amos. A quick powwow with my wranglers revealed that no one had seen him since we had taken the trail from our Wall Lake camp. With sinking heart I remembered tying up his halter shank and turning him loose when we'd packed him, so that he could graze while we loaded the other horses. Obviously he had wandered out of earshot of the bells and had not heard us leave. There was no telling where he might go in that rough country, and his pack could get him into serious trouble.

Then, too, he was a walking photography store, and the valuable contents of his pack belonged to my guests. The thought of losing the exposed film he carried made me break out in a cold sweat. This was the third week of a twenty-one-day wilderness trip, and now a successful expedition might come to a gloomy end. Quickly I dispatched a wrangler to find him, while I took the rest of the outfit over a range of mountains to a timberline camp perched on the rim of Boundary Creek Valley.

In the meantime, Amos came down out of the basin onto the main trail leading over Akamina Pass. Here he got the scent of strange horses blended with those of the trail mates he was following, and even that confusing mixture was fast fading on a dry wind. Coming to a three-way fork where a short-cut trail headed for Cameron Lake in Waterton Lakes National Park, Amos stopped in momentary indecision. Here he could double back over the long trail of the past two weeks on the British Columbia side of the divide; he could follow the main trail over the summit into Alberta; or he could take the short cut to Cameron Lake. He chose the main summit trail and so missed the wrangler riding hard up our back trail.

With only the musical tinkle of his Swiss bell for company, Amos hurried down off the pass to where the trail ended abruptly on a highway buzzing with Sunday-afternoon tourist traffic. Again he was faced with a puzzling choice of directions. To the east, outside the far rim of the mountains, lay the home ranch and familiar pastures. To the south was a vast stretch of peaks beyond the dead end of the highway at Cameron Lake. Most horses would have headed home or panicked, throwing the pack to the four winds. But not Amos; the wheels of intelligence were turning coolly in his wise head as he turned south along the shoulder of the highway, ignoring the cars in his patient search for the missing pack train.

Earlier in the season I had taken him up this road to pick up some supplies at a warden's cabin not far from the lake, Amos remembered the place and turned off the highway, coming to a halt before the cabin door. The warden was preparing his supper when he heard the bell outside. He opened the door and was greeted by a soft nicker. Amos shook his head as though asking, "Seen a pack train? I've lost one somewhere around here." The warden rubbed his ears and led him back to the corral, where he threw him some hay. Having recognized Amos, the warden saddled up a mount after supper and led him over to my camp on the shore of Cameron Lake.

I was never so happy to see a horse and a pack, both safe and sound. From what the wrangler and the warden told me, I pieced together the story of Amos's adventure and marvelled at his cool-headed solving of a situation that could have been a disaster. To Amos, it was just another challenge to his intelligence, another adventure in a long, colourful career of service.

I raised Amos and broke him to pack as a two-year-old. In his youth he was a rollicky type, loving nothing better than to shake me up in a wild bucking spree. Not out of meanness; it was just a way to let off excess steam.

Once, though, his exuberance got us into an embarrassing jam. That summer I had taken out a Boston family on a wilderness trip – a completely new experience for them. They were the kind of people I wanted for steady customers, so I was anxious to please them. One morning, as I was saddling Amos, I could see by the look in his eye and the slack droop of his near ear that he was going to buck. Some of the guests were nearby, and I decided to give them some western entertainment.

I stepped into the saddle, and Amos, with a little squeal, dropped his head and soared while I sat up straight and pretty. Our course took us right through the camp and, in no time at all, between two trees, where the lady of the party had her clothes-line strung. The line caught my saddle horn and broke at both ends. We went out of there with flags of feminine apparel snapping in the wind on both sides.

Up to then, Amos had only been horsing around. Now, scared out of his wits, he really came apart, and I had a tough time staying with him. With a great soaring leap he took off the bank into the creek, where the lady herself was fly-fishing for trout. We blew the pool wide open right under her nose, then dashed on for a quarter-mile before I got the snorting, wild-eyed Amos stopped.

Considerably chastened, I rode back, gathering up various items of trampled apparel. At the stream I saw the lady sitting on a rock, her head down and her shoulders heaving. I thought she was crying, but when I placed the bedraggled laundry at her feet with an apology she looked up through tears of laughter.

"Please don't say another word!" she gasped. "I'd have come all the way from Boston to see it!"

Never in his life has Amos bucked with a pack. If anything goes wrong with his load on the trail, he stops and waits for someone to come and fix it – a rare packhorse indeed. He is greying with age around the head, and does only light work now, but he has never missed a trip since we both started in the outfitting game twenty-four years ago.

His bosom pal is a big packhorse called Sally, who is another equine character. Three parts Clydesdale and one part cayuse, she is 1,600 pounds of gentle power and good horse sense. From her flowing tail to the fierce-looking moustache under her Roman nose, she is a model packhorse. For years she has held the responsible job of carrying the valuable cook boxes so necessary for building good meals on the trail.

But for several years after I broke her she was an irresponsible, incorrigible clown. Carrying two hundred pounds of canned stuff as though it were so much corn flakes, she'd hoist her head and tail and circle the whole pack outfit at a dead run. This and other equally carefree antics generally wore the labels off the cans in about two days, reducing the cook to tears. Sometimes Sally's pack hit a tree and the contents went flying. I tried various disciplinary measures in attempts to settle her down, but Sally accepted them stoically, as though saddened by my lack of humour. None of them had the desired effect on her harum-scarum ways.

Then I became aware of a habit she had that gave me the key to cracking her crust of irresponsibility. She loved to walk up over a little tree, bending it down to scratch her belly. So I began regular scratching sessions, which she accepted with delight. From then on she was my slave – I could do no wrong. When her high spirits prompted her to go romping off, I'd roar at her and she'd subside, coming back into the line like a well-trained dog.

Now when I step out in front of the tents to admire the view, I often hear heavy footsteps approaching to the tune of a bronze bell. My view is suddenly blocked by a great horse as Sally nudges me gently with a shoulder and sidles into position to get that itchy place in the middle of her broad belly scratched. When I hit the required spot, she half closes her eyes in an ecstasy of joy, twists her moustache in an equine leer of pure satisfaction, and lets go a sigh that can be heard for yards around.

The pack train, one of the oldest forms of transport known to man, is still employed by western guides and outfitters to take guests far back into relatively untouched wilderness on hunting, fishing, and sightseeing trips. It is made up of a string of pack- and saddle horses numbering anywhere from a dozen to fifty. The packhorses carry the gear and supplies necessary to make life in the wild comfortable. The true wilderness guide-outfitter does not lead his packhorses on a rope, but turns them loose with their loads to trail behind a lead horse ridden by the head guide. A well-trained and reliable pack outfit will traverse incredibly rough country safely.

There are as many facets to a horse's character as there are to a man's. In the make-up of a pack train it takes all kinds of temperament. There are the leader types and those that prefer to follow, even a "caboose" – the one that insists on bringing up the rear. Many packhorses have their favourite spot in the line and will fight tooth and hoof to preserve it. Some horses are born timid and uncertain of themselves, others are full of fire and courage, and still others are lazy to the marrow of their bones. Rarely do you find a truly stupid horse. The occasional outlaw is often one of the smartest who has been twisted by mishandling, for a man has to know more than the horse to teach him and sometimes the man fails to measure up.

In training and working with horses, I have often been aware of a sympathetic link of understanding – a sort of telepathy between man and beast. Often I have sensed what they intended to do before they did it. And sometimes I think they know me better than I know them.

One fall, to meet an emergency, I had to trail a bunch of forty horses across ninety miles of country, and do it alone, starting out at sun-up. I had bells on the leaders of the various bunches that prefer one another's company even in a close-knit pack outfit. They knew the trail better than I did, but because our route traversed ranching country with numerous wire fences and open gates it sometimes was not easy to keep them together.

By riding my best horses and changing mounts frequently, I made good time. At dark I kept on, and now it was up to the horses, for there is a limit to hard riding at night. Somehow they seemed to know what was required of them and gave me little trouble. The bells were in different keys, so I could spot a bunch getting out of line and know the horse leading it. A sharp command usually brought them back into line. I gave them their time to pick the trail, just pushing enough to keep the stragglers at the rear from falling too far behind.

In the black dark we crossed two rivers and a stretch of timber. At midnight I headed them into a pasture on my father's ranch, seventy-five miles from where I had started, and not a horse was missing. Next morning at dawn we hit the trail again and arrived at the destination before noon. Such a ride would have been utterly impossible with horses I did not know – or with horses that did not know me.

There have been times, I'm sure, when my horses doubted my sanity. Generally they put up with my eccentricities, but once they acted on their own initiative to correct a situation, and we all had a bad time. We were on an October hunting trip on the west slope of the Rockies in the Flathead country of southeast British Columbia. It was the shank of the trip, and we took advantage of a fine day to hunt high for goats. When we came back in the evening, I noticed that the horses had hung around camp all day, as though expecting something.

We tied up a night horse and drove the rest out to pasture in some beaver swamps not far from camp. Next morning the tents were sagging under a foot of snow brought in by a raging blizzard. To make matters worse, we had only the night horse. The rest of the bunch had departed for the home ranch forty miles to the east over the Continental Divide. They had known the storm was coming and that we should have been on our way out. I bitterly regretted not getting the hint, for it took us a week to get them back through snow that was piled in seven-foot drifts and lay thirty inches everywhere else.

Only one horse in hundreds has the qualities for a good leader in a wilderness pack outfit. I have been particularly fortunate, for I have had two outstanding leaders. There was Elk, a big, handsome grey with lemon-coloured freckles. Tall and powerful and weighing about 1,300 pounds, he combined cool-headed courage with great stamina. Through sunshine and storm he carried me across thousands of miles of mountain trails, and never in all the years I rode him did he question my decisions. Most of the time I left the choice of trail to him, but occasionally in some tricky spot it was necessary for me to choose. His co-operation was always faultless. This is extremely important, for a show of fear – or even momentary indecision on the part of a lead horse – will telegraph itself the whole length of the pack train, causing confusion and even danger.

Elk's cool courage, when the chips were down, was something to marvel at, and I will never forget one spot where his willingness to face danger got us out of a bad fix. I had contracted to guide a party of geologists through a stretch of trackless wilderness on the upper reaches of the Flathead River in British Columbia. It was the roughest kind of country, a large part of it strewn with fallen logs, the result of a fire. Some of the area was so bad that even moose shunned it, and it was desperately difficult for horses.

One fine August morning I was leading two geologists up the slopes of a ridge toward a peak at the far end of a twisted mountain valley. It was hot and dry, and the last thing I expected to see was a bear. But suddenly I spotted the familiar outline of a grizzly on a rimrock a quarter-mile above as we wound through a stretch of down timber. Generally bears make themselves scarce at the sight of riders, but this one started our way at a slow lope. Knowing how shortsighted grizzlies are, I was unconcerned at first, thinking he was just curious and would turn and run just as soon as he saw what we were. But the closer he came, the faster he moved.

There are times when a bold attack is the best defense, even when the odds are heavy against it. So I drew my Colt .44, reined Elk around, and spurred him straight at the charging grizzly as I gave out a war whoop. Without the slightest hesitation the horse plunged over the logs, closing the range swiftly. About half a jump from being sure my bluff had failed, I saw the grizzly suddenly skid to a stop fifty feet away. He was well above us on a rock ledge and looked utterly ferocious as he swung back and forth, chomping his jaws and growling.

Elk faced the bear as motionless as a marble statue while I loudly told the big bruiser what I thought of him, hoping fervently that I wouldn't have to use the pistol, which now seemed about as potent as a peashooter. Had Elk so much as flinched, anything could have happened. But he stood like a rock, and finally the grizzly began to cool off. His back hair settled down, after several of the longest minutes of my life, and he moved back a few feet to a big boulder, where he lay on his belly like a big dog and looked us over. Finally he headed up the mountain at a walk and disappeared.

With the grizzly gone, Elk, who had given no sign of worry, let out a gigantic sigh that creaked the saddle under me. Such courage and acceptance of a rider's judgement is a rare and wonderful thing.

During a thunderstorm last summer Elk took shelter under a big spruce on a steep mountain meadow. When lightning struck the tree, he was killed instantly. The thunder, rolling and booming among the peaks, played a fitting requiem for him.

His successor is making a fair bid to equal him. Ace is a powerful black, as active as a cat, and the best climber I've ever ridden. But his special talent is his memory for trails. His qualities of leadership are accented by a natural arrogance resenting any interference from me in choice of ground, and I have to be careful how I bend him to my wishes. Too pointed insistence on my part sparks his temper. But once over a trail he never forgets it. I have seen him find and hold a trail under the most trying conditions.

Three seasons ago we finished a hunting trip on a high plateau a few miles across the British Columbia border. I had another party coming in immediately; so I left the tents and stoves set up to save extra packing on the return trip. But before we could get back, a short, fierce blizzard blew in from the north, slowing our schedule for the return trip.

It was dusk and we were still miles to the east of the divide, with a rugged 8,000-foot pass between us and the camp. Breaking trail with Ace, I had to choose between making camp in the snow without tents and going over the pass in the dark. If there had been plenty of horse feed, I would have camped, toughing out the night around an open fire, but there was none. My guests, Warren Page and two of his friends, were game to try for the pass and our camp, so we kept going.

But as we swung the outfit up the long switchbacks, bucking deeper and deeper snow, we ran into the heavier gloom of fog, and I began to regret my decision. At timberline, though, we suddenly ran out of the dark fog into brilliant moonlight, which was encouraging except that it revealed a chilling sight. Here the trail climbed up along a steep mountain-ridge crest and wound across a ledgy face through a shallow saddle; then it went up past the ragged edge of a steep-pitched boulder field to the summit. A single slip could mean disaster; it was an ominous picture. Up here the wind had drifted the snow, completely hiding the trail and sculpting the scrubby trees in bizarre forms of ghostly white.

Ace stopped to catch his wind and I sat sizing up the mountain ahead. Then the big black began working out the trail. How he did it is still a mystery to me, but he casually broke trail up that first pitch and over the tricky shelves and through the snow-choked scrub without one hesitant step. At the rim of the saddle he rammed through a shoulder-deep drift and halted on the ridge comb. When I looked back at the string of horses behind me I could have cheered, for every one was moving steadily, without a sign of concern.

But the worst was yet to come, where the trail staggered along the broken fangs of the drift-choked boulder field. Again Ace moved out. With head held low he eased into his work carefully while I rode with a loose rein, giving him complete freedom. The trail lifted around a point of leg-breaking boulders, and there he suddenly checked and pulled back, then reached out and probed the snow with his hoof. For a moment I thought he had lost the trail, but when I got down to feel for it with my feet I found what had stopped him.

A flat slab of rock had slipped across the trail before the storm and lay at a steep angle. Hidden by snow, it would have thrown any horse stepping on it. But somehow Ace had detected it in time. Kicking the snow away, I slid the rock down slope and remounted. From here on the trail to the summit was easy. When I reined in Ace at the top, the sky was a faultless canopy of stars, cleaved by snow-shrouded peaks lifting in great ranks through soft masses of moonlit valley mist. Faint and far away a coyote mourned in a high, lonesome solo.

Ace broke the spell with a gusty snort and a toss of his proud head as he started down slope toward camp, to the accompaniment of the pack-train bells' soft music. If a man is honest, he knows what he owes to his horse in a place like this. Reaching forward, I stroked his arched neck – a salute to a courageous heart.

Seppi | A Hunting Dog

For some unaccountable reason, I have two speeds as a shotgun artist. I either play grand opera on the twin tubes of my 12-gauge over-and-under Browning, or blast ineffectual holes in the sky with no more damage to my targets than if the shot had been left out of my cartridges. There is no rhyme nor reason for it and I have come to accept it as a personal shortcoming for which there is no cure.

Certainly it is not bad stock fit, for the Browning is good and I am equally erratic with other guns. I once won three jackpot trap shoots with three different borrowed weapons in the same afternoon. A reasonably consistent rifle shot, it is my fate to be a most unpredictable type with a scattergun.

This was one of my bad days.

Seppi, my German shorthaired pointer, had been finding cock pheasants all afternoon and each of them had winged his way to safety with chilled sixes going wide to inspire acceleration. Seppi had also found and pinned down a fine covey of Hungarian partridge. True, they had flushed into the wind, towering and

From *Field, Horse and Rodeo* (January 1963)

spreading on an updraft to offer a tough shot. But I had small excuse for missing, for they had flushed within easy range and there must have been at least eighteen birds providing a choice of targets. The shooting had been wonderful, my dog had worked like a field-trial champion, but my game pocket was empty as a greenhorn's wallet after a session of card-sharp poker.

Now Seppi was twenty yards ahead of me working out some weeds along an irrigation-ditch bank. His tail was vibrating like a hummingbird's wing, spelling pheasant as clearly as if the bird had been lit by a neon sign. Suddenly he pivoted to spring in one smooth bound across the six-foot ditch, twisting as he landed to creep ahead for forty feet. There he came to a classically statuesque point, with only the tip of his tail quivering ever so little, and I knew he had the bird pinned down. It was so pretty it almost hurt.

Easing closer, I could plainly see the long barred tail of a cock sticking out of a clump of thistles not a foot from his nose. The layout posed something of a problem, for just beyond was a row of willows. If the bird jumped while I was on the opposite side of the ditch, he would likely dive over this. If I nailed him in the clear, the close-bunched shot would make hash of him. If I waited there might be no chance to shoot; so I decided to cross the ditch.

It was empty, but slick with mud. When I stepped down the steep sloping bank, both feet shot from under me and I came down on my hip pockets in the greasy clay. Holding my gun high, I came up standing just in time to see Seppi lunge and grab the cock in mid-air as it flushed. He killed it with one crunch and brought it to me rather apologetically. But the gleam in his eye belied the apology, telling me plainly as words he was fed up with this bungling and damned if we were going home skunked.

That was the first pheasant he caught and killed, but not the last. A couple of times since, when the ammunition companies have obviously failed to put shot in my shells, he has chosen to take a hand in putting some weight in the game bag. Happily, he has chosen to kill cocks so far; but the law of averages is going to catch up with me one day when he chomps a hen, which are rigidly protected here. I wonder what the game warden will say when I tell him my dog killed it?

A badly trained dog maybe? It is not for me to criticize, for Seppi and I worked into the upland gun-dog sport together and I concede that his techniques are far more polished than mine. Anyway, we are not unduly concerned about the more refined points of the game. We hunt for fun, enjoy each other's company, and we could not care less about our various eccentricities.

Seppi is my first pointer. He was presented to me when about a year old by my good friend Felicien Philippe, and I will be forever grateful. He not only gave me a truly great dog, but introduced me to canine character and also to the wonderful sport and enjoyment of gunning game birds over a pointer and all-around hunting dog.

I was furthermore most fortunate in having "Phil" Philippe's guidance in training Seppi, for without his vast store of sporting-dog knowledge and his tremendous background of experience to draw from, my dog might have been a failure. Most certainly my hunting would not have been so enjoyable.

Phil was born a Frenchman, educated in Italy, growing up by necessity in a highly cultured atmosphere in the city of Florence, and by choice, at every opportunity, in the rugged Swiss Alps. From an early age his every waking hour was largely concerned with the outdoors and the pursuit of sport with rod and gun. As a young man, he left off his passion for fishing and hunting to volunteer for service with the International Brigade, where he served with distinction for four years through World War I.

After the Armistice, he went to Germany to live, and shortly developed into an internationally recognized outdoor writer and editor for one of the biggest publishing companies in Berlin at that time. When Hitler came to power, Phil's naturally fearless, independent, and outspoken ways got him into trouble and he was forced to flee to Italy, leaving everything behind him.

It was not long before he was appointed game commissioner under Mussolini's regime and established twenty-five game refuges and national parks, stocked them with game, and organized a very efficient wildlife-conservation service for that country. While doing this, he owned and trained the great Axel, a superb German shorthaired pointer, which won the International Field Trial Championship and also the International Bench Show Championship. Competing against the finest dogs in Europe, this was a tremendous feat and one that has been rarely, if ever, duplicated.

But then Mussolini began goose-stepping with Hitler and again Phil was forced to flee, this time to America, with only the shirt on his back and a fine gun. What was Europe's loss was our gain, for Phil, a most versatile and artistic personality, proceeded to develop a new glazing technique for putting hand-painted outdoor scenes on fine china. In his studio in the Catskill Mountains of New York State and later in Alberta, he turned out some truly great art. His plates are the prized possessions of all who own them. He is now semi-retired in Pasadena, California, where he still does a limited amount of fine china art. A man with an historic past reading like a great adventure story, Phil has done a great deal to illuminate the name and the popularity of the German shorthaired pointer.

Sometimes fate and circumstance do strange things, affecting people's lives. As a direct result of the trials and tribulations resulting from the Hitler-Mussolini partnership in Europe, I came to acquire a great friend and hunt with the finest dog I have ever owned.

On one side of his family tree, Seppi is a grandson of the great champion, Axel. At first he was a roistering, devil-may-care rebel with an unlimited capacity for having a good time and getting into trouble. He was never penned, for we kept him as a house dog and he enjoyed the open country of our ranch joining the edge of the Rocky Mountain wilderness of Waterton Lakes National Park. Hunting came as natural to him as breathing and keeping him under control was not easy. He was partly trained to mind the whistle and I proceeded with this by working him on a long line and checking him, when he found reason to lapse. He is a strong-minded, tough, active dog, and during that early training he taught me as much as I taught him.

When the next hunting season rolled around, I gunned sharptail and ruffed grouse over him. Ruffed grouse, most numerous around our home, are difficult for a young dog to handle in thick cover, and harder yet for me to hit consistently in the heavy brush with my choked barrels. If taken close enough to offer a clear shot, they are usually ruined by the charge. If allowed to get out where the shot spreads, they have a way of ducking behind trees. Seppi had trouble getting them to hold and suffered with my erratic shooting; but on his own without any special instruction by me, he worked out a system. He began to circle the birds, putting them up towards me so they offered a better shot as they towered against the sky. Our percentage of hits went up and often we came in with my game pocket bulging with the limit of five birds. From the beginning, my percentage of lost birds dropped to zero. Seppi rarely fails to find a wounded bird and almost never misses a dead bird dropped into heavy cover.

I never realized what really fine game birds sharptail grouse can be until I hunted them over a pointer. They hold fairly well and they are much easier to hit than ruffed grouse, because they frequent open park country, prairies, and stubble. Seppi's regard for my shooting rose a bit hunting these birds and he found the retrieving easier.

One day, we jumped a flock of sharptails on the open edge of a grove of willows and aspens. They jumped at extreme range, giving me just one shot, which connected. Seppi was bringing me my bird when someone else shot at the same flock on the far side of the grove. Delivering the bird, Seppi streaked away through the trees and came proudly back with a second bird a few moments later. He had hijacked another hunter's game, which we duly returned with apologies. This is a bit of skulduggery he still indulges in on occasion with a fair portion of arrogance that is comical.

Inevitably he came to meet a porcupine and fortunately this adventure occurred close to home. With his usual brashness, he grabbed the phlegmatic beast by the back and got his mouth loaded with the agonizing quills. Many miles from the nearest vet, I had no choice but to perform the necessary operation myself. Without anaesthetic it was a salutary lesson for my dog and a most nerve-wracking experience for me. A big active dog, quick as lightning and hard as nails, he was mad with pain and fought me like a demon, tooth and claw. I rolled him up like a mummy in a heavy tarp, straddled him and went to work. When the job was finally done and the last quill was pulled from his jaws, we were both shivering wrecks. We sat back and glared at each other, like mortal enemies too tired to fight each other any more. I reached out a battered hand to ruffle his ear and spoke to him softly. The fierce fighting lights in his eyes went out and he put his head on my knee whimpering for sympathy.

Skunks were something else. From the very first time he encountered one of these high-powered beasts, he considered them fair game for fun. He got himself liberally doused, but seemed immune to the stinking essence. Somehow he managed to close his nose and eyes to the charge on contact and proceeded with his hunting, where most dogs would be so utterly blotted out they could not separate bird scent from skunk smell for twenty-four hours. He never tries to kill one, but seems to think them prime sport. When he got himself shot with both barrels, his popularity with the family understandably fell, and he found himself sleeping on the porch. Fond of his comforts, he took this to heart, but it did not detract from his love of playing with skunks. I prevailed on him to desist while we were hunting birds, but at every opportunity, he continues to play with them on his own time.

Through long practice, he developed a technique that is almost foolproof for dodging their fire, which he demonstrated to me one day.

We were out for a walk one fine spring evening, when I spotted a big boar skunk promenading across a meadow ringed by aspens with his plume set at half cock. Seppi was off to one side investigating something and I did not think he had noticed the skunk, until he suddenly shot into the open. Streaking in fast and quiet, he ran right up close to the animal from behind. With his nose not more than a foot from the potent exhaust pipe, he let out a sudden great roar and dodged. The startled and demoralized skunk shot without looking and missed the dog clean. He swung for a second try, but this also missed, for Seppi was circling fast, roaring and whooping. That skunk never did work out a system of lead necessary for wing shooting. For a while he resembled a revolving lawn sprinkler. Seppi was hugely enjoying the caper and only desisted when I called him off in self-protection, for the atmosphere in general was getting so stiff one could have almost carved it up into chunks and built a fence out of it.

Seppi came to me, tongue rolling out of the corner of his mouth in a devilish grin, beside himself with delight. He was a bit high with scent collected off the grass, but proceeded to scrub himself as good as new by rolling and wallowing in the loose, fresh dirt of a pocket gopher mound. He has the business of goosing skunks down to a fine art.

When Seppi was still little more than a pup, but with considerable bird-hunting experience, I began to appreciate what an intelligent and versatile dog I owned. One day I came into the yard to hear the high yipping bay of a trailing hound ringing from a small willow swamp back of our buildings. It was Seppi on a hot trail giving tongue as he circled the swamp. As he swung back, the flat bark of a little .410 gun put a period to the baying and my heart sank. The boys were hunting rabbits with him and I groaned inwardly, thinking of all the jackrabbits he would be chasing in the pheasant country on the prairies. Using a bird dog for hunting rabbits is bad business usually and a first class way to ruin a good dog. But when my two oldest sons, Dick and Charlie, came out of the woods with a big snowshoe rabbit in hand, Seppi stalking proudly beside them, I did not have the heart to scold them.

My fears were groundless, for the first time we jumped a big jack in the pheasant country, Seppi stopped instantly on command and no more than glanced at the big hares for the rest of the day. He knew when I wanted birds and left other game alone. To this day, he can be trusted to trail rabbits in the morning and point birds in the afternoon.

But breaking him of running deer was an entirely different story. I had had him about six months when we jumped a couple of does one fine morning not far from the buildings. Seppi immediately gave chase, completely ignoring my whistle to come back. His hackles were up, and it was easy to see this was no light-hearted game, for every line of him spelled "Kill!"

He has always been an exceptionally fast dog, so it was virtually impossible to run him down in the act of trailing deer. My only hope was to cut across a circle and head him off. Had it not been for his baying, I would have lost him completely. As it was, he came closer to running me to death than catching the deer; but it was only when he gave up the chase I was able to catch him. I gave him a whipping, but was far from sure it would do any good.

That same summer we moved to Waterton Lakes National Park, where I had acquired a livery and trail-riding business as a supplement to my outfitting pack-train work. Naturally we took

Seppi with us, but I was concerned about him, for the park authorities are very touchy about loose dogs running game. I could have
kept him tied or penned, but felt this would turn him into a mean
dog; so I prevailed on the park officials to let me keep him loose.

There were deer everywhere in herds and if ever there was a
heaven of concentrated temptation for a dog inclined to run them,
this was it. For some time Seppi was a model of good behaviour,
but I could see their presence was a strain, for when they were
close, he would stand trembling with a cold fire burning in his
eyes. This was a different thing than the desire to point birds, chase
rabbits, and play with skunks. There was cold-blooded murder in
the air and I knew one day the flames of desire would flare, with
hell to pay. I could only hope for some luck, for without it I would
surely lose my dog. No man can tolerate a dog that makes a habit
of running deer in a park or out of it in this country.

When the blow-up came, it exploded out of the blue and it
could not have been more fortunate. I was standing in front of the
corral gate, having just finished catching some horses, with my
lariat coiled in my hands. Two fawns suddenly burst through the
yard at a tearing run with Seppi hot on their heels. He was driving
them hard, for their tongues were out and he was closing fast. The
fawns shot by within feet of me and I doubt if Seppi ever saw me
until my quick-thrown loop snapped shut around his neck.
Throwing him hard, I doubled the hard twist rope and gave him
a sound whipping, which he took without a whimper.

The next day a doe, probably the mother of the fawns, put on
the finishing touches. I was walking to the barn when I heard a
whine and a thudding of hoofs in the corral at the back. Running
to investigate, I found Seppi flattened out on the ground close
against the barn wall with a big doe pounding him to a pulp with
her hoofs. Had I not driven her off, she likely would have severely
injured or killed him, for he was making no move to defend
himself – just lying there soaking up terrible punishment. He was

the saddest, sorriest-looking dog I have ever seen. Every square inch of his hide was pounded full of dirt, even to the end of his short tail. Next day he was so stiff and sore, he whined every time he moved. When a deer went by the yard gate, he looked at it with an expression of utter disgust, as though the mere sight of one was nauseating. Seppi never chased another deer.

Hunting and rambling with my dog promoted an interest in the origin of the German shorthaired pointer and I read everything I could find about the breed. However, nearly all the best historical accounts are written in German and have not been translated into English, so my research was somewhat limited. A query to Phil Philippe brought a letter containing the most comprehensive and condensed history of this type of dog I have seen. He says:

> The origin of the German shorthaired pointer can be traced back over two centuries. His forefathers were a breed of heavy, coarse-haired, slow-moving, short-ranging pointer dogs called "Aldeutsche Vorsteh-Hund" – Old German Pointing Dog.
>
> According to the most reliable sources, this breed of dogs originated by crossing south European, probably Spanish, pointing bird dogs with hounds of French, English or German descent. There is no way of telling if other breeds were used for the creation of this German dog, for no records were kept and no stud books were known at that time. But it is certain that the Germans were the first to realize the need for an all-around gun dog: pointing or retrieving birds and small game on land or water, plus an ability to trail crippled big game like deer and boar. This idea was in opposition to the English tradition of breeding special dogs for each type of hunting; setters and pointers for pointing birds, spaniels and retrievers for bringing back shot birds and hounds for hunting foxes from horseback.

Hunting in Britain has always been considered a sport, exclusively the privilege of the wealthy. In opposition, the Germans had a more realistic and ethical concept of killing game. At a very early stage, they merged hunting activities with conservation. Even to this day hunting in Germany is not considered just sport, but a serious activity of harvesting a game crop and eliminating weak and old specimens as part of a game management program. Nor is it indulged in only by the rich, for any man with sufficient knowledge of hunting will receive plenty of invitations to hunt on privately leased hunting lands at a very nominal fee. Old traditions and severely ethical principles rule the conduct of the hunter. The hunting dog is trained and kept as an indispensable auxiliary and companion of the hunter. The dog has to perform his duties under all circumstances to assist his master to conform with hunting codes.

The British, once the masters of breeding domestic animals, usually kept their hunting dogs in kennels owned and operated by the owners of the estates. They created beautiful and famous breeds of pointers and setters, solely bred for the purpose of finding and pointing birds, mostly grouse. But never has any English breeder tried to produce an all-purpose gun dog, as the Germans have done for over two centuries.

When the first English pointers were imported into Germany, hunters and dog breeders were impressed by their outstanding features, beautiful proportions, short dense hair, long range, speed and stamina in the field, keen nose and stylish pointing. As early as 1840, the first Old German Pointers were crossed with English pointers. The groundwork for the German shorthaired pointer was thus established.

The results were very gratifying. The problem ahead consisted of development through wise selective breeding, a standard for the new cross-breed – an all-around gun dog with the outstanding virtues of the original breeds: the German shorthaired pointer.

By 1878, the standards for the different breeds of hunting dogs were finally established by a convention of delegates from many hunting dog clubs. From then on all pure bred dogs were registered in the German Stud Book.

The very active German Shorthaired Pointer Club began to encourage selective breeding after set-backs caused by the revolution of 1848. They bred to type for pleasant conformation, endurance, speed, stamina in the field, woods and water. They put particular emphasis on intelligence and versatility.

The breed was a hit and was considered an outstanding all-purpose gun dog in Europe long before specimens were introduced into America. I sometimes wonder how many present-day German shorthaired pointer owners in America know what a versatile dog they have in their possession.

In 1878 many different clubs founded a new and unique organization for field trials of the all-purpose gun dog. This organization, literally translated from German, was named "Union of Clubs for Field Trials of All-Purpose Dogs for Hunting." There were three kinds of trials introduced: derbies for young, partially trained dogs; fall trials for more advanced dogs, and full trials for the establishment of championships. The requirements for these last were so severe, that only the most outstanding performers stood a chance of winning a prize. Dogs placing in the prize classes were automatically registered in the "German All-Purpose Gun Dog Stud Book."

The full trials required good performances afield with birds: fast, long-range pointing and retrieving of birds and hares, rabbits, and foxes and the retrieving of waterfowl from deep water. Dogs were also required to trail, find, and retrieve crippled small game, and also trail wounded big game on a long leash. If the hunter is unable to finish the animal, the dog must pursue the crippled alone and hold it at bay till the hunter comes up with it. If the dog finds the game dead, he must either return to his master and lead him to it, or stay at the spot and bay until the hunter finds him. This last performance is highly rated and is called "Totverbellen" – giving tongue to the dead. Finally, the dogs were also tested in flushing in heavy cover, where pointing is useless. As a final test the dogs must catch and kill quickly all types of vermin encountered. Of course perfect obedience and control was of paramount importance in all tests.

The German shorthaired pointer met all these requirements in the final phases of breed development and has been recognized in all countries where these dogs are used, as the top all-around gun dog. Quoting from the *Complete Dog Book* published by the American Kennel Club in the chapter dealing with the German shorthaired pointer: "When adaptability, as well as excellence of performance is considered, then the German shorthaired pointer is without peer, for he will do and do well the many duties, which hitherto were considered possible only through the use of individuals of different hunting breeds."

Hunting big game with a dog in Alberta is prohibited, but Seppi had plenty of opportunity to display his versatility and talent. As a house guard in Waterton Park, where black bears are sometimes a problem to be dealt with, he proved himself equal to any situation.

One afternoon our little daughter, then a year-old toddler, was playing on the lawn in front of the house. Her mother and I were some distance from her when we saw a big black bear emerge from the cottonwoods outside the yard fence and start straight across the lawn. I am sure the bear had nothing in mind other than crossing our yard, but his path was directly in line with Anne, and any sudden move or noise on her part could have been dangerous. Before anyone could move, Seppi appeared like a canine thunderbolt from the shady side of the house, and before the bear knew what was up, the roaring dog had a mouthful of his rear. The bear bawled and swapped ends to fire a slashing haymaker at his attacker. Seppi was not there when it arrived and again the bear found his rear under vicious attack. He left hurriedly with Seppi worrying his heels. On the edge of the trees he ran over a sapling, which snapped up behind him and smacked Seppi squarely on the end of the nose, knocking him flat. Scrambling to his feet, half blind with pain and bawling with rage, the dog went back looking for more fight. However, the bear had gone, but our dog had proved beyond a doubt his speed and courage. That night he got a very special feed and basked under much petting and admiration from the whole family.

Although Seppi rarely goes looking for trouble with bears, he hates them, and when one comes close to the buildings, it is instantly under attack. If Seppi has had one bear fight, he has had a hundred. Unquestionable proof of his outstanding agility and speed, he has never suffered anything but one or two slight grazing scratches in his many close-quarters battles with bears. Once he had a very narrow escape.

He tore into a two-hundred-pound black bear in our yard at Waterton one day, and after a short flurry, the bear lit out running towards the lake a couple of hundred yards away. It came out on the beach close to our sons, John and Charlie – then boys nine and twelve years old – with Seppi hot on his heels. Had the boys not been on the scene, the chase would likely have ended there, for the bear took to the water to swim across a small bay. No doubt excited by the boys' presence, Seppi went completely berserk. Any other dog would have circled on the beach to circumvent the bear as it came out, but Seppi went just far enough to reach a little spit of gravel running into the lake, raced out to its tip, and plunged in to meet the bear in the water.

He grabbed the bear by the ear and both animals immediately sank from sight. What went on under water is anybody's guess, for they stayed down for some time with bubbles bursting on the surface over them. On the beach, the two boys were beside themselves with excitement and fear for the dog. The bear came up first and headed straight for shore. Seppi surfaced a moment later blowing and snorting water out of his nose, as he swam after the bear. When they beached, the bear turned and jumped on the dog, before he could get entirely clear of the water.

Completely unmindful of possible consequences, nine-year-old John leapt into the battle and grabbed the bear by the ears trying to pull him off the squirming, fighting dog. The bear turned with a snarl and lunged at the boy. But Seppi was on him like a flash, rearing like a maniac and jerking fur off the seat of his pants in mouthfuls as John dodged away and Charlie came streaking in swinging a driftwood club. Fortunately for all concerned, the bear lit out for tall timber and climbed a tree. Seppi emerged the victorious hero, strutting with pride and grinning a toothy grin. Neither boys nor dog received so much as a scratch, which was more good luck than good management.

But it was in the hunting fields that Seppi truly shone, as he reached maturity. His ability to adapt himself to various conditions and circumstances is a constant delight while hunting with him. He is far from perfect in many ways, but nevertheless he is the best dog I have ever hunted over on upland game.

On a bright October morning, Fred Sharpe, Ducks Unlimited naturalist, and I were hunting the irrigation country near Brooks, Alberta, when Seppi found a flock of sharptails among some willows ringing a dry slough on the edge of a wheat field. As the birds got up Fred dropped one and I winged another, which planed

down to fall in the wheat stubble on the side of a knoll. I sent
Seppi to get this bird, but when he reached it, he pointed instead
of picking it up. Fred was closer to the dog than I, so he went
over to investigate. I was puzzled, for Seppi had never pointed a
wounded bird before.

When Fred came up to the dog, a big ring-neck cock flushed
from under his nose and Fred dropped it just as it cleared the top
of the knoll. Seppi went after it, but again he pointed on reaching the spot. The cock's tail was sticking up out of the stubble and
this time I was sure Seppi was making a fool of himself. Walking
up to him, I was dumbfounded when a fine covey of Hungarian
partridge flushed from around the dead pheasant. Much to my satisfaction, two dropped, cleanly killed. Seppi retrieved the birds
and then I sent him back for the sharptail. It was running and
had gone a long way in the interval. He trailed it to the edge of
the field out on to a road, then down the borrow pit for several
hundred yards, where he nabbed it in a patch of weeds.

Without him we might easily have missed seeing the pheasant
and the partridge and one grouse would surely have been lost.
Such a mixed bag in so short a time is most unusual even in
country where mixed bags are commonplace, and the incident
stands out in the pages of memory.

On that same trip Seppi hunted ahead of four guns for six days
without a break. He lost only one wounded Hungarian partridge,
which fell into a thick bramble patch loaded with bird scent, where
it may have crawled down a hole. We hunted ducks as well as
upland birds, and while enjoying some jump and pass shooting
along a canal bank one day, Seppi displayed an amusing bit of skulduggery, which backfired.

George Mason, a local businessman, was with us that afternoon
with his fine Labrador bitch at heel, a well-trained retriever that
would be hard to beat. We were walking along the weed-grown

bank of a big canal, where ducks were almost continually jumping and trading back and forth overhead. Occasionally a pheasant or a flock of Huns would get up to add spice to the hunting.

Seppi was never fond of cold water, and as all of the downed ducks and some of the upland birds were falling in the canal, George Mason's little Lab was taking the lion's share of retrieving. This was fine with my dog, but he was missing out on some of the glory. To correct this discrepancy, he began sneaking down through the weeds on the canal bank, meeting the Lab as she emerged from the water, and taking her birds away from her to deliver them to me. I wondered how long she was going to stand for this state of affairs. About the third time he hijacked her bird, she followed him up the bank with a determined gleam in her eye. As he gave me the plunder, she piled on him. He made no effort to fight back, but accepted her chastising like a gentleman. I checked George's instant concern and we let the bitch worry him a bit, as she was mostly noise and not very savage about it. After they had settled their differences, Seppi reformed and took his share of the water retrieving.

This was one of many hunts we have enjoyed together. Seppi is getting to be an old dog in his eleventh year, but his eyes still shine and his mouth looks like that of a dog half his age. He is slowing up a bit and his joints creak slightly after a long day afield in cold weather. Every so often during the winter, we give a lynx or a bobcat a run to keep in shape. Certainly he is an all-around hunting dog – the best I will likely ever own.

Right now he is sitting in my favourite armchair contemplating me with all the gravity of a judge. There might be some question, whether I own him or he owns me. Neither of us are very concerned about it. We have had a lot of fun and adventure. Given a break with Father Time, we will have a lot more.

Encounter at Grizzly Gulch

John Ewing and I scrambled the last fifty feet up onto the top of a little shoulder that jutted from the side of Panorama Peak. There we looked out over the tumbled expanses of Grizzly Gulch. Peaks, canyons, big timber, and new snow blended with the blue sky and bright sun to form a picture typical of the wild reaches of southeastern British Columbia in September.

My outfit had been out ten days with a party of three sportsmen from Greeley, Colorado. This was Bill Farr's second trip with us, and he and his two friends, John Ewing and Bob Noffsinger, had had plenty of climbing. The weather had been hot and dry, which made hunting tough. We'd spent most of the first week right on top of the ranges, seeing many goats and several grizzlies. Bob and Bill had got billies, and Bob missed a shot at a black bear, but John had not fired a shot at anything. Now he and I were out for the day with Bill and Dave Simpson, one of the guides. We were all determined to find John a trophy.

It might seem futile to hunt an individual animal in such a huge, broken piece of country, but that was exactly what we were doing.

From *Field and Stream* (December 1957)

That morning we'd left camp near the top of Starvation Pass, where we had weathered out the first snowstorm of the season. Two days before the storm, Bill had killed a huge billy goat not far from Little Bear Lake, in a hanging basin on the rim of the gulch. While he and Wenz Dvorak, the head guide, were skinning out the goat, another billy had walked out on a shelf a thousand feet above and stood looking down. He was as big as a donkey and carried an impressive set of horns. Wenz is a veteran of forty years in the mountains, and about the coolest man I know, but when he described the goat later that day there was an unusual gleam in his eyes. Any goat big enough to get Wenz excited is worth looking for, so we were out to try to find him for John Ewing.

We'd ridden through the basin near Little Bear Lake and tied up the horses in the timber half a mile or so farther up the basin. Then we split up. John and I climbed straight up the mountain, while Dave and Bill ascended into the back of the basin.

After a long hour and a half of slippery footwork through a tangle of snow-covered blow-down timber and snowbrush, John and I sat down on a dry slab of rock in the sun. We were glassing the mountainside for sign of the big billy when a curious sound drew my attention. At first I was not sure of its direction, but then it came again clearly through the still air – a distinct sharp sound, as though someone were hammering on a rock.

John heard it, too, and asked me what it was. At first I was stumped, but then I remembered that a party of oil geologists were camped in Akamina Valley, a few miles to the north. When the peculiar sound came up to us again I suddenly decided I had the answer.

"Rock hunters!" I muttered disgustedly to John. "They *would* have to show up in here. Big help on a goat hunt."

In all the years we had hunted that area, we had never run into any interference before, and I couldn't help a feeling of vast disappointment as I scanned the basin trying to locate our unwelcome visitors. I swung my glasses along the edge of the big timber that bordered the clearing around Little Bear Lake, trapped in a natural bowl at the foot of the mountain 1,500 feet below – and a grizzly walked into view! It was a big silvertip. As it walked over to our horse trail, I distinctly heard the *chock-chock-chock* of the hammering. Then the big bear let out a hair-lifting roar. Immediately afterward I heard the hammering sound again.

John had his glasses glued on the bear, and he suddenly exclaimed, "That racket we've been hearing isn't rock hunters – it's that bear chopping his teeth together! I just saw him do it!"

He was right, and for the next half-hour we were treated to a sight I'd never seen before – a picture complete with sound. The bear stalked back and forth along our horse tracks, repeatedly roaring and snapping his teeth. It was an awe-inspiring sound, leaving little doubt in our minds that this particular grizzly was mighty put out with our intrusion into his territory. It was very unusual behaviour for a grizzly, but the explanation was obvious. He had located the carcass of Bill's goat and was laying claim to it in no uncertain fashion. We had probably ridden right past the big animal in the morning as we entered the basin, and that thought sent a little chill up my back. If he had jumped us on the trail that snaked through boulders and down logs we'd have been in trouble – real trouble.

"That's the meanest bear I've ever seen," I told John. "I think we should turn this goat hunt into a bear hunt and go down and bust that old bruiser."

"Just fine with me," John answered. Then he added, "I'll bet this is a relative of that grizzly you were telling us about the other night. Grizzly Gulch is well named!"

He was referring to a story I had told one night at the fire – a true tale of how Grizzly Gulch got its name.

In the spring of 1908, my father-in-law, Bert Riggall, who was later to become one of Canada's most famous guides and naturalists, was working with a drilling crew that was prospecting for oil near some seeps in Akamina Valley. His job as tool dresser had two attractions for Bert, who had recently come from England into the raw new land of western Canada. It paid him a fair wage in hard cash, which was a mighty scarce article at the time, and it also took him into the heart of the practically unknown wilderness mountain country of southeastern British Columbia. Bert had climbed the Alps as a boy and had an abiding love for high mountains.

So it was only natural that he spent all his spare time exploring amongst the peaks surrounding the oil camp. On every second Sunday, his day off, he'd take a lunch and head up into the wilderness country alone to explore the unmapped mountains. The only weapon he carried was a 7.63 mm Mauser pistol, one of the first semi-automatic types. It had a six-inch barrel and the magazine was a clip that hung just forward of the trigger guard. The gun was carried in a unique wooden holster with a spring-locking lid. This lid snapped open when a concealed button was pushed. The holster, made of a piece of hollowed-out walnut, could also serve as a quick-detachable stock for the pistol, turning it into a sort of short rifle. At the time this pistol was the last word in sidearms and Bert was mighty proud of it.

One Saturday evening in late August, Bert busied himself preparing for a Sunday wandering and exploring. He packed a lunch and carefully cleaned the pistol. After cleaning it, he placed the gun in its holster and set it on a table in the cook shack. A few minutes later he accidentally nudged it off onto the floor, and when he picked it up he was appalled to find that the holster lid had split off at the hinges. Only a man who loves fine equipment could appreciate Bert's feelings. And no one could know that the broken lid was going to save Bert's life.

Next morning at dawn, he headed up a wild, heavily timbered valley that led into the high peaks south of the camp. The narrow gulch was choked with down logs, snowbrush, and bogs under a heavy growth of spruces and firs. The going was heavy, and Bert used many of the down logs as pathways through the brush.

At noon he came out into the clear at the foot of a pass. Here avalanches that came down every spring had cleared a series of broad, open swaths. These natural clearings are carpeted with berry brush, and as he climbed the pass Bert counted five grizzlies feeding on the huckleberries. At the crest of the pass, the tremendous vista of Starvation Valley came into view, with its lakes, glacier, and rugged flanking mountains. For two hours Bert climbed and explored, viewing the country from various ridges and shoulders. Time passed swiftly, as it has a way of doing in such country, so it was late afternoon when he finally turned back down the pass toward camp.

He travelled fast, being anxious to get through the timber in the lower valley before dark. As he went, he kept a wary eye peeled for bears. Their sign was everywhere, and in many places along the watercourse the brush and lush grass was trampled flat into broad, intercrossing bear trails. On reaching the timber he continued to travel as fast as possible, and again used the down logs for natural boardwalks so he could avoid scrambling through the interminable snowbrush. In one place he found a whole series of logs lodged; by jumping from one to another he was able to travel several hundred yards without coming to the ground. Finally he leaped up onto a particularly large fir tree and clattered along it for about seventy feet before coming to a big branch. He swung around it and continued for a few steps more, then came to another branch blocking the way. For a moment he paused undecided, then jumped down four feet into the brush.

When he hit the ground, things happened fast. Like a giant jack-in-the-box released by a spring, a huge grizzly came out from under the log right in front of him, and stood towering on its hind feet and snorting angrily. The bear was practically within touching distance, and for a moment the picture was a frozen tableau of mutual surprise. The bear had been sound asleep and was confronted by a man. The man had been in a hurry to get home and was confronted by a bear. Bert moved first by reaching for his gun. Without a wasted fraction of a second, he swept the pistol up out of the open-top holster, thumbing off the safety catch as he drew. Just as the bear was lifting a giant paw to strike, Bert rested the pistol in the crook of his upraised left elbow and fired at a spot just under the big animal's muzzle. The grizzly stiffened and then came down like a falling tree. Bert had to throw himself backward to avoid having the big animal fall squarely on top of him. For a few seconds he stood tensely with the pistol cocked and trained on the grizzly, ready to shoot at the least sign of life. But the big animal had died instantly. The little jacketed bullet had hit it in the thorax and penetrated deep into the throat, where it had smashed the atlas vertebrae that joined the spine to the skull.

Bert stood for a few moments and gazed thoughtfully at the obstructing limb on top of the tree trunk. If it had been a few feet farther along, he'd have jumped squarely on top of the bear, with no chance to defend himself. He put the pistol back into the broken holster that had allowed a fast draw, when seconds were as precious as life. Feeling mighty lucky and not a little shaken, he continued through the gathering dusk to camp.

It was Bert who gave the canyon the name Grizzly Gulch, and it stuck. To this day the valley is a favourite range of the big silver-tips — just as wild now as it was back in 1908.

John and I turned back down the slope, swinging up into the basin behind the shoulder to avoid the dripping brush. On the way we picked up Dave and Bill, and together we returned to the horses. Riding single file down the back trail through the timber we reached a screen of alders on the edge of the clearing by Little Bear Lake, where we dismounted to look for the grizzly. Most of the snow was gone and the flat seemed to be empty. Swinging the glasses slowly along the edge of the heavy timber on the far side of the flat, I searched for some sign of the bear. The field of the binoculars had almost completed the swing, and I was scrutinizing a knoll beyond the lake when I spotted the grizzly.

He was lying like a big dog on his belly with his head up, and he was near where the horse trail emerged from the trees. The bear was over four hundred yards away, so we slipped down through the alders to a washout that cut the flat in half where the overflow ran out of the lake. We had good cover as far as the lake, but once there we were still three hundred yards from the bear. Our angle of view had altered; now we were looking at a small piece of him between two giant trees. Since a wounded grizzly is pure dynamite in timber, we'd have been asking for trouble in big raw chunks to try a shot from that spot. So we eased out onto the flat below him, using some small spruces for cover.

When we had gone a hundred yards he must have heard us, for he suddenly stood up at full height on his hind feet looking our way. He made a picture to remember, framed between the towering spruces against the blue sky, with the outline of a thousand-foot perpendicular cliff behind and to one side. It was a wild and beautiful sight. We froze and waited. The grizzly dropped to all fours and we heard that ominous chopping of teeth as he came walking out onto the slope diagonally toward us.

"Get set!" I whispered.

Bill and John fanned out abreast and sat down with their rifles ready. When the bear reached a patch of broke boulders fifty yards from the timber, John cut loose with his .25-06. Instantly the grizzly swivelled on his hind feet, slapping at the rocks beside him. As he slewed our way, Bill's .300 Weatherby roared. Then things came apart in a hurry. Tumbling and bawling savagely, the bear came down through the boulders like an avalanche. Both Bill and John fired at him as he came, but the bullets went high, throwing dust off the rocks. The shooting got so fast I lost track of it, but just as the grizzly cleared the rocks a hundred yards away, a bullet caught him flush in the shoulder and his roaring trailed off into a choking bawl and silence. We all sat there tensely watching, but he didn't move.

I glanced at Bill and John; both looked as though they didn't quite believe what they had just seen and heard. Little drops of sweat were standing out on their faces.

"By gosh!" John exclaimed finally. "I'm sure glad he wasn't twins!"

"You can say that again!" Bill muttered, as he stuffed more ammunition into his rifle.

We walked over to the grizzly and gingerly approached to within a few yards. Dave chucked a rock at him but he didn't move. John had his grizzly, or so we thought. We have a standing rule that when two hunters fire at the same animal, the trophy goes to the man drawing first blood. So we dragged the bear out into the sun and photographed John with it, for we were all sure he had hit the grizzly with his first shot.

Then we skinned the bear out, and found only two bullet holes. One had struck the hip and ranged forward into the body cavity lengthwise; the other had smashed the shoulder. We recovered parts of both bullets – and both were .30-calibre.

The grizzlies of Grizzly Gulch have a reputation of being ornery bears, and this one lived up to it even after he was dead. He wouldn't even stay with the man who was supposed to have had him for a trophy.

High Country Honeymoon

People, whether they realize it or not, have always been influenced by other forms of life associated directly or indirectly with them in their environment. Primitive man always was and still is, in various parts of the world, a hunter depending on his success with many kinds of weapons ranging from fish hooks to bows and arrows for means of life.

Contrary to the conviction entertained by those who tend to support complete preservation, classing the hunter as a blood-hungry barbarian, a throwback from so-called civilization to the savage, the true sportsman hunter, really loving the game, is an asset to wildlife of all kinds. It is these who dip deep into their private bank accounts to support the causes of organized conservation and without them such organizations that are dedicated to wetlands restoration, many forms of research and other valuable projects would be nonexistent.

To practise complete preservation in any society is the next thing to impossible, and furthermore contrary to nature. People who advocate it are not really very consistent and tend to overlook

From *Horns in the High Country* (1973)

a valuable facet of outdoor recreation, plus the fact that we are not really so far along the trail from the primitive that we have lost the built-in characteristic of wanting and needing to hunt.

Among the wide variety of people, of many walks of life, finding their way every year to my door from all corners of the world, there are some who abhor hunting, will not eat meat and subsist on vegetation because they sincerely feel this is best for them. This is fine and I cheer them for it. It is the privilege of any individual, but as in the case of expounding one's particular brand of religion, I personally feel rather strongly against such a belief being thrust down someone else's throat.

Besides, while a few purists go as far as to wear canvas and rubber footgear and a string for a belt, there are others sufficiently hypocritical to wear leather footgear and hold up their pants with a strip of the same material. These are the noisiest of the lot, and on more than one occasion have had a turn at me.

I have often tried to analyze my own approach to hunting in such a way that it could be explained to others who might justifiably question the ethics of a conservationist who enjoys such recreation. It is not an easy thing to do, because I truly love to be around animals ranging free and undisturbed and certainly do not look on wildlife as just something put there for my enjoyment or to be killed. Perhaps it can best be defined thus: conservation in its truest form is a situation where man and nature work in harmony together. Hunting, properly managed and conducted with decent ethics, is most definitely a part of that harmony; for it is of no detriment to any species to take a part of each year's crop, a portion of the natural increase, to keep it within bounds of the restrictions of wintering range. It is equally necessary to maintain a very important phase of recreation. Man is inherently a predator, whether or not he chooses to recognize the fact, and because he is somewhat predatory he needs this outlet. It is the establishment of good ethics that counts. Under such discipline and awareness, he can be a powerful and successful influence towards the preservation of the environment and the continuance of the wildlife he pursues.

Why do I hunt the wild things I love? In fact my guns are hung up and now used largely for putting holes in targets, but I still enjoy singling out a buck in the fall and taking him to add to the winter's food supply. It does something for my ego as a provider for my family – a certain pride in the heart of man since he first picked up a stone to throw it and bring down a bird or animal for food way back there when a fire stick was the means to make a fire to cook it. Besides, we are very fond of fat, prime venison. Although we don't think of it in that way, it can be classed as rent paid by one animal for the food and shelter many others of his kind enjoy inside our fences. Also I have many friends who are hunters, and they are the salt of the earth. I still very much enjoy taking the trail with them in big open country and sharing a fire and the contents of a frying pan, stew pot, and the brew from a tea pail.

There are few families alive who have benefited more from their association with wildlife and the kind of people who love to hunt than those who share my roof. The advantages we enjoy go infinitely deeper than mere money gained from our activities afield; no question, they began when we were still in the cradle. But it was not till we were old and experienced enough to observe the richness of our surroundings that we became aware of them, and by one means or another began answering the calls of destiny.

Many, many years ago when I met and married Kay, my destiny took a turn for the better. It was June and I was trailing a string of forty-five horses north from this ranch to our base camp on Dutch Creek near where the Oldman River twists its way east through the gap in the Livingstone Range out onto the rolling reaches of the Alberta prairie. The hills and valleys along the front of the Rockies were lush and green, the sun warm and the breeze redolent with the smell of flowers and new leaves on the aspens and willows. On the ridge tops between the many streams across our path, one could sit his saddle and see the mountains stretching from south to north – blue and mauve in the distance. The sound of the Swiss bells on the horses played music in accompaniment to the sound of hoofs: muted on the grass, then drumming on hard trails. The timing of the bells chimed slowly when we walked up the steep slopes and over rough ground, but picked up its rhythm when the horse herd broke into a long reaching trot on the flats.

At first the horses were spooky and fractious after the winter's complete freedom, but after two long days on the trail both men and animals were once more a well-organized unit, blending together with the smell of hot dust and sweat in their noses. There was a certain anticipation of mountain trails ahead stretching through summer and fall till snow and cold sent us back to the home ranch for the winter.

I knew a feeling – a satisfying awareness that my personal trail held promise, although it did not stem from accumulation of much property. For about all I owned in the world besides what I stood up in was my saddle and bedroll, the contents of my war bag, a few horses, traps, and various gear. This was the beginning of my third year as a guide, packer, and rough string rider, and experience was telling me something of the zest going with being fairly good at what I was doing. For three years I had been attending a kind of outdoor school under the direction of Bert Riggall, a man who was a great teacher without being aware of it. The horses had added their bit to the education, as well as the association with many highly educated people. The school of the Rockies is one of hard knocks on occasion, but it has its definite compensations.

When we came jingling into the corral at Dutch Creek on the evening of the second day with ninety miles unrolled behind us, camp was set up and waiting. Bert greeted us as we pushed the horses through the gate. After unsaddling, I left my trail partner to tie up a night horse and headed for the cook tent suddenly aware that I was starving. At the door of the tent I was happily greeted by the girl who reigned over the place. I had not seen her for two days and it seemed like two years, which speaks for itself.

Bert's daughter, Kay, had been born in a tent and grew up on horseback. She had worked on the trail as cook for the outfit since she was fourteen years old and had an uncommon amount of experience for her years in about everything from keeping city people happy in wild country, to treating an axe cut in somebody's foot, or making a sick horse well again. Her smile was serene and her temper about as even as a woman's can be. Many times, I have seen her get off her horse in pouring rain, help set the cook tent up, and have a sizzling hot supper ready for a dozen people in about forty-five minutes from time of arrival.

Kay and I had been working on the same crew for two years, so we knew each other. There is no place where you get to know anyone quite as well as while camping in all kinds of weather on wilderness trails, especially in the fall high up in bighorn country. For there the blinds are lifted, the true character of a person is revealed, and there is no man or woman who can manage to hide much of importance about themselves. There is something about living in the open among high mountains in all kinds of weather under canvas with the smell of campfire smoke in your nose that strips away all pretense.

To make a long story of fun and adventure shorter, after four solid months on the trail with various parties that summer and fall, Kay and I were married on a fine October day at high noon in front of the big windows of the lodge here at the ranch and headed out on our honeymoon. Did we take off for the city and the bright lights? We did not. We saddled up nine head of hand-picked horses and headed back into the mountains for a month's sheep hunt. We did not care a whoop if we shot a ram, but we knew the quest would take us a long way, we would have a wonderful time with nobody to think about but ourselves. The hunting was strictly an excuse for the going, but if we were lucky we would come back with the winter's meat.

We travelled in leisurely fashion following the streams up between the mountains under brilliant skies with the lower slopes all painted in yellow, gold, and red. We pitched our tent on mountain meadows in the evenings close to a stream, and while I tended the horses, Kay cooked supper. We ate from a folding table sitting on pack boxes with our aluminum plates gleaming in the light of candles, and what was just plain good food tasted like a feast prepared for gods. We lay snug in our eiderdown robes at night drifting into sleep with the soft murmuring of the river in our ears accompanied sometimes by the music of Swiss bells in the distance, or the faraway lonesome singing of coyotes.

Sometimes we took our fly rods and went fishing with the barbs of our hooks broken off to make releasing the trout easy. At one camp we checked the sights of our rifles by shooting at a white spot on a boulder projecting from a bank 250 yards away across a bend of the river.

It was just after sunrise and Kay was getting ready to shoot from a prone position behind a rolled-up sleeping bag when we spotted two riders coming up the valley. They were cowboys from a big ranch outside the mountains making their fall round-up of the cattle grazing here all summer. We knew them and, after the usual greetings, they asked what we were shooting at. When I pointed to the target, they both looked at Kay, and one said, "Hmmm," softly to himself and there was a slight note of skepticism in it. I just nodded and grinned at her as a signal to go ahead and shoot, while our visitors stepped off their horses to watch.

Kay rested her left hand holding the forestock of the little .250 Savage over the sleeping bag, snuggled her cheek down firmly on the stock, and squeezed off a shot. Dust flew from the mark on the rock. She levered a fresh round into the barrel and fired again. Again the bullet kicked up dust from the same spot. Casually she stood up to let me take my turn. The cowboys were looking at her with awe and admiration, for there are few things that impress this kind more than good shooting.

As they stepped up on their horses, the skeptical one swept off his hat in a graceful bow from his saddle and said, "Some shooting, ma'am! Good hunting!" Then turning to me he added, "Congratulations! But take care you don't ever make her mad enough to take a shot at you, because if she does, she sure as hell ain't going to miss!"

With that they whirled their horses and were gone.

There came a day when we rode high above timberline along the crest of a ridge, searching for bighorns in a series of basins. But all we could find was a bunch of ewes and lambs and a few juvenile rams. We watched them a while from above, our saddle horses ground-hitched behind us over the rim out of sight, but there were no big rams in the vicinity. A mile or two of country was covered like this, and then we ate lunch on top of a rocky point while glassing the surrounding country. About a mile away, I spotted a big mule deer buck with a fine rack of antlers as he got up out of his bed in a patch of shintangle to feed along a strip of low brush at the foot of a rock slide. We needed meat and here was a chance to get it, but the buck was in a very open piece of country with very little cover for a stalk. While we finished our sandwiches we looked the problem over and decided the only way to reach the buck was to come down from above him on the far side.

So leaving our horses we made a great circle way up around the head of the canyon. Our swing took us more than an hour and finally brought us to a place directly opposite where we had first spotted the buck. The only wind was from the thermals lifting up the slope in our faces in the warm sun. Making use of the folds of the slope we headed down. Then we came to the long stretch of coarse rock slide above the patch of scrub where the buck had been feeding. A slight bulge just over the spot hid it from us, but our hobnailed boots would telegraph our approach long before we could come within range.

There was just one thing to do: sitting down I took off my boots and hung them over my shoulder. Not hesitating a moment Kay did the same and together we went gingerly out onto the broken stuff in our stocking feet. One thing about going over rough rock with nothing on your feet but a pair of heavy wool socks, you are inspired to proceed with care and are consequently very quiet about it. So we went down across the slide as silently as a couple of Indians.

Finally we came out onto a tiny grassy spot within sight of the scrub willow, but no buck was in sight. Combing the place with the glasses, I examined every little detail of it with great care. The lenses picked up the dull gleam of a polished antler point sticking up from behind a boulder a hundred yards below.

Whispering to Kay to get ready, I threw a rock down the slope. The buck must have been aware he had company, for he soared out of his bed in a great leap and went bounding down the mountain. After half a dozen jumps, he paused to look back and there Kay dropped him with a quick shot through the heart.

The echoes of her shot had not died when another, much bigger buck exploded out of some shintangle not twenty yards to my right. He took me completely by surprise and by the time I got swivelled around, was flying in great jumps down the mountain. Swinging the little 7 mm Greener-Mauser like a shotgun, I swept the sight past his nose and closed my hand on the trigger. The bullet caught him in the ribs on top of a great bound, raking through at a forward angle and dropping him so dead he never kicked.

Both bucks were hog-fat. There was something mighty satisfying about cleaning them out and cutting up the carcasses so they could be packed on horses; the days were growing shorter and the nights sharp with frost, reminding us of the long cold months ahead when fat venison would taste mighty good. I hung the quarters in a scrub pine to cool.

As we were closer to camp than to the saddle horses, I suggested to Kay that she walk down the canyon to the tent pitched at its juncture with Savannah Creek, while I made the long climb back up to the horses and brought them around the way we had come. To this she readily agreed and she disappeared down the valley with her rifle slung over her shoulder. Little did I think that the day's excitement was far from being over.

Some time later, when the sun was just beginning to dip behind the mountains to the west, I was skirting the face of a steep grassy slope along a narrow game trail with Kay's horse trailing behind. I was still more than a mile from camp, relaxed in the saddle with my mind on the hot supper that was waiting ahead, when the game trail lifted a bit to skirt the top of a low bank rimming a hole full of brush. There was a spring bubbling up among the willows with a big lone spruce growing beside it. My horse was a big, black, quarter-bred Kentucky mare, and when she got right above the spring hole, there was a sudden great snort from something hidden in the brush below and another from the mare in reply. Then a big grizzly reared up, and the horse promptly blew up. Being very allergic to bears, she swung her nose uphill and reared straight up on her hind legs. Swivelling in the saddle and drawing my rifle in the same motion, I was looking down over the cantle squarely into the grizzly's face. The mare was apparently going to try to kill the bear by falling on him, and wanting no part of such recklessness I swung off her. At the same time she gave a big jump and I came down from a great deal farther up than I planned with my rifle clutched in my hand. The landing shook me plenty and slowed me down, and by the time my eyes came back in focus and I got somewhat better organized, the bear was just disappearing over a bulge on the slope below heading for tall timber in great bounds. When I looked back toward the horses, it was to see them hightailing for camp on the dead run.

Somewhat chagrined and disgusted, I followed. About a quarter of a mile from camp, Kay came riding to meet me leading my horse. When she saw I was still in one piece and not even limping, her face lit up, and when I explained what had happened she laughed.

"Hurry up, bear hunter!" she said. "Supper will be burned to a crisp."

Whirling her mount she headed back on the gallop. Lifting my horse into a run behind her, I couldn't resist howling a war whoop of sheer exuberance. It was fun to be alive. This was adventure raw and wild; we were up to our ears in the middle of it.

At supper Kay told me how she had come down through timber along the creek; big branchy white pines loaded with cones, and the ground beneath all torn up by grizzlies digging up squirrel caches. That year the white pines in that part of the country bore a heavy crop of nuts, and as they always do, the squirrels had gathered from miles around to reap the harvest. The same moccasin telegraph had told the grizzlies and they too came, not to take the nuts from the cones in the trees, but to rob the squirrel caches. Kay reported the ground was literally ploughed under the trees and that she had come a mile ready for trouble, parting the greenery ahead of her with the muzzle of her cocked rifle.

Next day when we went back with horses for the meat, we crossed the tracks of four grizzlies, but none had touched our meat.

Grizzlies did not interest us enough for us to go out of our way hunting them, so again we packed to head up onto the slopes of the main range of the Rockies just a mile or two east of the Continental Divide.

It was a wild and secluded place we chose for a campsite, our tent snuggled in close to a grove of big pines on a bend of a little creek with snow-streaked peaks towering up behind. It was a dream kind of hunting camp with shelter, water, lots of dry firewood for the cutting, and plenty of good grass for the horses along a chain of meadows flanking the meandering stream. Apart from an old Indian trail marked with blazes made with knives, round-backed instead of flat like those slashed by a white man's axe, the valley looked like nobody had visited it for years. Except for the hooting of a great horned owl in the trees back of the tent, it was very quiet that evening as we ate supper by candlelight.

Next morning it was blowing hard, but it was warm so we went out to have a look for sheep. A couple of miles to the west, the trail lifted steeply out of the timber into a series of alpine meadows just under the talus fans of a big basin. The wind was sporadic but very turbulent, alternating between periods of flat calm and wild gusts that came roaring and twisting through the timberline spruces and larches. Overhead, the sky was full of flying, wind-torn clouds scudding eastward on the blast of a southwest gale. Up high the wind was consistent in its direction but down at our level it was sucking back under the cliffs, very erratic and promising trouble if we had to make a stalk.

Sheep trails crisscrossed the slides, some heavy and looking freshly used, but when we tied the horses and climbed up for a closer look, the freshest sheep sign we found was two or three days old. In this kind of weather tracks age fast, which can be misleading, but when we glassed the slopes no sheep were in sight. We climbed down to remount and head up onto a ridge dividing this basin from the next one to the south.

Tying the horses again in a little grove of scrub fir lining a pocket, we climbed to the crest and there ran into the full blast of the wind. Crawling on hands and knees we bellied down to glass the deep basin revealed below. The wind was terrific, stinging our faces with bits of herbage and dirt, sometimes forcing us to flatten out with eyes tight shut for protection. Overhead it was booming and slatting off the top of the cliffs as though popping giant sails.

Directly across from us at a fairly high level where a strip of slide rock lay trapped between cliffs, there were a couple of snow-filled gullies showing the tracks of sheep. These tracks looked fresh, so we endured the discomfort and continued to search in the intervals allowed by the wind. We would not dare to try any kind of stalk across the ledges along the front of the mountain on a day like this, for it would be far too dangerous. But the rams would likely be low in this kind of weather, if they were here at all, and that was where we directed our glasses.

We were about to give up, when I saw a flicker of movement in a strip of brush away across the basin, low near the timber in the bottom. Then the outline of a big pair of curling horns showed up against a patch of yellow leaves, and a moment later six rams filed out of the willows to begin feeding on a strip of grass. Two were young with half-curl heads. Three more carried horns close to a full curl. The leader was a magnificent old ram – the kind that makes the pulse of a hunter jump. If they had been warned of our coming they could not have chosen their feeding ground with a better eye to strategic location. It looked like an impossible place to approach, particularly on a day like this with the wind rolling and curling back under the lee of the mountain in all directions. It was not only being stirred by the sheer force of velocity, but it was warm, and this compounded thermals into the boiling cauldron brewing a hunter's nightmare, and my experience knew no precedents from which to draw comparisons. There were two things that were sure: these rams would be gone if they caught our scent and if they saw us they would be rapidly departing through a hole in the scenery. My memory was fresh with an example of their keen eyes.

Earlier that fall, Bert and I had been hunting in this same general region with our old friend Franklin Crosby, who was the complete antithesis of the kind of hunter who lives to kill. For over twenty years he had been coming from Minneapolis to hunt with Bert for a great ram to the point of making an annual pilgrimage of it. Time and again he had passed up chances to take good rams, for he wanted a very special kind of trophy — a huge old buster of a ram close to the end of his life trail.

He generally hunted with us alone. Over the years he and Bert had become very close friends, a fact soon apparent to me upon my joining the outfit. My role on these expeditions was that of horse wrangler, packer, and apprentice guide. I was warmly aware of being accepted and welcomed by these men as a third member of the party, invited to trail in the hunting and given full credit for my ability with horses and knowing how to climb. If there was one thing I had trouble understanding it was their philosophical, easygoing, and enormous patience. Time and again they looked over good rams and turned them down without a flicker of disappointment showing on their faces. Neither of them seemed to mind if the bag was empty at the end of a long trip; they just planned another. Being young I did not realize at first that they were enjoying themselves just looking, not caring a whoop if anything was shot; something that comes with experience and savouring good company in hunting camps scattered across the Rockies. Sometimes I wondered if we ever would find a ram that would get these two excited.

Then came a day in September, delightfully cool and clear, when the three of us topped a ridge above timberline to glass a deep basin below very much like this one. Lying prone on a natural overlook among some scattered rocks to hide our heads, we combed the place thoroughly through three pairs of the best binoculars until I was personally sure that I had minutely examined every boulder, clump of brush and tuft of grass not just once, but at least three times. Although some of the trails on the talus fans at the back of the basin looked dark and sharp cut as though from recent use, not a living thing was in sight.

A big lone billy wandered into view around a shoulder a peak above. I gave it a cursory glance or two, but we were not interested in goats.

Then Bert grunted and got to his feet to lead the way out across a wide open stretch of steeply pitched mountain meadow covered with bunch grass. We had gone about fifty yards single file when he suddenly dropped as though shot between the shoulder blades, and we came down flat behind him an instant later. I could hear Bert swearing softly and fluently to himself and knew he had seen something mighty unusual. Then my eye caught a flicker of movement in the bottom of the basin about seven hundred yards below amongst a mess of boulders. Slowly turning my head for a better look through the glasses revealed five rams – all real patriarchs – and then I knew the reason for the swearing. All five were big but the largest was an animal to stop the breath. He was big all over, a deep charcoal grey, and his mahogany-brown horns were massive, swept well back in the curls and coming around in a full swing with the broomed tips about even with the bridge of his Roman nose.

How we missed seeing them earlier is still a profound mystery to me, for they were in plain sight, though bedded deep among the boulders. I could have wept, for here we were pinned down in the open like a trio of rank greenhorns, and it looked like we would have to stay anchored till dark or the sheep decided to move. Every eye was fastened on us, and as big rams will often do, they did not even bother to get up on their feet. Then the big herdmaster rose to give us a long hard stare, but when we did not move, he lay down again, calm and serene.

I had the taste of bitter hopelessness in my mouth feeling sure we were beaten without a hope of doing anything about it. Incredulously, I heard Franklin Crosby chuckle softly to himself behind me, obviously amused at the joke that was on us. It was almost more than I could stand.

But Bert had other things in mind. Hissing to get our attention, he softly told us to slip out of our rucksacks and jackets, prop
the bags up against anything handy, and drape our jackets over
them. He set his packsack up against a little tree about two feet
high, wrapped his jacket around it, and then tied a red bandanna
to the tip of the tree above, where it swayed and fluttered in the
breeze. Motioning for us to keep flat with out noses in the grass
roots, he squirmed downhill into a bit of a trough leading back
and down at an angle to a tongue of shintangle scrub. We trailed
along wiggling like snakes as close to the ground as we could get.
It was slow going and a long crawl. When I finally dared sneak a
look at the rams, they were still bedded down with every eye still
fixed on the beguiling flag Bert had left behind.

It is amazing what hard work such a crawl can be even when
downslope, and by the time we reached the screening scrub and
could sit up, we were wringing wet with sweat. Fifty yards farther
and we were in heavy timber, where Bert led off at a trot straight
toward the rams. Finally he slowed to a walk again to lead the way
out to the edge of a meadow for a quick look. He nodded at our
hunter with a smile, took the shoulder-high alpine stock he always
carried and placed it cross-wise in a gap between two branchy
pines to make an improvised armrest. Beckoning Franklin to sit
down behind it and take his shot, Bert lifted his glasses to watch.

Through my binoculars I could see the big ram a bit beyond
and up the slope from the rest. He was lying broadside but a bit
quartering toward us with his eyes still fixed on the decoys. Our
friend took his time to steady down, then aimed very deliberately
and fired. The bullet popped on the rocks, throwing up a puff of
dust six inches below. It was a long reach for the little 7 mm
Mauser, close to three hundred yards, with the ram seeming to
offer a much bigger target than he really was, for we were looking
downhill at him. At the shot, he leapt to his feet and bounded a
few jumps straight away up the slope at an angle to come to a stand

looking straight away with his rump patch showing white against the dark grey rock.

"Hold right between his horns a foot over his tail," Bert murmured softly.

As calmly as though he was in a shooting gallery, Franklin Crosby chambered a fresh cartridge, aimed, and fired again. This time the unmistakable plop of a bullet striking flesh came back to our ears. For a second the ram stood motionless, then turned slowly downhill weaving on his feet to suddenly collapse and roll over dead.

We were jubilant as we made our way across to the ram and Bert whooped when he got a close look at the horns. This ram was truly a buster – big, burly, and fat. Our friend had collected a trophy of a lifetime, one of the biggest and oldest I ever saw killed. It was the one having sixteen annual rings on its horns allowing one for brooming, and as sure as we stood there in our boots, we had witnessed a master sheep stalker at his best, improvising and making use of his knowledge of sheep and available cover.

Now Kay and I were confronted with a similar prize but a different kind of dilemma. We had plenty of cover leading directly to the rams, but we dared not use it, for if we tried, the rolling and eddying wind currents would most certainly give us away. Our best and only chance would be to circle wide and come down on them from the top of the buttress ridge above them, so we headed for our horses. While the hurricane roared I led the way in a great circle down and across the valley below picking a circuitous trail through the heavy timber. It was a bit hair-rising here and there when we heard the thunderous crash of a big tree coming down. Striking a heavy elk trail, we made better time across the bottom and up the far side. Finally we rode into a comparatively sheltered spot amongst a scattered grove of larches in the lee of a knoll. There we tied the horses and proceeded on foot. At timberline we came out among some low scrub and swung down at an angle over a steep slope to a bench overlooking the place where we had seen the rams. On hands and knees we crawled out through a belt of scrubby fir and sat up for a look. The rams had vanished.

Very carefully examining every foot of ground through my glasses, I finally spotted the top edge of a big curling horn showing over the rim of a gully. The rams were lying in the bottom of the wash just beyond out of the wind. With rifles ready, we waited for them to move. Perhaps half an hour went by, when a puff of wind must have blown down to them from above giving them our scent, for they suddenly exploded into view heading straight up the mountain on the dead run past us. The big ram was in the lead.

"Take him," I said softly.

Kay aimed from a sitting position while I watched to spot her shot. But nothing happened, and when I looked to see what was wrong, it was to see her frantically taking the safety off. She had been trying to shoot with it on, something never too good to calm the nerves. Now the rams were at our level and passing like race-horses at about 150 yards. Kay shot but her bullet went a good foot behind the ram's tail, powdering rock in a puff of dust.

"Shoot before he gets behind those rocks," she implored.

Picking the ram up in my sights I swung with him and fired, but the steep angle fooled me and my bullet went under his belly. Now the rams were flying and I committed an error. For a frac-tion of a second I looked down at my rifle as I bolted another car-tridge. In that short interval a ram just behind the big one took the lead, and without even looking at its horns I swung my rifle past its nose and killed it stone dead in mid-stride.

The instant I pulled the trigger, I knew I had shot at the wrong ram. "Damn if I haven't killed the wrong one!" was all I could think to say. "Quick! Take him!"

But the rams had gone behind a rock spur and when they reap-peared they were about three hundred yards away. There they all stopped to look back, bunched up close together with the big one standing a bit to one side.

"You can anchor him there," I told Kay. "He's the one on the left."

"But I might wound another one," Kay said. "No, I've missed my chance. Let's let them go."

I did not argue, for the choice was hers. Besides, she was smiling and unconcerned as she watched the sheep running in a string across the trail on a talus fan toward the far side of the basin.

We dressed out my ram, propping it open to cool. I piled some brush over it to keep off eagles and magpies, then took the head down to the bottom where I hung it in a tree. Climbing back to our horses we headed for camp, planning to come back with a packhorse in the morning.

Next morning it was snowing a blizzard out of the north and the driving wind had the cold dry smell of the Arctic in it and the feel of winter. I found the horses humped up, cold and miserable, in a patch of timber a mile or so down the creek from camp, brought them to the rope corral and caught a couple. Kay wanted to come with me but I knew what it was going to be like at timberline, and persuaded her to stay in camp.

Leading a packhorse I headed out. It was a wild day at timberline with flying snow sometimes cutting visibility to fifty yards. By the time I reached the ram, skinned it out, cut it up and packed it, there was a foot of snow on the ground and it had turned mean-cold with no letup in the wind. When I reached camp in late afternoon, the warm tent was welcome.

By the following morning it had almost stopped snowing but the sky was lead grey and the temperature way below zero; so we holed up to weather out the storm. The tent was warm and cheery and there was plenty of wood to keep it that way. We had brought some good books and Kay had some wool for knitting. She alternated between reading, getting meals, and knitting me a pair of socks, while I cut wood, kept track of the horses, and took my turn at the books. Once, I rigged up my fly rod, much to her amusement, went up the creek to a beaver pond and cut a hole through the ice with my axe. Using a wet fly, jigging fashion, I soon had enough fat cutthroat trout for our supper, although my line froze solid in the guides of the rod.

Watching her knit as she sat in a comfortable improvised chair, while the fire crackled cheerfully in our sheet-iron stove, I had the wonderfully satisfying feeling of knowing a remarkable woman. If either one of us had been shading some opinions about the other, they would have come out during that three-day storm. Being storm-bound in a mountain camp was not new for us, but this was the first time we had shared one alone. There is not much of importance two people can hide from each other in such a spot with the wind moaning cold among the trees and peaks; no friction between personalities that can remain secret, for this is the supreme test.

It was the beginning of a long, adventurous, sometimes worrisome though happy trail called marriage. Like all people we have had our share of troubles, but when the chips are down these fade to nothing and we can still look at each other and smile after nearly thirty-five years.

If I were to design a coat-of-arms for our family, it would feature a mountain flanked by a grizzly and a bighorn ram, for our tracks have been entwined with theirs and the mountains have been our home and talisman from the very beginning.

PART THREE

WITH ROD AND REEL

As a boy, Andy haunted the streams and creeks around the ranch. He explored them, fell into them and, yes, he caught fish. He was largely untutored and free to use any means of corralling them he could devise. Mountain rivers and creeks are seductive. They have always enticed young boys and girls with their beauty and their song. That song, once heard, signals a lifelong love affair that compels the hearer to return again and again to listen to the music and to pursue the denizens who dwell beneath the sparkling waters.

Andy was introduced to fly fishing for trout by summer guests wielding fine bamboo rods. It was not long before he became not only a proficient fly fisher, but an ardent one. Andy's stories reveal the special joy he finds along wild rivers or on the shores of remote mountain lakes stalking feeding trout.

The Wilderness Fisherman

As a boy of a size "somewhere between weanin' and chewin' tobaccer," as Charlie Wise, an old friend and mountain trapper, would put it, I ran the gamut between tickling trout, noosing fish with a loop of snare wire tied to the end of a stick, throwing a bait to them big enough to keep a good-sized cat fed for a day, presenting an impaled grasshopper on a snelled hook, and angling with hand-crafted artificial flies so small it was difficult to see them well enough to tie them on the hair-like tippet of the leader.

To those who have never heard of tickling trout, I will explain: it is an old English and Scottish poacher's trick, which I learned from reading a classic entitled *Lorna Doone* and from the further instruction of our old friend Lionel Brook. It is only possible in small streams or in such places where one can reach into a hide with a hand. By the use of much patience and practice it is possible to slip a hand under a fish and stroke its belly, which lulls it into allowing the fingers to be slipped under the gill covers and clamped shut. The fish is then thrown out of the water onto the

From *Trails of a Wilderness Wanderer* (1978)

bank. I might add that very few people have the patience to master the muscle control necessary for success. On one or two occasions when I was hungry and had nothing much to work with but my hands, I used this method with success. One time I took a fair-sized Dolly Varden out from under an overhanging ledge and cooked him on a flat rock over a fire without anything else to garnish the result. My father and I ate well off that fish and enjoyed what would have otherwise been a very hungry ride.

Snaring fish is largely illegal and justifiable now only as a means of survival. All one needs is a piece of brass or copper wire from fourteen to eighteen inches long. For small fish only one strand is necessary, but for larger kinds this may be too light and then two or three strands must be twisted or braided together. The snare is tied on the end of a light pole with the loop open. It is a matter then of just carefully slipping the snare over the fish's head, jerking it shut just back of the gills, and swinging the captive out on the bank in the same motion. Of course this can be done only in clear water where fish are within reach. In the smaller streams along the mountains in summer we took whitefish in this manner, when food was the first consideration.

When someone came who was likely to stay for a meal, my mother, upon finding her pantry a bit short of something to serve quickly, would send my brother and me to the creek for some fish. In half an hour we would usually be back with all the whitefish we needed. Just to see if it could be done, I once snared a ten-pound great northern pike with an ordinary braided cotton shoelace tied on a forked willow. It is a good way to get a meal in wilderness country if one has no better way, but there is absolutely nothing sportsmanlike about it.

The early settlers along the foot of the Rockies did not use nets. A net is expensive to make or buy, and this means of taking fish was largely unnecessary, for few people needed or wanted that much fish. Dynamiting was another means of taking fish practised by a very few. It was frowned upon by most everybody, for it destroyed everything in a section of stream and was extremely wasteful. On rare occasions dynamite is still used by unscrupulous types. The only time in my life I was ever tempted to throw down on a man with a gun was when I caught three coal miners dynamiting trout.

We were coming back through the Rockies with the pack train in August, after a camping trip on the Flathead River in southeast British Columbia, when I rode back to an overnight camp alone to get my spurs, which had been left hanging in a tree. That morning we had passed three coal miners on a fishing holiday hiking down the trail with packs on their backs. Where the trail rimmed a deep gorge not far from our campsite, I heard the unmistakable boom of a blast from down in the bottom. When I left my horse and climbed down to investigate, I came out of a fold in the cliff face within ten steps of this trio of tough-looking characters all busy retrieving fish killed by the blast. At their feet among the rocks were several large Dolly Varden trout. Upon my somewhat smoky query as to what they thought they were pulling off, they turned in momentary astonishment. But this did not last long. Two of them started toward me with that flat, stone-hard look men get in their eyes when they are closing in on one of their own kind with nothing good in mind. I was wearing a long-waisted, heavily fringed, beaded moosehide jacket, which somewhat camouflaged the gun belt and holster strapped around my hips. In the holster was one of old Sam Colt's historic "equalizers" – a famed .44-calibre single-action six-shooter, and at that moment I was very glad to have it within reach. I didn't touch it, however, but just peeled back my coat out of the way and hooked my thumbs in the belt. The atmosphere and general climate around there changed very fast, and the gentlemen in front of me acquired the look of those who were all set to club a rabbit and suddenly found they were declaring war on a grizzly bear. They did not try to run, but melted down to size while I read them the riot act. Had I not been over a hundred miles from the nearest conservation officer and in no position to lay charges, I would have been delighted to turn them in for prosecution. As it was I hazed three chastened men back up the trail and escorted them out of the province of British Columbia with a solemn promise of what would happen if they chose to come back. I never saw them again.

I carried that pistol for years, with a special permit to make it legal, putting up with its weight and inconvenience with the thought that some day I might need it to discourage a bear that might decide to chew on me or kill a horse if someone got a foot hung up in a stirrup. In all the thousands of miles of wilderness country it was never needed except on that day, and, strangely enough, to protect myself from some of my own species. Had I not been carrying it, I might have bluffed or fought my way out of a tough spot, but likely not without some considerable expense one way or another. As it was, the episode amounted to very little, nobody got hurt, and perhaps some good was done – all of which may boil down to some kind of moral in the context of some modern-day questions.

When I was still little more than knee-high, I can remember my father putting a set-line in the St. Mary's River to take fish for the table. A set-line, or trot-line as it is called farther south, was generally anchored on each shore and adjusted so that the length of the line lay across the bottom of the river. At regular intervals a shorter piece was tied to this line – each with a big hook on the end. The hooks were baited with a piece of raw meat or a small fish. Such a line was usually attended with a boat, and with it a considerable number of fish could be taken at once. But where no boat was available, the trot-line had a heavy weight attached to one end for an anchor; the other end was attached to a stake or tree limb along the shore. This was the kind my father and mother used for northern pike, walleyes, and other fish found in the river. There were very few trout in the lower reaches of the St. Mary's, but plenty of coarse fish, including the occasional enormous sturgeon, Lake Winnipeg goldeyes, ling, or burbot, along with millions of various kinds of small fish.

It was always something of an adventure to haul in a set-line. Mother would shriek with excitement as she pulled in a malevolent-looking monster of a pike with a mean gleam in his eyes and a set of teeth that would do justice to a small alligator.

The pike is a predatory fish looking something like a freshwater variety of barracuda. It will eat about anything small enough to get down its throat, and has been known on occasion to choke on something too large to fit. Small fish are its usual prey, but it will also take small animals and birds if the opportunity arises. I once saw a mother mallard moving her brood from a high-ground nesting site to the Waterton Lakes. When she came to the river with her brood, she headed for an island in mid-stream, but before she had gone more than a few feet, a V-shaped wave headed her way at high speed from one side. There was a sudden heavy swirl and a duckling straggling a bit behind the small flotilla was suddenly not there any more. At first the mother duck was unaware of the deadly menace stalking her family, but when another duckling disappeared, she sped into a flurrying scramble. The surviving young ducks almost ran on the surface in their efforts to keep up to her, but in spite of her efforts to get her family out of reach of the big fish, half the brood was gone by the time she reached the shelter of the island.

I once dressed a northern pike weighing perhaps five or six pounds that had just eaten a young muskrat before it took my spoon. Another time I found a half-grown ground squirrel in the stomach of one.

At Grandfather's ranch one afternoon following a heavy thunderstorm, I found a barn swallow's nest knocked down from under the eaves of one of the buildings. There were four almost fully

grown and fledged young swallows lying drowned in the wreckage of the mud nest. Not really knowing why, I picked up the dead
birds and carried them down to the river, where I casually tossed
one into the water. The heavy current swept it down around the
end of a submerged reef of coal projecting from the bank, where
there was a sudden electrifying explosion from the depths and
the bird disappeared. The next swallow that went floating along the
same route had a fairly substantial hook impaled in it, which was
bent to a wire leader tied to a stout braided cotton line. My rod
was a peeled willow, to which I clung with both hands with the
butt braced against my belly.

There was still a lot of slack line coiled in loops and bends on
the surface when there was a sudden flash of a big fish and the
water flew as the floating bird disappeared. The line went shooting out toward the middle of the river at high speed, and there
was barely time to get my legs braced when a huge pike ran into
the end of the slack like a suddenly snubbed bronco at the end of
a rope. Up out of the water the big fish jumped in a great tail-
snapping leap, ending up in a big splash as the tight line jerked it
down. The pike was hooked deep in the gullet, and when I finally
hauled it out on the sand bar and quieted it with a stout club, it
appeared even bigger than it had in the river.

It was a handsome fish in a tigerish sort of way and all the load
a ten-year-old could manage. When I picked it up by a gill cover,
its nose came up even with my shoulder while its tail still dragged
on the ground. It was never weighed, but over the intervening
years it still lingers sharply in my memory as being one of the
biggest fish I ever caught. It was about the closest I ever came to
taking pike on a dry fly – although many times some good catches
have been taken on a floating plug made of wood or plastic – all
painted in gay colours and armed with treble hooks. Even though
these pike were taken on light tackle that would have made my
peeled pole of that day on the St. Mary's look like a telephone

pole by comparison, that battle stands out as being a combat of sheer strength between a small boy and a big fish – primitive, fierce, and unforgettable.

I once knew a trapper who in the spring tended a line by canoe along a river collecting beaver and muskrats. It was a wild, uninhabited piece of country, and his only contact with the outside world was a small village upstream a few miles, where a railroad crossed the stream.

Upon running short of some supplies, he paddled up to this place one day to replenish his stock. Along toward evening he headed back downriver, loafing along with the current, carrying his canoe silently on its way. It was a very pleasant, balmy evening and the man was enjoying a good cigar as the canoe slipped past groves of silent spruces and cottonwoods under a rich canopy of stars studding the night sky. Taking the cigar from his mouth he knocked the ash off into the water, exposing the glowing coal on its lighted tip. Before he could put it back in his mouth, a great pike came lancing up out of the river and closed its teeth on his hand. He threw the fish in the canoe and managed to extricate his fingers from its mouth, but not before suffering bad lacerations. He went on to his camp, but the wound somehow got infected and did not heal for a long time. This man still carries the scars to prove that pike sometimes snap at anything when hungry.

The pike is generally not considered to be of top eating quality; but if carefully filleted and skinned, then deboned by pulling the forked sidebones out of the fillets with a pair of pliers, it is delicious when caught in cold water. Its flavour can be greatly enhanced by sprinkling the raw sides of the fillets with a teaspoon of rye whiskey as they fry.

The walleyes rarely achieved a weight of more than six or seven pounds. These were delicious fresh from the river fried in bacon grease. John and I had our best luck with them as the water cleared after a heavy rain – especially following the spring flood. If one was caught, there always seemed to be more in the same hole, for they ran in schools and fed like hungry wolves.

Almost every time we went fishing in the St. Mary's, we caught one or two Lake Winnipeg goldeyes, a Canadian fish found nowhere else but in Lake Winnipeg and the Saskatchewan drainage. The goldeye is a pretty fish, with large silver scales and bright gold eyes. It grows up to sixteen and seventeen inches in length and sometimes attains a weight of two and a half pounds. We occasionally caught them on the surface with a floating grass-hopper, but more often with a polished copper Colorado spinner or a small minnow while fishing for pike or walleyes. The goldeye is a tasty panfish when cooked fresh, but reaches gourmet heights when smoked.

The first time I ever set a line in the river all night I hooked a fish I had never seen before. When I went early in the morning to haul in the line there was something heavy and sluggish at the other end. Bringing in the line revealed a great ugly fish, almost as long as I, with a slippery smooth scaleless hide coloured in yellow-green mottles against a lead-grey background. Its tail was rounded instead of forked, as were all its ventral and pectoral fins. Running most of the length of its back was a long, ragged dorsal fin like a piece of wet limp leather. I had captured a monster of a ling with a great potbelly and a mouth like a cavern.

The ling, or more correctly the burbot, is a kind of fresh-water cod. It looks like something held over from another era in the evolution of life on earth – a time when strange and wonderful animals wandered among the steaming swamps – and quite likely it is. By trout standards of good looks, it is a most unappetizing-looking fish, and more than one modern-day bait fisherman has thrown such a catch away. Nothing could be more wasteful, for the ling, upon being skinned, filleted, and properly cooked in bacon fat, is a most delicious fish, almost indistinguishable from fresh cod; its meat is sweet, snow-white, and rich, with only a few large bones.

Although the huge sturgeon was a very rare catch on the far western reaches of the Saskatchewan drainage, every so often a set-line fisherman would catch one of these fish. I recall a coal miner hooking and landing one on the St. Mary's that was about as long as himself and weighed in the neighbourhood of seventy pounds. As sturgeon go it was only a baby, but a monster of a fish just the same, which warranted headlines in the local newspaper and gave the fisherman a measure of fame for miles around.

Food came first and sport second among the early settlers where catching fish was concerned. The rivers and creeks teemed with fish then, and while there was no kind of refrigeration to keep them for very long, smoking and salting were the methods employed to preserve fish for winter use. Some of the ranch women also canned fish in Mason jars with a light vinegar sauce, which softened the bones and kept the meat perfectly for a long time. For the most part fish were eaten fresh.

Up in the streams under the face of the Rockies we found a different world, where my brother and I not only enjoyed the ultimate in piscatorial adventure, but also learned to appreciate and practise sporting methods of taking fish.

Down either side of the great rugged mass of Drywood Mountain the north and south forks of the Drywood flowed clear and sparkling cold to join on our ranch. We called the north fork Butcher's Creek, and the other Carpenter Creek, after two ranchers who lived along the banks, while below the forks it was the Drywood as designated on the map. These creeks flowed over brilliantly coloured rocks of every shade, where sun and shadow played in the swirling currents, and cutthroat trout, whitefish, and great Dolly Vardens lurked and fed – vastly exciting, undulating shadows moving under graceful overhanging willows, aspens, and cottonwoods.

Later the rainbow trout was introduced, and we found the added thrill of fighting a great sport fish, which leaps high out of the water when hooked.

There was a smaller stream – the middle fork of the Drywood – that flowed down from between the shoulders of the mountain through miles of aspen groves, and this was a beaver haven, with chains of dams providing small boys with fishing grounds like something dreamed up in paradise. These ponds were stiff with cutthroat trout, so many they rarely grew beyond half a pound in weight, and so eager for food we saw them sometimes strike at a bare hook. Once I remember taking a good catch with aster blooms for a lure and another time with fragments of puffball. Mostly we used grasshoppers for bait at first, and stalking trout in the bushy, tree-bordered dams was a kind of careful hunting for individual fish hidden in innumerable hides. Mere catching of fish soon palled, so we laced our angling with the excitement of seeking and catching the biggest ones. We also progressed from bait fishing to taking fish with a fly.

Our first rods were crude, the traditional willow poles so often portrayed as the choice of small boys. These were heavy, awkward, and not much fun to wield after an hour or two of fishing. We substituted light cane poles – eight or ten feet cut from the tip of a binder whip shaft used when these harvesting machines were drawn by horses. Such a pole cost about fifty cents and was a vast improvement over a crooked willow. Then we progressed to the lighter and handier telescopic and jointed-steel bait rods then sold by every hardware store and mail-order house. The best one I ever owned cost ninety cents at Eaton's – a Canadian mail-order house equivalent to Sears Roebuck. It was light, whippy, and strong; it collapsed into three sections for carrying, and it lasted a long time. We also used steel telescopic bait rods with sections that pushed down into each other, so the rod could be more easily carried through the bush. But most of these rods had the habit of either

jamming or coming apart, so they usually ended up stuck or sol-
dered at full length. When carrying such a rod we usually just
wound the line up on the reel until the hook caught in the tip
guide, and this practice once caused an explosion of unexpected
action in a most unusual way.

We had spent the day fishing Carpenter canyon with some
neighbour boys and were riding down the valley in later afternoon, our saddles hung with bulging fish sacks and our rods in
our hands. One of the boys was riding a big, lazy, sleepy-looking
white horse that had a habit of poking along as though reluctant
to put one foot ahead of the other, his tail at half-cock, and breaking wind at every other step or so. He was about as inelegant as a
horse can get. At one point along the winding trail a fly lit on his
big, ugly nose. He stopped abruptly to wipe it off on his front leg,
and at this point the rider coming behind, also half asleep, ran the
tip of his rod up under the horse's tail, where the hook caught on
the edge of his equine exhaust pipe.

The results bordered on sheer magic. That old white horse
came alive with a great snort and a thunderous sound of exhaust
as he went straight in the air like a three-star rodeo bronc. The
reel on the surprised fisherman's rod screamed as line tore off it,
and that startled individual helped the uproar into a resounding
crescendo by rearing back on his rod as though fighting a leaping
tarpon. About the third jump the white horse threw his rider into
the tops of the trees along with his sack of trout, and then ran
away, still impaled by the hook and trailing a length of broken line.

It took the three of us a good half-hour to run down that horse.
Several times we managed to get close, but somebody's horse
invariably stepped on the line, which launched another stampede
for distant places. When we finally managed to get hold of him,
we were still faced with something of a dilemma, for the hook
was still imbedded in a very tender part of his anatomy and trying
to remove it was a barefaced invitation to get your head kicked

off. Somebody hobbled him with a halter shank, and then we tied
up a hind foot with a lariat so he was standing on three legs. A
jacket was employed as a blindfold to keep him in the dark. Then
some crude surgery was carried out with a pocketknife without
benefit of anaesthetic. The operation was successful, but ever after
that when we went fishing with the boy who rode this horse and
he began to poke along holding up the line, all someone had to
do was pull a little line off a reel behind him. At the sound of it,
the lazy white horse would tuck his tail down and take off like a
scalded cat. He was henceforth endowed with what might be
termed a conditioned reflex.

Sometime around 300 B.C. the first references to "luring fish
with feathers" was made. Likely the first artificial lures of this kind
were minnow imitations used in jigging or trolling in salt-water
by fishermen in the Red Sea and Mediterranean.

Another historic reference cites the third century A.D., when
a naturalist by the name of Aelian wrote about fly-fishing in his
scroll *De Natura Animalium*. In a chapter entitled "De Peculiari
Quadam Pisatu in Macedonia," he says:

> There is a river called Astraeus flowing midway between
> Berea and Thessalonica, in which are produced certain spotted
> fish whose food consists of insects which fly about the river.
> These insects are dissimilar to all other kinds found elsewhere;
> they are not like wasps, nor would one naturally compare
> them with flies called Ephemera, nor do they resemble bees.
> But they are impudent as flies, as large as Ant Hedon, of the
> same color as wasps and they buzz like bees. The natives call
> this insect the "Hippurus."
>
> As these flies float on top of the water in pursuit of food,
> they attract the notice of the fish, which swim upon them.
> When the fish spies one of these insects on top of the water,
> it swims quietly underneath it, taking care not to agitate the

surface, lest it should scare away the prey; so approaching it, as it were, under the shadow it opens its mouth and gulps it down, just as a wolf seizes a sheep, or an eagle a goose, and having done this it swims away beneath the ripple.

The fishermen are aware of all this; but they do not use these flies for bait because handling would destroy their natural color, injure the wings, and soil them as a lure. On this account the natural insect is in ill repute with the fishermen, who cannot make use of it. They manage to circumvent the fish, however, by the following clever piscatorial device. They cover a hook with red wool, and upon this they fasten two feathers of a waxy appearance, which grow under a cock's wattles, they have a reed about six feet long and a line about the same length; they drop this lure upon the water and the fish being attracted by the color becomes extremely excited, proceeds to meet it, anticipating from its beautiful appearance a most delicious repast; but as with extended mouth it seizes the lure, it is held fast by the hook, and being captured, meets with a very sorry entertainment.

So goes what is likely the first historical reference to taking fish with artificial flies – a very graphic and revealing description of an insect and the means of copying it in order to take trout. Sport fishing was very likely born this way, for no man could fish with such delicate tackle without some practised skill; nor could he see fish coming up through clear water for his hand-tied artificial fly without some feeling of meeting a wild thing on its own terms and enjoying the contact as much for the experience as the possible kill.

Sport fishing on the Alberta frontier along the tributaries of the Saskatchewan was something that grew on the people through contact with English remittance men and visitors from those parts of the world where a certain protocol had been developed in the sports of fishing and hunting by the necessity of conservation and population pressures.

Several centuries ago, British landowners had set up certain rules and sporting traditions in the development of game management in that country, which was second only to the system practised in Germany at that time. Over the intervening years the Germans still maintain the lead, for their refinements of sporting manners, traditional rules, and protocol afield and along their streams are the ultimate. Here in North America we too have come a considerable distance in a comparatively short period of time, but we still have a long journey ahead before we can match our management programs with those used by European biologists and foresters. North American authorities defend our system by saying that the same kind of program as used in Europe will not fit here, which is true to a point, but the framework of principle and knowledge involved will hold anywhere. To a large extent our government fish and wildlife departments are more interested in the harvest and the resulting income from sale of licences to sportsmen for the privilege of hunting and fishing than they are in the development of true appreciation of sport and safety. They pay lip service to stream pollution problems, but do nothing to really get at the roots of the trouble. If a licence purchaser does not know the difference between a rifle and a shotgun, he still has the legal right to go hunting.

The first artificial trout fly I used was a snelled Royal Coachmen wet fly, bought at the local hardware store more because it was very pretty than because I thought it could take trout. But the trout of my favourite beaver pond went hog wild over it, chewing it to rags in no time, but not before I had taken plenty of the biggest ones for a feed for the whole family. From then on I was a confirmed fly fisherman, although my steel rod was anything but delicate and my money supply did not include enough for a stock of store-bought flies. To solve this deficiency, for my first homemade fly I pulled some feathers out of an outraged Plymouth Rock rooster and proceeded to tie something out of red wool, Christmas-tree tinsel, and ordinary sewing thread. It was born looking like nothing ever seriously contemplated by a purist and made a splash like a drowning chicken. But, amazingly enough, it caught trout. As a matter of fact, the first time I used it, my heart missed a beat when a great Dolly Varden struck it hard, no doubt mistaking it for a small bird that had fallen into the creek. The big fish smashed into it in clear water within two feet of my toes as I stood on a low undercut bank rimming a deep pool, and I came within a whisker of falling in over my head. Thus a fly fisherman was born.

The first really good fly tackle I ever saw belonged to a judge of the circuit court, who for years spent his summer holiday camped by the creeks on our ranch or the adjoining one belonging to Butcher. The Judge, as everyone called him, was a Scotsman by descent, with a great love of camping alone in the midst of the wilds and a taste for whiskey. My first acquaintance with him got off to a very poor start, although my intentions were good and I very likely saved his life in the process even if it was crudely done.

During July and August the big Dolly Vardens came up the mountain creeks from the rivers; their September spawning grounds were along the bars and riffles near the headwaters. Hunting and catching these beautifully coloured big fish was a never-ending source of excitement, and they were wonderful eating besides. So every evening when I rode down into the valley to bring in the milk cows, I went along the banks of the creek looking down into the pools to spot these fish as they lay on the bottom. The Dolly Varden, like its very near relative the eastern brook trout, has a distinctive and sharply contrasting border of ivory-white along the leading edges of its pectoral and ventral fins, a colour that often gives it away to sharp eyes even when hidden by logs or overhanging ledges. If I located one or two of the big fish, I came back early the next morning properly armed for their capture.

One particular evening I came to a big pool at the forks, and as I rode up on a gravel bar dividing the creeks at their junction a surprising sight confronted me. There in the middle of a fast riffle dropping into the pool sat a somewhat portly gentleman in long waders. The waders were awash, for the creek was running cheerfully over the top of them at the back, and the man was in grave danger of being swept down into deep water, where he would doubtless sink like a stone. It was the Judge.

For a moment or two I just sat there on my horse in astonishment, not fully aware that he was in real trouble. But when he turned to look at me, his expression gave away his fear, and it became instantly obvious that he was pinned down by the weight of water, virtually unable to move.

I was only a kid weighing perhaps ninety pounds, while the Judge in his present predicament with his waders full of water, likely weighed two hundred fifty. To attempt to drag him out, as one would normally do, was just asking for trouble. Had I been afoot, the problem would have been near insurmountable; but I was astride a wiry little cow horse with a great love of snapping things on the end of a rope. Just as naturally as one would reach for his hat upon entering someone else's house, my hand dropped to the coiled lariat hanging on its strap on the fork of my saddle. Before the Judge was aware of my intent, the mare came splashing out toward him and a loop sailed out to drop and be jerked up snug around his arms and chest. In the same motion I dallied the rope around the saddle horn, and then with a great deal more enthusiasm than diplomacy my mount spun on her heels to head for dry ground. The Judge came sliding out of the creek backwards, somehow managing to hold his rod out of harm's way, and when I checked my horse he came to a stop head down in a hollow on the gravel bar. He was instantly inundated by a rushing flood issuing from his waders. He came up on his feet muttering thick Scottish words of import not found in courts or churches as he shook off the rope. My horse took one horrified look at him and bolted, which was probably just as well, for at that moment I doubt very much if the Judge was entirely cognizant of my good intentions.

The Judge's fine split-cane English fly rod had survived the action unscathed, but a few days later it met an ignominious end.

My friend Butcher, in a burst of enthusiastic extravagance that summer, had purchased a brand-new, magnificently appointed McLaughlin-Buick sedan – a grand car with an arrogant profile to its general outline and a powerful engine under its long bonnet. It was a favourite model of rum runners during Prohibition, a famed "Whiskey Six," a fast, rugged machine that would stand up to use on the sketchy roads of the times. It had one idiosyncrasy of design – the reverse-gear position was that of low gear in most other cars, so new owners who had learned to drive ordinary ones sometimes found themselves going backward instead of forward as expected.

Naturally Butcher was delighted with this new toy and drove it into our yard to show it off. Only my mother and I were at home, but we were a satisfactorily appreciative audience as he explained and pointed out all the finer points of his new car.

Finally Butcher turned to me, "Come along and open the gates for me. We'll go visit the Judge."

So I sat on the big leather-upholstered front seat beside him and away we went down a twisting wagon trail into the valley where the Judge had his tent pitched. The Judge was warm in his welcome and very interested in Butcher's new car. He uncorked a full bottle of whiskey to celebrate the occasion as he and Butcher exchanged the latest accounts of happenings in the country well laced with humorous comments. Being too young, I was not invited to join them in a drink, but I sat enthralled as they laughed and chuckled at various stories. As the talk proceeded, the bottle was passed freely back and forth, its potion being slightly diluted with creek water in large glasses. By the time Butcher was ready to leave for home, he was feeling no pain.

He shook the Judge's hand with decorum and settled himself with immense dignity behind the steering wheel of his car. The door banged shut as the starter whirred and the engine caught in a throaty purring of power that spoke of many horses waiting to be turned loose. Butcher threw the shift lever out of neutral into gear and let up on the clutch pedal, whereupon we began to go backwards.

The Judge had been standing by the car as this happened, and he came trotting along beside the open window to pronounce with a certain judicial firmness of tone, "But Mr. Butcher, you are going backwards!"

"Nonsense, Judge," Butcher replied, "I am in low gear."

About the time the Judge opened his mouth for some further comment on Butcher's mechanical misconceptions and direction, there was a vast clatter of various things, a ripping of canvas, and some lurching as the car went over a six-foot bank to land with a great crash in the creek. The engine stalled and Butcher opened the door to get out, but he changed his mind when he saw cold water lapping the floorboards of his vehicle. Somewhat sobered but still firmly in command of things in general, he started the motor again and drove straight down the bed of the stream to a low place in the bank where the trail crossed. There he swung the car back up on the beach and returned to what was left of the Judge's snug camp.

Together he and the Judge stood solemnly surveying the wreckage. The tent was flat and torn, the sheet-iron sheep-herder's stove looked as though a very large elephant had stepped on it, and the rustic table and bench the Judge had so carefully constructed were all kindling wood. Sorrowfully the Judge reached in among the rags of his recently neatly pitched tent and picked up the fragments of what had been a beautiful, very expensive fly rod. But the crowning touch to the gloom was the sight of an almost full case of fine Scotch whiskey smashed as flat as a pancake with only a rich aroma left to remind them of its sweet potency.

With a typical rebound of good spirits, Butcher took the Judge's arm and said, "I'm dashed sorry, old man. Rotten luck, what?" and then added with a Shakespearean flourish, "Come, we must not stand here mourning. Let us go repair the damage and celebrate in royal fashion a friendship welded even stronger by the whims of fate!"

We all got into the car and drove to my house, where I got out to watch them go on toward town in a swirling cloud of dust. The "repairing and celebration" lasted for three days, and their trail took them about 180 miles north to Calgary. There Butcher bought the Judge an even better English fly rod, a new tent, and complete camp equipment of the very best quality, all of which was brought back and put into use at the site of the wreck.

One evening I rode past the Judge's camp on my way to get the cows. All traces of the wreckage had been removed and the place was again neat as a pin. The Judge invited me to get down and come into the tent. As he showed me the various items of his new equipment with obvious enjoyment, he was warm and friendly.

Finally he turned and drew himself up as though making some kind of dissertation in court, and his words poured out in a rich Scottish accent that still comes back to me forty-odd years later with clarity and poignancy.

"My boy," he said, "apart from the fact that I give you my belated thanks for possibly saving my life, albeit in a somewhat unusual and unexpected fashion, I welcome you as a friend. Let's you and I remember that clouds of adversity most generally melt into sunshine, given a bit of time, and that which may seem like disaster may well be the source of better things." And having got that statement of profound wisdom off his chest, he cleared his throat with a great harrumph, grinned like a boy at me, and invited me to share his supper.

Many times after that we met by the streams, and the Judge introduced me to the art of fly fishing for trout. His was the first real fly rod I ever held in my hand, and under his direction I learned how to let the smooth silk of a fine-braided fly line go shooting on its own weight through the guides, so the fly came down lightly on the water with all the guile necessary for enticing the most wary fish. Thus he opened a door revealing something of worth and enjoyment in living – a door still open, which has led me to much adventure and exploration.

Although it was some time before I contrived to get a fly rod of my own, its ownership was a means of continuation and enjoyment of a wonderful kind of sport. Like many of the old-timers in the country then, a large percentage of fishermen today still feel that fly fishing is either a somewhat inadequate and impractical sport, or one that is too hard to learn; so they never try it. Actually, with about half an hour of rudimentary instruction, almost anyone can learn to cast a fly well enough to catch trout. In good time a person can proceed toward refinements that make the game more enjoyable. Apart from basic necessities, such as a proper rod, reel, and line, all one needs is four or five different patterns of flies in two or three sizes, although few dyed-in-the-wool fly fishermen will admit it. However, sooner or later, most of us use dozens of patterns; and if we have progressed to the point of hand-crafting our own flies, the collection of materials used can represent a fair cross-section of the fauna of the world. Fly fishing can be both an art and a science combined, for it entails not only a considerable study of insect life but also delicate artistry in copying various kinds in fur, silk, and feathers. It is a game that can be as simple or as complicated as anyone wants to make it.

Beginning with that first monstrosity tied with sewing thread, wool, and chicken feathers, my adventures among mountain waters took me into a phase of sport I had not known existed – a delightful combination of the development of equipment, art, and sheer love for the game. Through it I met many people from many corners of the world, the kind who enrich one's enjoyment of living by mere contact with them, the breed one enjoys trading talk with around the flickering light of a campfire. At the same time I encountered fish – individual trout – that time cannot erase from memory. In perfect recall focus are bright mornings when the snow-streaked peaks stood out sharp and clear against the vivid blue bowl of the sky, birds sang in the nearby groves of wilderness timber, and the air was tangy with the smell of pine and spruce and silver willow.

I remember one of those perfect days when everything seemed just right. My creel hung comfortably heavy on my shoulders after two full hours of fast action on the creek. The sunlit hills rolling gently to the foot of the Rockies were a mass of soft greens mingled with moving cloud shadows, and the trees sang softly in the breeze to the deeper accompanying overtones of the mountain stream. I was about ready to head for home. More out of habit than anything else I slipped quietly down through a grove of tall aspens and cottonwoods to a special place where a big pool lay against a timbered low-lying bank on a bend for another try at a mighty trout that made this place his home.

This was a giant fish – a rainbow trout – a real old tackle-busting he-trout, with a hook in his lower jaw like a salmon and a temper like a wild stallion. Over the course of three seasons, he had taken my fly several times and then broken off. My luck was bad with this fish, mostly because it was nearly impossible to keep him out of the network of roots under the overhanging bank where he had his lair. Fish for him with tackle heavy enough to hold him and he would ignore the lure as though it didn't exist. Work the kind of leader it took to fool him and he broke it every time. If trout could hold degrees, this one had his Ph.D. in survival. He was more than simply smart: he was uncanny.

The first time I saw him was when a puff of wind lifted my back cast high and hung my last remaining fawning Royal Coachman in a tree twenty feet from the ground. That fly had been doing well for me and I was loath to break it off; so leaving my rod against a rock, I scrambled up the cottonwood.

After loosening the fly and letting it drop onto the gravel bar, I looked down over the pool spread out as clear as glass at an angle where surface reflections were nil and every detail of the bottom was in sharp focus. A half-dozen fat cutthroats hung a foot or so above bottom ahead of a school of thirty or forty whitefish. There was the small dimple of a rise where the slow current eddied around the foot of a big cottonwood beyond. For a moment nothing was visible in the black shadow beneath the slanting tree trunk, but then a big, dark-green shape took form in a patch of sunlight.

At first I couldn't believe it was a trout — it was just too big; but then the thing moved, and an enormous rainbow drifted lazily to the surface to suck in another floating natural; I almost fell out of the tree.

Maybe I scared him down with a sour cast or perhaps the big trout just quit feeding, for in spite of working on him till almost dark, I could not get as much as a curious look out of that fish.

A few days later I came back and floated a Brown Bi-visible over his hide. This time Lady Luck smiled a little, for the rainbow rose and engulfed my fly with the confident movement of a big trout that is completely fooled. But the smile was brief, for he fell on my leader in his first wild jump, breaking it like so much cobweb. Those were the days when we used diamond-drawn silk-worm gut for leaders, with a relatively low tensile strength. In waters like this the odds were very much in favour of such a fish.

That was the last of him for that season, but the following summer he was back under the tree again, and I renewed acquaintance by sinking the barb of a tiny Grey Adams in his jaw. This time I stayed with him until the second round, when he dove behind a root, leaving me standing up to my knees in the riffle shaking like a leaf while I tied a new leader on the end of my line.

Another day I stalked him during a shower, when big drops were pounding the surface of the pool after a long, hot, sultry afternoon. The sudden change of temperature seemed to waken the trout, for they began to feed in a frenzy of action. Twice as I worked to tie a new fluffy Bi-visible on my tippet, the shattering rise of the big rainbow threw water in the air. His broad back and dorsal fin came right out and once I got a good look at a tail as broad as my hand. I was having trouble with my knot, for the sight of him brought on a mild case of buck fever. Keeping the fly dry was utterly impossible, but I hoped it wouldn't matter. Shooting it upstream, I let it come down half drowned toward the trout. It swirled in a bit of eddy and the giant trout came up·with his mouth wide open to suck it in. Like a tyro, I struck too soon and too hard, and once again the battle was his before it even started.

On and off all winter I saw that big rainbow in my dreams, and by the time the water cleared after the spring flood I was back armed with my experience and some specially selected leaders that I had tied and tested for just this purpose.

Now I was cool and bound to take plenty of time before making any move. Coming to the edge of the trees across the pool from his hide I stood among knee-high hellebore and cow cabbage watching a hatch of drakes dancing on the surface. Wondering if the big trout was back from wherever he went in winter, I watched several small trout rising steadily upstream from where I was standing, then swung my attention to the foot of the big tree across the pool. As though in welcome, a big shadow detached itself from surrounding gloom to come up through the gin-clear water for a bug.

Then I heard the click of a reel coming from the tail of the pool: the place was already taken by another fisherman. Standing a few yards below where the pool broke over the edge of a fast riffle, a stranger was fast to a lively cutthroat with his light fly rod dancing in a graceful curve. He seemed as unaware of the big trout as he was of me. I stood motionless to watch.

The cutthroat came reluctantly to net and after killing and creeling it, the stranger dried his fly with several false casts as he made a step or two upstream. Again the shadow moved under the tree, and again there was little to give away the size of the fish, for there was only a tiny dimple of disturbance on the surface and a sound like a bubble bursting. But the fisherman saw it, and with flawless form shot his fly a little above and a shade to one side of the rainbow's lair. Holding my breath, I saw it settle like dandelion fluff and dance jauntily down the current without the slightest drag. Just short of the tree the fly spun through a couple of tiny swirls in a fairy dance, and then it vanished as the water boiled in response to the stranger's strike.

Like a short-grass bronc with a burr under the saddle and a tin can tied to his tail, the trout came lancing up into the sun amid a shower of water drops in a wild end-swapping leap that almost put him high and dry on a litter of driftwood along the bank. Somehow the leader held as the snappy little rod turned the big fish to the middle of the pool, where he jumped again – once – twice – three times in quick succession. Each time he jumped I saw the stranger throw slack to him, and I knew I was watching a master; for that is a trick known to few Rocky Mountain anglers and practised by fewer still. The hardest thing I ever learned to do was deliberately throw slack to a big rainbow jumping on a short line. It's a crucial move, for it greatly reduces the chance of a broken leader or a thrown fly.

The rainbow had more tricks in his bag, which he brought out with sizzling speed. Time and again he made stampeding rushes up the pool, while the angler used the rod and current to wear him down. Several times he bored deeply toward his hide, but the gallant little fly rod bent to the grip as it turned him back. Once he jumped right at the man's knees, but when the spray settled the rod still danced in a fighting curve.

Finally the trout's rushes slowed to a weary slugging, which was still dangerous but without the smash and drive of his first efforts. I felt like cheering – maybe a little like crying too – as the man worked him slowly down toward the net. Grudgingly the big trout rolled on his side and slid head first into the open meshes. The net was too small for him, but it didn't matter; the fish was completely exhausted, too tired to even wiggle.

I was reaching for my camera in my jacket pocket when I saw something beyond belief. The man downstream carefully slid the rainbow from the net, held him up for a brief admiration, unhooked him gently, and, while the trout worked its gills gathering a reviving supply of oxygen, stroked him as he held him upright in the current. Then with a certain majesty and a slow swirl of its tail, the big trout headed back for its hole under the bank.

"Well I'll be damned!" I said to the world at large.

It was the stranger's turn to be surprised. "Where did you come from?" he asked.

"Right here for the whole show," I told him. "Why did you turn him loose?"

The man smiled and replied, "I've been taking a crack at that big bruiser every time I get the chance for quite a while. Hooked him several times but he always beat me. Killing him seemed like a kind of fool way of celebrating. Anyway, it's fun to know of a place where there is a really big fish."

"You're right," I said, as I went over to introduce myself and shake his hand. "That was some fight!"

Several guiding trips with the pack train kept me away for the rest of that summer and fall, and no chance came to go back that season. I never saw the big trout again. Maybe someone caught him. Or perhaps a mink killed him. It could be that he changed his living place for another pool, where he finally died of old age. Whatever happened, that big trout taught me much, and if the man who caught him and turned him loose should see this book, I would like him to know that he also showed me something of value. It is possible to have your cake and eat it too; but sometimes it is much better to forgo the latter pleasure for the sake of keeping alive something of great beauty for a while longer.

Over the years my trails have led me through some of the wildest and most rugged reaches of the mountains all the way to the tundra prairies of the high Arctic. I have fished British Columbia's Bella Coola in April near spires of peaks hung with snow and clear, blue ice, when its bottom was literally paved in places with big fighting steelhead, their flanks like molten silver, fresh from the sea. I have known the indescribable feeling of one of these fish tearing the river wide open as it plunged and ran in its wild bid for freedom.

I have cast a tiny dry fly over northern waters so stiff with pastel-shaded Arctic grayling that it was merely a question of which fish got to it first. The kind of fly couldn't have mattered less; the size of the fish one hooked depended on its proximity to the lure and its speed.

Once a small ten-incher was fighting in fast water at the foot of a falls when up out of the depths came a great char – a lake trout that had taken to the river – and engulfed the grayling, the tiny fly, and a good portion of the leader. My rod weighed a mere two and a quarter ounces, and the resulting battle threatened to smash it a dozen times, but the eight-pound fish finally rolled over in defeat.

No matter the thrill, when the campfires flicker at night and the little red gods dancing in the flames encourage recall of the past, I see trout coming to crude lures presented by boys lucky enough to have been in places where boys should grow up.

There My Stick Floats

One of the west's wild rivers, a magnificent stream full of mystery and beauty, strong in its current, placid in its pools, and still reasonably pure in its waters, winds down between folded hills, blue and silver in the sun, alternating fast white water and slick runs with quiet holes. Beyond the hills the Rockies rise, tall and craggy, their expressions strong in profile, enduring since the earth's crust split to heave them slowly up towards the sky.

For two hours I had been fishing, standing thigh-deep in the river and enjoying the powerful tugging of its current against my legs – soothing medicine to wipe away the tension. There are few things as satisfying as plying a finely balanced fly rod and line in presenting a hand-dressed fly to feeding trout. While a full creel has no part in the witchery, mine hung comfortably heavy on my shoulder – sufficient promise of a delicious breakfast when the sun rose again.

The fishing was only part of the river's wealth. There were signs of mink and beaver along the edges of sandbars. Elk, moose, and

From *Andy Russell's Campfire Stories* (1998)

deer tracks showed here and there, and in one place the big paw marks of a black bear were printed deep in the mud beside a spring. Earlier in the evening, while the sun was still up and the world still warm after a long hot day, I had come down a steep bank along a little trail. It led me through a pocket close by the river and filled with berry brush higher than my head. As I made my way into it through a patch of tall fireweed, the leaves rustled noisily in the breeze, muffling my footsteps. There was a sudden explosive snort and a great crash as a huge whitetail buck with antlers like a rocking chair leaped from his bed into flight, so close I could have touched him with the tip of my rod. My thoughts had been somewhere else, and the suddenness of it made my pulse jump a bit, but doubtless less than his at having me almost walk on his tail. Later, as the evening cooled and I was standing knee-deep in water at the tail of a pool, I watched a doe browsing delicately among some saskatoon bushes, alternating choosy nibbles of leaves and twigs with enthusiastic mouthfuls of the luscious ripe fruit.

The sun dipped down onto the far rim of the mountains to the northwest, throwing long shadows of trees and promontories along the opposite bank. I shot my line upstream to drop a tiny fly where an eddy curled by some big rocks. There it danced, light-footed as a mayfly, when suddenly the kerplop and splash of a diving beaver sounded behind me. Swinging my head to look, I let the fly drift unattended for a moment and missed the strike of a good trout. The beaver surfaced to swim towards me, full of curiosity, his whiskers working on each side of his face like an animated moustache as he tried to get my scent. My chuckle triggered another great tail-smacking dive that threw water in all directions.

My attention to my fishing had been broken again, but such is a love affair with a beautiful river, and now I stood contemplating it, full of wonder at all the life it had known over the long reaches of time before I was born. It was to places like this that the first white men came, some of the old mountain men – free trappers adventuring in search of beaver. They may have stood here braving the dangers of wrathful Blackfeet just for the privilege of looking at new territory and taking some skins. They had seen the ancestors of my beaver, the deer, and other game, their spirits lifting as mine did at the sight of a flaming sunset over the mountains.

For a few mystic moments the shadows of Old Bill Williams, Jedediah Smith, John Fitzgerald, and other long-gone mountain men stood close beside me, contemplating the river, leaning on their long rifles with the breeze stirring the fringes of buckskins redolent with the smoke of a thousand campfires. A peeled beaver stick floated by in the lazy current, bringing to mind something just beyond the edge of recall – something heard or read long ago.

Then a great horned owl suddenly broke the silence from some cottonwoods across the river. "Who? Who? Who?" it called as though questioning my thoughts.

Then I remembered. It was Old Bill Williams, of course! When something pleased him or he liked a place, he would say, "Thar my stick floats!" And come to think of it, there my stick floats too.

People Along the River

From the home ranch near Waterton Park to our base camp
on Racehorse Creek inside the gap was about ninety miles.
We made an average of two round trips a season trailing
forty-odd head of loose horses. It was a two-day ride each way,
which took us across a number of tributaries of the Oldman, just
a few miles east of the mountains. At first there were two of us
making the trip, but later I persuaded Bert Riggall that I could
trail the bunch alone, for I liked the work and knew the country
well enough to make it easy. When a bunch of horses become
accustomed to one man, they handle even better than with two
riders. A lone rider doesn't get his concentration sidetracked, and
can better anticipate problems before they happen.

Well into the shank of an afternoon one long, hot day, I was
heading south up out of the Crowsnest River valley past a bench
inside a rancher's field. There was an open gate leading to the
field, and perhaps hoping I would stop and camp for the night,
the leaders of the bunch trotted through it and fanned out to feed.
I was riding around to haze them back out onto the road when

From *The Life of a River* (1987)

I suddenly noticed an old hidden teepee ring of stones, which the Indians had used to hold their tents down in this windy country. I soon found that it was only one of about a hundred such rings on the bench, and they had been there a long time, for many of the rocks, six to eight inches through, were barely showing in the sod, and it takes a lot of years for sod to build up around surface rocks of this size. Sitting there on my horse, it was easy to visualize the big camp that was once pitched here with probably three to four hundred people. Old buffalo-hunters, these ones, people who had ranged up and down this valley before there were any white people.

It was not the first time that I had found teepee rings along these rivers, nor would it be the last. But it was always a thrill, like riding into a historic review of the past, when this was all unfenced, open country with buffalo dotting the hills on an ocean of grass running far beyond the horizon, and halfway across the continent. It was something to think about as the horses jogged on south toward the Castle a few miles farther.

It was evening when I came down to the river, the horses spreading out at the near edge of the shallow crossing to drink. For some reason known only to herself, old Cee-Cee, the lead mare, turned upstream instead of heading into the river and led the bunch under a steep bank. I rode up along the top of it to head her off and stepped my horse out near its edge to yell at her and turn her back. Immediately I smelled smoke and to my amazement saw a stovepipe sticking out of the ground almost under my left stirrup. At the same time a voice down below yelled, "Get the hell off the roof, before you come through!" My horse jumped sideways just as a man appeared on a little shelf a few feet down the bank against a clump of willows.

My surprise was complete as I sat there on my horse looking at him. He was of medium height and indeterminate age, with a face as brown and wrinkled as a sun-cured prune and a pair of eyes that were clear blue and sharp.

"Seeing as how you rode out on my roof, you might as well get down and come in, Russell," he said with a grin. "I've seen you cross down below with that string of broomtails often enough to know who you are."

I stepped down, and picked up a rock to shy ahead of old Cee-Cee with a yell to go with it. She plunged into the river and headed across. The idea of a cool swim must have seemed like a good one, for the whole bunch followed her across, including the packhorse. My sleeping bag was on top of the pack and out of the water, which was a comfort.

Climbing down to where my unexpected host was standing, I grinned at him and shook his hand. Although I had not seen him since I was half-grown, I knew who he was. For Bill was something of a legend; hunter, trapper, cowboy when he felt like it, and on occasion there were rumours that he was a moonshiner. He was a crack rifle-shot and spent a large part of every winter ranging far and wide across the hills hunting coyotes for their skins.

"Got a nice bull trout this afternoon," he told me. "It's about suppertime. When you get your camp set up, better come and have a bait."

I accepted his invitation and went to my horse and rode back down to the crossing. By the time I had caught and saddled a fresh horse and spread my bed under a tree, the sun had dipped behind the hills. Riding back across the river, I hobbled my horse on a little meadow among some aspens and climbed down to Bill's dugout. The door stood open and Bill was busy at the stove. The inside of the place was neat and the walls and roof were lined with old weathered rough planks that looked as if they had once been the flooring of a bridge. They were supported by a log centre beam and two side beams, each of which were held up by three stout posts. The stock of a rifle peeped out of a buckskin case hung on two pegs set into one of the beams, and a miscellany of equipment was tucked under the bunk at the back of the dugout.

The table was a couple of wide boards on two oak barrels, and on the well-swept board floor a row of stone crocks stood along the base of one wall with a coil of copper tubing over them.

When I had washed off the dust in a wash-basin on a shelf outside the door, Bill poured a measure of clear liquid out of a jug into a cup and handed it to me.

"Sample some of my white mule to celebrate," he said, "seeing as how you're the first to ride on my roof."

He poured some for himself in another cup, and by way of a toast he laughed and said, "Here's to your ornery old packhorses and mud in your eye!" whereupon he downed it in one gulp.

I took a sip and almost choked, for that so-called white mule had a kick like one – pure liquid fire.

"Don't be scared of it," Bill grinned, "it's pure stuff filtered in charcoal to take out the gook. Make the hair grow on your chest!"

I took another cautious sip and thought it would more likely burn the hair off.

We had a good supper of fresh fried trout, Dutch-oven bis-cuits, and boiled new potatoes, topped off with canned peaches, which we ate off our knees as we squatted outside where it was cool. Then we lit up smokes and sat back to trade some stories.

That was a fascinating evening, for Bill was in an unusually loquacious mood. He told me about riding north to Canada from the States many years before through this country along the Oldman – a fugitive from a gunfight with a rancher who had some vengeful relatives.

"I kept right on going to hell and gone beyond, away north into British Columbia. Figured on staying there, but it wasn't in the cards. I remembered this country and came back. Been here ever since."

He had a real love for this mountain and foothill country and knew the river from its headwaters to away down on the prairie. Like me he had come to know it and to love the spirit of its movement through feeling the push of it against his legs. We had both fished it, and trapped beaver up along the creeks in spring. We could talk about it, though there was no need. Like the Indians, we had looked and learned something about how to really see and feel its power. Like the smell of campfires burning under a starry sky, or the whispering and roaring of the wind in the trees and among the high rocks, it was something we shared in our blood.

Bill told me that, more out of the challenge of it than anything else, he had been making the odd batch of white mule on and off for several years. He had been careful where he sold it, going far enough away so his still wouldn't be easy to find. When he had dug out this place, he had planted the willows outside to hide the front of it. In winter the snow drifted down deep over it; he had a log cabin further up the Castle, where he lived most of the time.

"But lately," he told me, "I been having bad dreams about windows with bars on them, and wake up in a cold sweat. Reckon a couple of close shaves with the Mounties started it. Got a feeling that landing in jail would kill me. I been free as the mountains for too long. If you had come a couple of days later, this would be only a hole in the ground. I'm quittin' while the quittin' is good!"

When I rode down the trail toward the home ranch the next morning, I knew I had met a real character. Bill lived for more years after that visit, enjoying the mountain trails, and with no more bad dreams about bars on windows.

There are few straight lines in the designs of nature: almost everything about it is a combination of interwoven curves, subtle sweeping outlines of form and motion. Some are obvious and some are hidden, and the understanding takes time. A river is the ultimate proof of it, for the water lifts and eddies, swirls and curls back on itself, jumps and falls in a myriad of interwoven patterns so simple and yet complex. This complexity will always be a real challenge to a fisherman presenting a tiny lure of fur, feathers, silk, or tinsel, so that it will drift naturally without dragging and giving itself away for the fraud that it is. The skill involved with fly fishing makes it an art, and sometimes an exasperation. It is not enough to tie the fly so that it closely resembles the insect on which the trout is feeding; the good fisherman must present it with sufficient skill and delicacy to make it irresistibly attractive to the fish. The eyes of a trout are sharp and discerning, and really big ones do not get that way by being careless.

It is not necessary to be a fly fisherman to truly love a river, but it helps. This love of rivers and the pursuit of trout has shaped and moulded some very special characters I met along the river.

There is Bob, who first came to know the Oldman while court-ing a rancher's daughter, with his mind on things other than fish. It took some time and concentration to persuade the girl that life with him would be utter bliss, during which he somehow did not elaborate unduly on the fact that at times she would be a fisher-man's and hunter's widow. She, being a smart girl, no doubt knew this already, and loved him anyway.

For a while Bob gallantly ignored the river, but one fine summer day they went on a picnic at a spot overlooking a pool, where they sat in the warm sun and wove dreams for a while, blind to everything but each other. Suddenly the quiet of the afternoon brought the unmistakable slurping sound of the rise of a big trout to his ears. He was suddenly totally alert, like a pointer dog with a noseful of the scent of grouse. A minute or two went by before that slurping sound came again, and this time he turned to see the rise beside a half-sunken driftwood log sticking out from the bank sixty feet or so up on the far side of the pool. Mumbling some-thing, he rushed to the car parked nearby and extracted from its trunk a cased rod and a fishing-vest with numerous pockets well stuffed with various things. With deft fingers he put the rod together, fitted his reel to its handle, strung the line through the guides, and then carefully tied a fly – a Letort Hopper – to the tippet of the leader. Without the slightest thought for his polished shoes or the sport slacks he was wearing, he went to the edge of the pool and waded out into the shallows at its tail until he was thigh-deep and directly below the end of the log. With consummate skill he worked out line with two or three false casts, at the same time stripping a bit more from the reel which he held in a loop with his left hand. Without breaking the rhythm of the rod, he gracefully shot the fly upstream, dropping it with delicacy and precision on top of the log. The gentle drag of the river on the line nudged the fly off the log into the water, where it floated with saucy daring on the surface directly over the trout's lair.

There was a quick swirl and Bob lifted the rod tip with a firm hand. A heavy rainbow trout exploded out of the water, fell back, and then came out again to tail-walk in a shower of spray before falling back to bore down toward the log. Bob did not yell – he is not the yelling kind – but he turned the fish out into the pool, where the dancing rod and the screaming reel told the story of its wild efforts to throw the tiny hook in its jaw. After a dramatic few minutes, Bob slowly backed out to the edge of the gravel bar, finally leading the tired fish to his feet. Stooping, he caught it by the gills and lifted it triumphantly out of the water.

Remembering that he had company, and with due regard for ·the girl's sensitivity, he turned his back to give the trout the *coup de grâce* on the head with a rock. He then carried it to her in triumph, and she, with shining eyes expressing admiration for his skill and daring, proceeded to throw her arms around his neck and give him a kiss of some duration. It was later that he became aware for the first time that he had forgotten to put on his waders.

Bob is a lawyer, and a bit of an eccentric, though inclined to dress in conservatively traditional pinstripe suits in his office. On the stream, he generally resembles a dignified bum, wearing clothes that are well marked by service, topped by a disreputable fly-strewn hat that looks as if it had been trampled by a herd of stampeding buffalo. He takes his fly fishing and hunting just as seriously as his law, but tempers it by writing delightful stories and articles about it. He purely loves the Oldman and regularly abandons his office to go fishing there at every opportunity. One can imagine his secretary answering a call at such times.

"Sorry, sir, but he is not in the office today. Where can he be reached? By four-wheel drive and waders somewhere in the Oldman River, I believe. It's trout season, you know."

After a lot of years, he is still married to the same woman, which says something.

One summer a few years back, Bob was fishing the Oldman near the forks when he came upon a boy about twelve years old sitting by the sawed-off stump of a big driftwood red-fir log. He was carefully counting the annual rings of the tree on the bevelled butt of the stump, which had been smoothed with a razor-sharp axe to reveal them. Filled with curiosity, Bob introduced himself and the boy gave his name as Rob.

"That's short for Robert, the same as mine," Bob told him and then asked about the log.

"Grandpa and I found it. It was washed down here on last spring's flood, I guess. He cut two gateposts off it. He thought it would be good if I counted the rings and found out how old it is. He says this big stump is about the best history book there is. I guess he's right. I've been having trouble with history at school."

"How's it going?" Bob asked.

"Pretty slow," Rob told him. "The rings are awful close together in some places. Grandpa says those are the dry years. See these ones here?" He pointed to some very fine rings not far under the bark. "Those are the dry years in the Hungry Thirties." Then he pointed to a dark ring farther down. "This was when a fire went through, burning the grass and brush."

He went on to explain how fir trees have thick bark resistant to fire and how it doesn't kill the tree unless it gets up into the green needles among the branches. "Grandpa says little fires on the ground are good for fir trees. They keep the brush down so flames don't get high enough to burn the top of the trees."

He had marked certain rings with a sharp pencil and noted dates. "This one I marked is 1905. That's when Alberta became a province. This one here is 1874 when the Mounted Police came and built Fort Macleod down the river. Here's 1877. That's when they signed the treaty with the Indians." Then he pointed positively to another ring: "This one is 1753. That's the year Anthony Henday came two hundred and seventeen years ago. He was the first white man to see the mountains. That's the last date in my book about this country. I guess I'll have to go back in Canada's history before 1753 now."

Bob could remember the dismally boring history books of his early school years. This boy had a smart grandfather who had seen a way to bring history alive for him, and at the same time open up an inquiring mind. As much as Bob had been around, up and down the rivers from the Red Deer River south to here, this was the first time he had really seen a tree right down to its heart. He asked how old this one was.

The boy pondered for a while. "I guess I won't know for sure till I count all the rings. But it will be easier towards the middle. You see, the rings are farther apart there. Trees like this grow faster when they are younger. But it must be close to eight hundred years."

"That will take you back into European history," Bob said. "Look, Rob, I've got a chain-saw in my Scout back about half a mile, and I think we can cut off this bevelled piece. It's too heavy to carry very far, but we can put it in the river and float it down to the car. Then we'll take it down to your place, for you to show at school. And I'd like to meet your grandfather and your parents."

It was mid-afternoon by the time Bob got back with the saw and cut off the required section of the stump. In the meantime, the boy had stripped down to his shorts and sneakers. They launched the awkward piece of wood into the river and Rob went with it, swimming with the smoothness of an otter in the deep places and pushing it along in the shallows. When it got stuck, Bob waded in to help him wrestle it free.

"This is the way Grandpa got the posts down," Rob said, "only he used his horse and rope. They were awful heavy. Kept getting hung up. Made ol' Baldy snort." He chuckled, then, "Grandpa cussed when he broke his rope."

When they loaded the piece of log into Bob's vehicle, and drove down to the ranch buildings along a twisted trail, the two thick posts were standing upright on each side of the driveway entrance in freshly dug holes. Rob's father and grandfather were there and the boy introduced them.

"I started out fishing today, but I got sidetracked in history," Bob told them. "This boy has been teaching me something I've never thought about before."

Bob had supper with the family, and when he drove to his father-in-law's ranch later, he knew that sometimes there is a lot more to fishing than just catching fish.

Joe shares the river with us. Like me, he was born and grew up on one of its tributaries, learning how to survive in the Rocky Mountain school of hard knocks while coming to feel the spirits of the wilderness and its rivers. A fly fisherman by choice and a mechanic and truck-driver by vocation, he is a big, lean man with rugged features, a sunny disposition, and wonderful skill. Whether he is handling heavy tools on some oil-well drilling site or plying his fly rod on some stream, his love for his work and play shines. He knows the Oldman up, down, around, and through probably better than any man alive.

Graduating from chucking bait with a willow pole to a steel rod and then to a fly rod, he learned to tie his own flies with whatever fur and feathers came to hand, an exercise that moved in his case from skill to sheer artistry. Joe knows a lot about the insect life in the river, a talent that does not run to Latin terminology but is nonetheless astonishingly well informed. He is always questing and experimenting; not being able to afford the kind of tackle he wanted, he began to make his own rods.

Joe is strong as a bear, with the big muscular hands that go with it, and it is purely amazing to watch the delicacy exercised in his making of a fine-tuned rod. Not a wrap of silk is a hundredth of an inch out of place, the guides are properly spaced for maximum shooting of the line, and the cork handle is shaped and dressed to fit the hand. When he has it set up to meet his critical eye and it has met the necessary balance with the chosen weight of line by way of some testing on the lawn of his backyard, he signs it "Joe Cutch" (a simplified version of his real name, which is as Italian as the Tiber River) at the base of the shaft just above the grip. After another coat of varnish, it is ready for the customer. Anyone lucky enough to own one of his rods knows that he or she has the best available, finely balanced and strong.

Regardless of where it flows on the face of the earth, a river is always the lifeblood of the surrounding country. A river with its valley is one of nature's greatest architectural designs of power and beauty, a living drama in which man struggles towards perfect adjustment with his environment. The Oldman is just one river among many, but nonetheless is vital to those who live along its course – a river with a long history, unique in its unspoiled wildness.

A few ranchers living along the river understood this and valued the Oldman highly. But to many of them, it was just handy water flowing past their homesteads, water to be used for irrigation of gardens and crops, and for drinking. When bad sewage-disposal practices of towns in Crowsnest Pass on the middle fork

rendered it unfit for drinking, people downstream resorted to wells
and springs without complaint.

For the most part, they took the river for granted. It was here,
it was always here, and it would always be here. In summer the
murmur of its flow lulled those who lived close to it to sleep. They
heard it, but did not really hear its message, just as they looked at
it every day and did not really see it. It was a fixture, unchanging
except for occasional floods that came over its banks. Sometimes
the ice went out at spring break-up time with a sudden booming
roar. Then there could be dangerous ice-jams that caused damage
to property, and these left miniature stranded icebergs weeping in
the sun till they disappeared. But for the rest of the year it was the
river, the Oldman, a wandering crooked line on the map. Very few
of the ranchers knew or cared that it was the holy river of the
Blackfoot people. Many of them had picked the stones of teepee
rings off their fields, a nuisance to be rid of.

But then there came a rumour of a dam to be built a few miles
downstream below the forks near Pincher Creek, and those who
lived in the valleys became worried. We knew that a possible site
had been surveyed years before, but many such sites had been abandoned as unfeasible. Two dams had been built, one on the Waterton
River a few miles downstream from the park and the other on
the St. Mary's River just below the town of Cardston. Both
rivers are important tributaries of the Oldman and were excellent trout streams, and both dams had flooded thousands of acres
of good land.

About the time of the first rumours, I spent a day with my fly
rod on the north fork of the Oldman, a mile or so above where
it joins the Castle and the Crowsnest. In early afternoon, I left the
stream to sit with my back to a big cottonwood, taking time out
from fishing for some lunch and a pipe. It was a lovely day, with a
gentle breeze and a few clouds running overhead. I was close to
being asleep when across the river I saw a girl riding a pinto

pony bareback with a guitar slung across her back. When she came opposite, she angled away to a clump of trees where she dismounted to tie up her horse. Then she took the guitar up the steep slope to a sandstone outcrop where she sat down on a ledge. For a while she remained motionless, looking up the river. Then she began to strum the strings and broke into song. It was too far away for me to hear the words, but it was an enchanting melody I had never heard before – a lovely addition to a perfect afternoon. Then a feeling came to me that I was intruding, so I moved away through the trees, back toward a spot where a good trout had missed my fly earlier in the day.

Wading out into the pool where the big trout lay, I stood watching for a while, the gentle current cool against my legs. Hundreds of stonefly nymphs were crawling up onto stones projecting out of the water above the pool, shucking their skins and drying their wings before taking to the air. Some of the big flat-winged insects were falling off the rocks into the water, others were landing on various plants along the river to gather strength before taking wing again on their egg-laying runs over the surface. This was the final stage of a three-year cycle, a moment fly fishermen dream about, when trout go into a feeding frenzy beyond anything like the normal. Some of the inch-long insects were even landing on me as I selected a stiff hackled bucktail replica from my fly box and tied it to the tippet of my leader.

A good trout rolled to one side of a boulder farther up the pool. Dropping the fly a bit upstream and slightly to one side of the spot, I watched it floating down in company with a live specimen, and knew a thrill of excitement when the trout took the artificial fly in a solid strike. It came out of the water in a cartwheeling leap, bored down deep behind the rock, jumped again, and then shot away across the pool. It was a thick-bodied, handsome rainbow, iridescent in the sun as it jumped again and again. When it finally submitted to being led down into the shallow water, I slipped the hook out of its jaw and watched it go swimming back to deep water.

The next hour was one of the wildest, most action-packed sessions I have ever spent. I used up more time cleaning and drying my fly than I did fishing, for the trout took it with reckless abandon almost every cast. When one got chewed beyond recognition or ability to float, I put on another, and the unbridled feeding went on. I lost count of the fish played and released. I tried every trick cast and type of fly presentation I knew, and the trout kept striking.

Finally, I worked my way down to a big pool where the river split itself on a huge boulder shaped like a Gothic church door sticking up a good three feet out of deep water. On my side there was a gravel bar and on the other a low undercut bank with a big willow overhanging it. For a while I just stood watching.

The stonefly hatch was slowing up, but the trout were still rising steadily. A couple of good ones were rolling a bit below and on each side of the boulder. Then, out of the corner of my eye, I saw a gentle, slow-rolling confident rise under the willow and against the bank. There was something about that lazy rise that spoke of a grand fish. But it was in a very difficult place to reach, for if the fly did not get hung up in the willow, it would be hard to drop it where it wouldn't drag and drown on the edge of an eddy. Big trout are shy of a dragging fly, and this one had to be sophisticated in the art of survival.

Tying on a fresh leader and a new fly, I waded slowly out into the pool downstream and across from the willow until the water was threatening the top of my chest waders. Working the line out in false casts, I shot the fly with all the power in my rod in a long cast that barely missed the willow, so that it danced on the far edge of a bulge in the slow current and floated jauntily to within six inches of the bank. Then it disappeared in a tiny rise no bigger than one made by a small fish. Muttering something smoky under my breath, I struck anyway — and the water flew in every direction as a massive rainbow came out of the river in a jump that came within a whisker of fouling the leader on a low-hanging branch. It shot out into the river toward the boulder and blew the river open again with another end-swapping jump. Then followed a move that took me completely by surprise, for the trout charged straight at me quicker than I could take up the slack and jumped again close enough to splash water over me.

For a long moment I thought it was all over, but then the slack came out of the line and I could feel the weight of the fish as it made a long run downstream with the reel howling in protest. As I backed out on the edge of the gravel bar, the trout slowly swam back upstream a way and then just stopped and hung there – dead weight. I manoeuvred down to a point a bit below and across from it and it must have seen me, for it suddenly shot back up the river. Finally, after several short runs, as it began to tire, I worked it up to my feet in shallow water, where I could see every detail showing against the coloured stones on the bottom. Keeping its head toward me, I slipped my fingers under one of its gill covers and lifted it up to admire it. It was by far the finest fish of the day and one of the finest rainbows I had seen in a lot of years of fishing along the front of the mountains.

I was about to slip the fly out of its jaw and release it when a voice behind me said, "Don't you like to eat them?"

Startled, I looked around to find an audience — the girl with the guitar sitting on her pinto horse with her long blonde hair hanging down her back and a quizzical little smile on her face.

"For sure," I said, "but I kept all I wanted back up the river. Would you like this one?"

"Oh, yes!" she said, "I'll take it back to the ranch where I'm staying. They'll love to have it."

That is how I met Lesley. She was staying with some friends on a ranch farther down the river. I dressed the trout and hung it on a forked willow stick. When I handed it up to her, I noticed a shadow cross her face and asked her if something was wrong.

"I've heard about the dam," she said. "I just can't believe anyone would drown this beautiful valley. All this will be under water, my friends say, and they will lose their ranch. Isn't there something that can be done to stop it?" She was near tears.

"So far, it's only a rumour," I told her. "But if it gets serious, some of us are going to try."

Take a Man Fishing

It was a fine August morning and I was busy checking over plans for an extensive pack-train trip into the Alberta Rockies with a party of sportsmen. Gordon, my youngest son, and his friend Bruce Briosi, a neighbouring rancher's son, suddenly appeared out of nowhere in the manner of boys, who are masters of well-planned aimlessness. They both were wearing the angelic expressions of twelve-year-olds who are either just getting into mischief or coming out of it.

"Hi, Dad," Gordon greeted me. "How about coming fishing with me and Bruce?"

"I don't know about that," I answered. "Where did you figure on going?"

"Francis Lake," Gordon replied with a rush of enthusiasm. "There's big rainbows up there and we've never been there."

"Not so fast," I exclaimed. "I'm busy and that's three or four days shot." But I was tempted. I'd been promising myself a trip to this high remote lake for years.

From *Outdoor Life* (August 1961)

With all the artful subterfuge of a boy, Gordon changed the subject without changing it. "Look," he said, as he fished for something in a shirt pocket, "I got a swell idea for a new fly that I bet those rainbows will jump out of the lake to grab."

While his friend Bruce watched with dancing eyes, he held out a handful of beautiful hackles for me to inspect. They were an odd colour, not black and not grey, but a curious translucent smoky shade. When I picked up one to stroke the hackles back along the quill, they stood out straight and stiff, the way top-grade dry-fly hackles should.

"Where did you get these?" I asked.

"Over at Bruce's place," Gordon replied innocently. Bruce suddenly snickered and both boys collapsed in gales of laughter.

"Gosh, he looked funny," Gordon gasped. "We pulled them all out of one side of his neck. He certainly was pretty mad."

"He jumped on the fence and crowed," Bruce added, "with feathers sticking out one side of his neck and nothing on the other. He sure looked funny."

The picture of an outraged rooster crowing his defiance with one side of his neck plucked naked was infectious. Gordon interrupted my chuckle to state, "You better come, Dad, and try out that new rod. You haven't caught a decent fish on it since you got it."

Temptation began riding me hard. Gordon was right. I'd acquired a little two-and-a-quarter-ounce fairy wand of a fly rod which had never been truly blooded. Reminding myself that man who is too busy to go fishing once in a while is just too busy, I began to bend a little. The ways and means of taking a few days off began to take shape. I've guided hunting and fishing parties in my home province of Alberta for the past twenty-five years, but it still offers small chance for active participation.

"Go tie your flies," I told the boys. "Maybe I can get away for the weekend after all."

Half the fun of going on an expedition is getting ready for it. Francis Lake is trapped in the spectacular peaks on the north rim of Glacier National Park just inside Montana in the heart of Waterton-Glacier International Peace Park. It is best reached from the Canadian side by taking a launch up to the head of Waterton Lakes across the international border and hiking up seven miles of mountain trail. So our preparations were designed to include only the bare necessities for comfort in high country, which could be carried on packboards by two boys and a man on a three-day trip.

Three light down-filled sleeping bags, the kind used by mountain climbers, along with a nine-foot-square, teepee-type tent made up the basis of our gear. To this we added a nested package of pots, plates, cups, and a frying pan. We took enough food to ensure two good meals a day without relying on trout, because the best way to go hungry is to tempt fate by gambling on plenty of trout to eat. Most of the food was dehydrated – this light and modern method of processing food is tasty and nourishing. When we had everything collected, we rolled up our gear and some spare clothing in waterproof tarps and lashed the equipment to our packboards. We had three good loads, with mine weighing sixty-two pounds, and the boys' averaging about thirty pounds apiece.

Gordon had also converted some of the rooster feathers into a dozen or so creations, which were really attractive, tied onto number-12 hooks. Using a white-and-black pair of coarse moose hairs, he first fashioned a ribbed body for his fly, set off by a jaunty two-toned forked tail. This was enhanced by generous wrappings of the smoky-black hackles at the shoulder, making a simple hackle fly that would float like a cork.

About noon the next day, we shouldered our packs at the head of Waterton Lake to head up-trail. For the first few miles, we wound through the shady depths of the great forest in the Kootenai Valley. Then the trail forked and lifted up a series of switchbacks to the mouth of a narrower side canyon which dropped down from our objective past sharp peaks.

The afternoon summer sun made us sweat, and soon each pack seemed to triple in weight. We slogged along, climbing steadily through the rank, almost jungle-like growth. Huckleberries were in profusion on the bushes everywhere.

We adopted a routine of fifteen minutes' hiking with five minutes' rest, and these breaks were a welcome opportunity to refresh ourselves with berries. Pound for pound, in proportion to my pack, the boys were carrying more weight, and I couldn't help but admire their cheerful plodding. But there is nothing like the promise of big trout at the end of the trail to keep one foot going ahead of the other, and we made good time.

The ever-changing vistas of the mountains provided many interesting sidelights. I spotted a whiskery old mountain patriarch of a billy goat perched on a crag watching us, the remnants of his winter coat fluttered in the breeze. The high basins flanking the canyon on either side were floored in new emerald green, for while it was August, early spring was just emerging from the winter snows at the eight-thousand-foot levels.

In several basins, my binoculars revealed the fresh earth of grizzly diggings, where the big animals had excavated for roots and ground squirrels. We climbed through strips of timber divided by open avalanche tracks down which millions of tons of snow had swept off the mountain slopes year after year. Some of the big trees standing on the edge of these tracks bore numerous scars from the terrific force of these thundering slides.

By the time the sun dipped behind a peak at the head of the valley a mile or two to the west, we were drawing on reserves of energy and stamina. The weight of the packs along with the heat and steady climbing made the promise of camp and a cheery campfire seem like paradise. So when the deep glints of the lake showed through the trees ahead, we threaded our way through the timber and dropped our packs with a feeling of tired satisfaction at a campsite just above the rocky beach.

In no time a small fire was dancing in a rock fireplace, and tea soon steamed alongside a frying pan filled with bubbling stew. After supper I pitched the tent under a big spruce, but it was only insurance against a possible shower, for we all rolled our beds out in the open. No one had any trouble getting to sleep.

A tiny crash of upsetting pots awoke us at sunrise and we reared up in our sleeping bags just in time to see a mule-deer doe go bouncing off through the trees. She had come to investigate our camp, and her inquisitive nose had upset the pots Gordon had stacked on a log the night before. Her fright didn't last long. She was back in a few minutes and hung around our camp for the rest of our stay.

Breakfast was a hurried affair in anticipation of the day ahead. While we ate, the early sun sparkled on wavelets of the deepest blue and lighted the face of a mountain across the lake, down which a two-thousand-foot cascade plunged into the water. Picking up our tackle, we circled the shoreline and headed for the brush-free slopes under the mountain where we could work out flies without getting our back casts all tangled up.

The boys followed the rocky shoreline, while I walked along the steep slope a hundred feet above, following a faint goat trail and watching for feeding trout.

There are two ways to fish a mountain lake with dry flies from shore. One method, favoured by most anglers, simply calls for finding a good location for casting and waiting for the trout to come within range of the fly. The success of this method depends largely on the occurrence of a general feeding rise, which may come only once during a day and then be of short duration. It demands what the boys call "kingfisher work" – unending patience – and the good fishing is well spaced with long periods of inactivity.

The other method, our favourite – which might be labelled "fish hunting" – is much more interesting. In every mountain lake during the daylight hours, there are always a few trout cruising the shallows close to shore, picking up insects that fall from over-hanging bushes and rocks. These trout are always shy, but they take a dry fly readily. They require careful stalking, extremely cautious manoeuvring for position on the part of the angler, and the delicate delivery of the fly. If the trout is feeding away from the angler, it is best to get ahead of the fish, and if the angler's path takes him over shelving rock ledges or loose slides, great care must be exercised not to dislodge any loose rocks that might fall into the lake.

From my vantage point on the goat trail, I spotted two fine rainbows cruising toward the boys, occasionally surfacing to lip down insects with tiny swirls no bigger than those made by fingerlings. Gordon spotted their lazy rising at about fifty feet and whipped out a short line to lay a cast ahead of them. Bruce dropped his fly gently a little to one side. Then both boys froze in rapt concentration.

From above I could see every movement of the trout and the flies bobbing gently on the tiny waves. For a moment it looked as though the trout were going to pass up the feathered offerings, but then one turned with a slow roll and engulfed Gordon's stinger. At the prick of the hook, the sixteen-inch rainbow took to the air in a wild flurry. Bruce struck involuntarily at the sight of him, and before he could correct his back cast the leader tangled in a shrub. He showed remarkable self-control in his patient unravelling of the tangle, for while Gordon fought his trout, the other darted in and out in plain view, trying to see what the hooked one had caught. Before Bruce could get his fly back into action, the second fish had prudently disappeared and Gordon was carefully playing his trout into position for landing. Leaving them to their fun, I moved to the foot of a cascade, where the plunging stream fell over rock shelves into the lake in foaming exuberance.

As though to greet my arrival, I saw the shadow of a two-foot trout rise from the depths to take a drowned insect. The sight of a big bull elk in hunting season or a fat buck within rifle range does not stir my blood much any more, but the rise of a great trout within easy casting distance never fails to generate in me a mild case of buck fever.

My fingers shook as I opened my fly box, and I came within an ace of spilling the entire contents, as I selected a fly. Choosing a favourite bucktail creation, fashioned to resemble a stonefly, I hurriedly knotted it to the 3X tippet on the end of my tapered leader. Whipping out twenty feet of line, I dropped it in the bursting bubbles at the foot of the falls. Instantly, the shadow rose to snatch the fly before it had moved a foot. I set the hook and felt the powerful head-shaking surge of a heavy trout, but then the little rod suddenly straightened and the line went slack. The knot had pulled out at the fly. Shaking at the knees, I sat down to light my pipe and tie on another. This time I gave the half-blood knot some extra wraps, which is something that I should have done in the first place.

My second cast dropped the fly on the edge of the froth, out to one side of the current over deep water. Letting it roll on a slack leader like a drowned insect, I watched it swing out of the foam and twitched it slightly. A good rainbow flashed up for it and my little rod bowed beautifully to its first strong rush. The fish lanced out of the depths like a spear, tailwalked a dozen feet, and bored away in a sizzling run. My fairy rod telegraphed every move up my arm, and I could feel each muscular surge of the hooked trout. I knew then that there had been many thrills missed over the years of angling with heavier rods. Certainly these super light creations require some care in handling, but they have something the heavier rods cannot possibly duplicate.

When the trout began to tire, I led it along the rocks to a point where a declining ledge let me climb down to the water's edge. But it was another five minutes before the trout was ready to gill. It was a fat, bright-hued female as shapely as a torpedo, much smaller than the one I had lost but still a very respectable trout. Nesting the glistening fish and the rod in a bed of yellow alpine mimulus, I took some photographs. My rod had been truly blooded.

Looking down shore, I saw Bruce fast to a fish. Then Gordon showed up over a rock in front of me, and I asked him how the new fly was working. With a grin from ear to ear, he held up a twin to the one I'd just caught.

"How do you like your new rod?" he asked.

Taking the hint from the envious glance he cast in its direction, I invited him to try it. On his first cast, he hooked a heavy trout which ran hard and deep toward the middle of the lake. Gordon turned him and began working him back. In the crystal-clear water off the rocks, we could see every move the deep-fighting trout made. We carefully released this one, for there was no point in taking more trout than we could use. This is trout fishing at its best.

Bruce joined us and we fished at the foot of the falls. For a while the action was sporadic, but then a heavy hatch of black gnats began to show up on the water. If was as though a fire had been lit under the lake; the whole surface began to boil with rising fish. This was a made-to-order opportunity for Gordon's new creation, which we had christened "The Rooster's Lament." We all tied one on our leaders. Gordon's prediction — that the trout would jump out of the lake for this fly — wasn't far wrong. We lost all track of time and the number of fish played and released. It was wild fishing, and while none of the trout were heavy they all showed a willingness to put up a fast and furious fight.

Finally, when we'd worn out or lost a good part of Gordon's latest invention, he suddenly announced, "Gosh, I'm hungry."

"Me too," echoed Bruce.

The day had gone like magic and the sun was dipping behind the mountains as we went back to camp. We'd kept three fish, which were soon cut in suitable lengths to fit the frying pan. There is no better-tasting food in the world than freshly caught mountain trout fried in bacon fat over an open fire. When we'd stuffed ourselves with two big helpings each, we sagged back contentedly against our bedrolls.

Flashing his warm smile, Bruce broke the silence by summing up the day. "I bet nobody ever had more fun," he said. Then turning to me, he added, "I'm sure glad you brought us up here."

With a deep feeling of appreciation, I recalled a slogan often seen in outdoor publications: Take a Boy Fishing. But somehow, in this instance, the shoe seemed to be on the other foot.

"You characters brought me on this trip," I gently reminded Bruce. "Thanks a million."

PART FOUR

HUNTING WITH
A CAMERA

When Andy decided to become a wildlife photographer, he was an experienced big-game guide and hunter. Almost immediately he discovered challenges he had never faced as a hunter. One of the first things he learned was that animals behaved differently towards him when he wasn't carrying a gun. They allowed him to get much closer, to witness their everyday behaviour. In the case of filming Grizzly Country, *he learned more about grizzly behaviour from facing the bear's charge with only a camera than he ever did over the sights of a rifle barrel. If you have a gun and a bear charges, most people shoot, period. What Andy and his sons learned was that not all charges were deadly; many times it was simply a warning not to come any closer. The narrative of their adventures, as they seek to understand the animals they observe, makes for exciting reading.*

Exploring with Cameras

F rom the very beginning of my experience with Bert
Riggall, it had been obvious that there were more ways
than most hunters recognized to hunt wild game. He had
shown the way to off-season stalking of all kinds of animals and
birds with a camera, the trophies recorded on film often being
more exciting to collect, and while the frying pan went neglected
even when success rewarded the hunter, there was no lack of
excitement. My initial experiments with a cheap folding Kodak
of a vintage once commonly sold in about every drug store in the
country proved beyond any shade of doubt that the successful
camera hunter had to be something of a naturalist, knowing the
animals well enough to anticipate their moves, and also a master
stalker. A good rifle is accurate up to ranges of several hundred
yards, allowing a proficient shot to collect a trophy way out there,
but at similar ranges my camera recorded nothing but unrecogniz-
able specks. To get a good close-up picture meant stalking to within
fifteen or twenty feet, and my early failures to get this close showed
me just how little I knew about the game. It was discouraging at

From *Horns in the High Country* (1973)

times, but not to the point of abandoning the idea. Something of animal psychology was being learned – not much, but still enough to show me that a whole new horizon of largely unexplored possibilities lay waiting. Failure after failure only whetted my interest and determination to master the game.

Compared to the array of equipment available today, the cameras of the time were awkward and cumbersome. The best available 35-mm models were imported from Germany and were very expensive. The variety of film available had just begun to include colour and there was nothing like today's assortment of black-and-white film. Film-speed ratings were comparatively slow and processors hated the small 35-mm format, so users of these cameras mostly did their own developing and enlarging. These cameras were considered play toys of amateurs; the professionals used big cumbersome view cameras. These took beautiful pictures, but they were very heavy and awkward to operate. When one tripped the shutter on some of these they made a racket like a bucket of bolts being dumped down a dry well, and quite often a skittish subject would jump three feet in the air while the film was being exposed. The resulting photograph was a blurry reminder to the photographer that his stalking ability had far surpassed the limitations of his equipment, in no way something to cheer his soul.

Bert Riggall and most of his contemporaries carried monstrous Graflex cameras all over the mountains. He had a big telephoto lens for his 4x5 Graflex with fine elements encased in solid brass that weighed like a cannon. Such an outfit was a fair load for a horse, let alone a man, and was anything but foolproof with its array of film holders and other accessories, but just the same he obtained some magnificent photos with it. The large format made darkroom work much easier.

Motion-picture cameras of the time were also anything but light and handy. Kodak came out with a light magazine-type 16-mm camera, but these had their faults, for the fifty-foot magazines were inclined to jam, and the cheaply constructed pressure plates of the returnable film holders had a nasty way of relaxing with age, allowing the film to get out of focus – a very unhappy thing to discover at the end of a prolonged trip where a prize piece of footage was concerned.

The first professional-grade 16-mm motion-picture cameras I saw were built like the proverbial brick outhouse – very heavy indeed – and when one used telephoto lenses there was always the problem of getting on film what you were looking at through the finder, for the finders were not of the reflex type that look through the lens, and so were subject to parallax. They had an assortment of mechanical pitfalls built into them to tip the unwary.

On occasion Bert and I guided both amateur and professional photographers using this type of equipment. Because being an adequate photographic guide meant knowing about the problems concerned, we learned something of such equipment and its use. As has been said before, a successful guide is someone very close to a jack-of-all-trades. Like the usual somewhat distorted picture of outdoor writers, we were supposed to be rugged philosophers, top riders, excellent shots, crack anglers, skilful whitewater men and outstandingly satisfactory to our women, as well as being fairly good at everything else our lives called upon us to try. Very few actually measure up to this blueprint, though the myth persists. Some of my most frustrating and astonishing experiences were with photographers.

There was the time when Franklin Crosby came out on a summer pack trip with assorted members of his numerous family, armed with a brand-new Bell and Howell 16-mm motion-picture camera. It was one of the first models of this rugged and very popular instrument, complete with turret head carrying three lenses. Naturally, it was spring-wound, and although it carried one-hundred-foot rolls of film, the length of sequences was limited to about eighteen feet. Even with its shortcomings in comparison to modern equipment, this camera was about the last word in such equipment at that time.

Franklin brought about a mile of film so he and his son, George, proceeded to shoot pictures in all directions. Nothing was safe from them: people and horses alike on that trip found themselves taking part in what might be termed a cinematographic binge. Naturally action was what was wanted, but our horses proved very self-conscious about performing on film. There were always one or two snorty broncos in the outfit that would ordinarily throw a high-winding fit at the least excuse; but if the movie camera was trained on them while being packed or mounted, their resolve to come all unglued and throw things in every direction seemed to evaporate. Almost every time they walked off meek as lambs. This of course was somewhat frustrating to the photographers, nor was it the only cause for tendencies to tears.

One day George and I spotted a huge old ram lying in a pocket beside a big snowdrift at the bottom of a cliff overlooking a mountain lake, where most of the party was fishing for trout. Understandably enough, George was immediately keen to stalk the ram with the camera and I volunteered to lend a hand.

There was a shallow ravine leading up the steep slope to the foot of the snowdrift, and when I looked this over with the glasses I was suddenly struck with a lightning flash of sheer genius. For this ravine had water in it which issued from the mouth of a cave in the snow – a tunnel carved by the stream and undoubtedly continuing back up to the foot of the cliff. If we crawled up this hole to its far end to the back we would likely find space enough between the snow and the rock to climb to the top edge of the drift, a position that would put us within feet of the snoozing ram.

Getting to the bottom edge of the drift was something else. But after crawling up along the water course scraping hide off our elbows and bellies on the sharp rocks, we arrived without spooking the ram. From there it was a very cool damp business making our way up through the tunnel, for its roof dripped copiously on us. We were wet and shivering when we came to the foot of the cliff, but sure enough, the way was clear to climb up along a ledge to a spot close to the ram.

George went first, and when he eased his eyebrows over the edge of the drift, he was within thirty feet of the sheep. With unusual calmness, he slid the camera into position and it began to whirr. Had I not been concentrating on the subject and noticed a bit more of other more important details, we might have avoided some considerable embarrassment. When the spring ran down, George carefully wound it up again and shot more film. Then the ram got restive and stood up to pose in very regal profile looking down over the country below. George rolled more film. Then the ram must have heard the camera, for he looked right into George's face, his eyes widening with alarm. The next instant it was heading away on a dead run with little puffs of dust at its heels. George tracked it through his view-finder like a professional.

I was just opening my mouth to cheer him for what was likely one of the best close-up pictures of a bighorn taken through the lens of a movie camera when he began to swear. He had taken the whole series of sequences with the lens cap still in place! Naturally the film was a total blank.

Near the end of the same trip his father had an unforgettable experience to round out their initial filming adventures.

We were packing up to move and about mid-morning Bert's dog gave chase to something down in some thick stuff along the creek. Next moment a small black bear went scuttling up a tall lodgepole pine, whereupon our friend moved in for some film. Bert went down a few minutes later to find out how he was making out, and Franklin complained to him that everything was fine except that the bear wasn't moving. All it was doing was clasping the tree about forty feet from the ground looking worried – not very satisfactory for motion pictures.

"I'll move him for you," Bert volunteered and proceeded to climb the tree after the bear with the idea of making it climb higher.

But the bear did not move in the expected direction. It just hugged the tree with eyes bulging with horror as it watched Bert's progress toward it. It had apparently been in a berry patch all morning and was stuffed to the ears, for it suddenly lost all control and berries and various muck came showering down all over Bert. Upon being attacked in this unexpected fashion, Bert beat a hasty retreat, whereupon the bear came sliding down right on top of him tail first all the way. And all the way, it continued to let go loads of digested berries in a continuous shower at point-blank range. When they came to the ground, the bear took off in great bounds for distant parts, while Bert took himself to the creek in an attempt to clean up. Fortunately he was wearing his hat!

Meanwhile, Franklin had joined the rest of us in such uncontrolled merriment at the whole ridiculous business that he had obtained scarcely a foot of film of the episode.

The Crosby family's enthusiasm for motion pictures of wild game was afire, and although we did not realize it at the time, George's zeal carried him to considerable heights of recklessness. There was a sequel to the ram and bear episodes surpassing anything yet experienced, and although the story is a bit off-trail it deserves telling. However, I did not hear about it for a long time.

Many years later I was visiting George in his home in Minneapolis, and during the course of some reminiscing about many experiences we had shared on numerous expeditions he and members of his family had made with us in the Rockies, he showed me various trophies. Among many other things hanging on the walls of his den there was a fragment of a canoe. It was a bit of the thwart, the V-shaped portion from the tip of the bow with a bit of broken sashcord hanging from it. When I asked George about it, he grinned and proceeded to tell me a story.

After they left us that summer when the new Bell and Howell camera was first tried out, they had taken the train east for some bass and muskie fishing at Lake of the Woods in southwestern Ontario.

One day he and his father went out to obtain some fishing pictures; Franklin with a guide in one canoe while George followed alone in another with the camera. It made a good combination to record some of the fishing sport available, and after an interesting and successful afternoon they headed back for camp.

At this time George left them to paddle back by a different route, hoping to get some deer and moose pictures when these animals came out along the shore to feed in the evening. On his way across some big open water he spotted a young bull moose swimming and immediately gave chase. It was not long before he caught up, but taking pictures and paddling proved to be something of a problem, for when he put down the paddle to shoot film, the moose swam quickly out of range.

But George knew something about the use of the lariat from his experience on the pack train and there was a thirty-foot piece of braided cotton sashcord tied to the bow of the canoe. So he quickly fashioned a running noose on the loose end of it, paddled up to the moose and flipped the loop over its antlers. Then he just sat back to take pictures to his heart's content while the moose towed him across the lake.

As can happen, his enthusiasm and excitement brewed some unawareness of important things, and before he realized what was happening, the moose came close to shore where it got its feet on solid bottom. It was only when the canoe suddenly picked up speed that George took his eye from the limited field of the viewfinder to find his camera subject heading at a splashing run for tall timber. Before he had time to do anything about it, the canoe hit something and capsized, whereupon George found himself sitting on the bottom of the lake up to his ears in water with the camera in his lap. At this point the moose disappeared, dragging the canoe at high speed.

George made his way to shore and trailed him a way. The trail was easy to follow for it was strewn with pieces of his canoe. The last sign he found was where he picked up the piece of bow thwart with a short piece of rope still attached where it had jammed under a deadfall. This was all he had left to record the adventure, for all the film was soaked with water and ruined. He proceeded to build a fire to dry out and was sitting beside it somewhat crestfallen, supperless and morose, contemplating the vagaries of wilderness cinematography, when a rescue party found him.

There are many ways to get into trouble while pursuing big game with cameras, and sometimes misadventure has a way of sneaking up on one in a most unexpected fashion.

There was the time I was guiding a professional wildlife photographer, one of the earliest and most successful of his kind. He is retired now, living a long way from the mountains where his adventure occurred, and to spare him possible embarrassment I will leave him unnamed.

He was a big, lean, and powerful man well over six feet tall, good company on the trail, and very keen about what he was doing, namely, putting a film together portraying pack-train life and its association with various kinds of animals. Amongst other things, he was particularly anxious to get some good close-range sequences of mountain goats in their spectacular surroundings.

Mountain goats are not an easy subject for camera work due to the country they call home, and even though they are not unduly shy or difficult to approach, the very nature of their chosen habitat offers a real challenge. Anyone attempting to get within close range of a goat sooner or later almost inevitably finds himself operating his camera with his hip pockets hanging out over a thousand feet or so of eagle thoroughfare, where if a slip occurs, it will not be the fall that hurts so much as the sudden stop at the bottom. It is no kind of country for a faint heart or shaky balance, for it can be exceedingly dangerous.

The danger is graded considerably by the experience and skill of the pursuing climber, but sometimes the best of cragsmen finds himself in a tight spot. When I was much younger and full of the stuff it takes to play with goats on their choice of ground, I was convinced that a man who was a good free-climber could follow them anywhere they chose to go. But one day I was trailing three of these whiskery mountaineers across a high face, where they led me down a ledge in a fairly steep incline. It took the goats around a bulge of the mountain and when I followed it was to find myself close-pressed from above by an overhang in a place where the goats had passed with ease. They were fifty yards ahead of me where the ledge had been wiped out for a few feet by water and icefalls in a perpendicular chimney. Never hesitating they blithely leapt the gap and proceeded on their way.

At this point I was beginning to feel that I would be much more comfortable somewhere else, but I was committed to follow, for the pack on my back and the nature of the ledge in combination with the overhang made going back extremely hazardous. I had been lured into a natural trap. The only way out was to trail the goats. When I came to the gap in the ledge and studied it I knew very well why goats climb so much easier than a man — they have four feet to land on instead of two and those feet are specially designed to stick.

There was nothing to do but try to mimic their jump, which I proceeded to do, landing on hands and feet goat-fashion. I skinned myself painfully in several spots but managed to stick to the rock. Then I climbed down out of there, a much wiser man. Now when

I see one of the whiskery ones looking down at me from the top
of some pinnacle, I am much inclined to say, "It's your mountain,
friend, and you are welcome to it."

Falling is not the only risk, for goats often double back directly
over the head of the pursuing climber and have the extremely
nasty habit of knocking loose rock down. Having trailed and
watched them innumerable times, I am tempted to believe they
do it sometimes with malice aforethought, or with a kind of grim
humour difficult to share. Any way you look at it, being on the
bottom end of a rock fall is no joke and can be very final. In any
event, wearing a hard hat is good insurance.

But guides and hunters are not normally morbid types or neg-
ative thinkers, and on this particular occasion my photographer
friend and I were not giving a thought to the possibility of trouble
as we stalked two big billies feeding in a shallow dip at the top of
some talus fans beneath a precipitous mountain wall about two
thousand feet high.

Our stalk took us up through a strip of shintangle into a little
ravine. This hid us fairly well to the base of the cliffs, where a
bulge of the mountain gave concealment in a traverse toward our
quarry. When we came within range my friend began to shoot
film through the gate of his Eastman Special, but he had barely
started when an eddy of wind gave us away. The billies instantly
elevated their short tails and proceeded to climb up and away
across the broken ledges of the face.

I knew that mountain like the palm of my hand and was
instantly aware of a possibility, for if the goats proceeded in the
direction of their retreat they might be pushed into an impossible
place where they could be cornered. Ahead and above them there
was a chimney with a smooth semicircular wall and an overhang
at its top. If they did not cross the chimney down low enough,
they would be committed to climbing into a trap. The thing to
do was to push them, for if goats are pressed and keep looking

back, it is possible to confuse them enough to haze them into such a place where the only way out would be back past us.

I pointed out the possibility to my friend, quickly packed his camera equipment into my rucksack, shouldered the heavy tripod, and led the way up over the steep rock hot on the heels of the goats. He came on strong, his eyes shining with excitement, and knowing he had considerable climbing experience I never gave him a second thought.

It was steep country but the rock was broken and rough enough to give good footing. Our Hungarian hobnails were clattering a merry tune as we scrambled in pursuit. The billies were out of sight, but pressing ahead I came within sight of them just as they were entering the chimney. Both looked back at me and obviously they were worried. Calling to my friend, I hurried, choosing a route carefully but swiftly as the billies dipped from view. Sure enough, when they came into view again, they were climbing into the blind chimney. Again I turned to urge my companion to hurry, but he was nowhere to be seen.

With a sinking feeling of dread, I back-trailed around a steep buttress wondering if he had somehow slipped and gone over the drop-off below. Then I saw him – plastered spread-eagle fashion on the face of a steep place I had just passed at a scrambling run. His complexion was almost pale green and he was hanging on with every fingernail, his knuckles white with the effort. His eyes were tight shut, and it was instantly apparent he was in the frightening throes of vertigo, a kind of nervous sickness brought on by an awareness of height that can put a climber into a paralyzing paroxysm of fear. I had seen it happen before and it is no fun for a guide and much less for the unfortunate victim.

Speaking to him quietly and reassuringly, I first found a place to safely stow my pack and the tripod. Taking a fifty-foot coil of rope out of the pack, I proceeded to help my would-be goat photographer down onto more hospitable ground.

Tying the end of the rope around him with a bowline knot, I passed the rest of the rope around a stubby little tree anchored firmly in the rock letting its free end hang down past him. Holding it to make sure he could not fall, I tried to talk him into moving, but he only groaned and hung on all the harder. So I literally pried him loose and slid him down to a ledge below, letting rope pay out as we went. He groaned some more and scraped his fingers trying to hang on, but I finally got him down to the limit of the doubled rope in spite of his best efforts to remain immovable. There was no tree for another belay at this point, but I found a projecting nubbin of rock that would do. Testing it carefully to be sure it would not crack loose, I placed my folded glove behind it to make a smooth bearing surface for the rope to slip on, and again slid the photographer down to the next available ledge, scraping all the way. He had me beat by forty pounds and was strong as a bull, which made the whole process somewhat complicated. I was sweating copiously in spite of a bitter cold breeze, when we came to rest a second time.

There another little tree gave me a third belay, and so we proceeded with me performing like a monkey on a string, prying, scrambling, and cajoling. It was a tough, exasperating business, but by one means and another we finally made it to a nice wide ledge maybe two feet across within a dozen or so feet of the top of the fine talus below. There I had no more belays, which did not matter much, for my friend could fall the rest of the way without doing himself much damage, the shale being pitched at a steep angle and lying deep and loose. So I left off being the solicitous diplomat and told him very shortly to open his goddamn eyes and jump. But this he refused to do, still imagining himself halfway between sky and earth.

So I resorted to other tactics. One way to shake someone loose from vertigo is to make him or her so scorching angry that fright is forgotten. On another day I had deliberately done this when a lady climbing companion had frozen up in a tricky place. She had reacted so well, I thought for a moment she was about to pick up the nearest rock and brain me with it. Then she took off like a goat and I was hard-pressed to calm her down before she broke her neck. Then she realized why I had been so unpleasant and we finished the climb good friends.

So without further argument I lit into the photographer, calling him every kind of yellow coward, a profound dissertation well spiced with some smoky, hide-peeling adjectives learned around cow camps over my youthful years. The therapy took effect and before long he was glaring at me in an extremely warlike fashion.

I wound up by telling him, "Look, you long-eared, awkward string of misery! Either you climb down off here under your own steam or I'm going to kick you down! And if you think I'm bluffing just try me out!"

By this time he was livid with anger and with a withering look he turned his back and walked off that place as though it was fitted with stairs. A few steps down the shale slope he looked back to see me coiling my rope and preparing to climb back up the face for his cameras. Realizing what I meant to do, he came back and begged me to leave the whole outfit – worth at least three or four thousand dollars – where it lay. Nobody, he told me, was going to risk his life to get that camera; to hell with it, there was lots more where that came from! I just grinned at him and headed up the mountain. By the time I got back, he was down where we had left our horses.

He was standing with his back to me leaning against his horse and did not even glance my way as I untied halter shanks in preparation to return to camp. Then he turned with a lopsided grin and stuck out his hand in apology.

I told him to forget it, that he was not the first one that had come down with mountain sickness, nor would he be the last. He really had nothing to be ashamed about, for vertigo is a nasty thing playing no favourites. Nor was I without blame, for I should never have taken him out on that face without some preliminary climbing to condition him. I learned something that day enabling me to avoid similar trouble since.

Twenty years ago it was evident to me that the wilderness pack-train business was likely doomed in this part of the Rockies, and set about making plans for changing a way of life that had become a family tradition for over half a century. Because I have always been convinced that happiness is doing something you enjoy, it was only natural those plans led me along wilderness paths. It occurred to me that wild country and the life it contained could be profitably shown to a host of people through the media of photography and writing. The transition would take time and tough going, but it at least would give us a chance to make use of previous experience, an opportunity to make a living in the kind of country we all so dearly love. It was not something that had to be started cold, for some of the skill had rubbed off the photographers I had guided. For several years I had been selling stories and articles to various leading outdoor and nature magazines. Besides, there had been plenty of experience talking to people across the campfires, interpreting the many adventures and things seen along the trails. So I had some considerable advantage over the rank beginner.

Apart from this, we had four boys, all about as full of steam and energy as boys can get. They had grown up close to the wilderness and had often spent time playing with sheep, goats, deer, and other wild things of the mountains. The two oldest, Dick and Charlie, were big enough to be restlessly looking for new worlds to explore and like all boys they needed an outlet for their energy and imagination. From the time they were big enough to safely handle the specially built little .22 rifle I had made up for them, they had been trained in the use of firearms, but photography was a much better outlet for their desire to hunt and would make an ideal developer for creative talent. Why not set up a wilderness-photography production company in the family and let them participate? There was no end to the subject material waiting to be tapped. When I suggested we go camera hunting, they were purely delighted.

For a start, I bought them cheap, fixed-focus, box-type Kodaks. Then I arranged credit for film at the local drug store and turned them loose. Little did I realize what would transpire. At the end of a busy season I went around to pay my bill and was dumbfounded at the size of it. But when I asked to see the pictures that had resulted from this unprecedented expenditure, my initial concern evaporated. There were many failures, but some were surprisingly good – sufficiently interesting and clear to warrant having some glossy enlargements made, and these were offered to a fairly high-circulation newspaper along with explanatory captions and some short columns in the nature vein. Quite a few were accepted and paid for, and ultimately appeared with full credit lines to the photographers. The editor was somewhat astonished later on to find out his new-found contributors were only ten and twelve years old.

It was not long before both boys graduated to using fine 35-mm Exakta cameras and were producing top-quality pictures.

In the meantime I had been shooting film for a lecture production through the gate of the newly acquired Bell and Howell 16-mm motion-picture camera. Every spare moment was spent afield. Every spare dollar was spent on film, and by the end of two years I had sufficient to splice together a film about an hour and a half long. It was a cross-sectional portrayal of about everything that walked, crawled, and swam within range of my camera. If not professional, it certainly contained something of the adventures of the photographer and reflected some of the stalking still accumulated over the years.

Bighorns formed the major portion of wildlife thus illustrated because they are spectacular animals living in picturesque surroundings and have always been a fascinating source of interest to me. They lend themselves well to such photographic study, being naturally photogenic; they live where backgrounds are rarely drab; and they respond well to human association. If one goes unarmed with an open, friendly mind among them it is not long before they accept close contact, a combination of characteristics that has led me along many fascinating trails.

But looking back on that first film from the perspective of years to enable comparisons to be drawn, I now wonder how I ever had the nerve to show it in public. It lacked a great deal in technical quality, but it was, if nothing else, completely authentic. It was fairly well exposed and most of it had been shot off a tripod, but the editing was ragged. However, I held it together with a running commentary, the experience gathered from entertaining around countless campfires shared with Bert Riggall and a host of friends. Though the film had its shortcomings, it afforded the chance to try out an idea.

A friend of mine with considerable theatrical production experience looked at the film, listened to my commentary, and decided that it was worth some effort. He booked up a series of eighteen shows in community halls, school auditoriums, and theatres around the country, and I was committed to sink or swim.

The opening show was in a large hall in the city of Lethbridge, where the boys accompanied me to participate in the festivities, as they had shot some of the film. It had been preceded by much promotional fanfare over radio and in the newspapers. I had butterflies fluttering under my ribs as zero hour approached; but when the doors opened and people flooded in to jam the place till it could hold no more, I knew that heady feeling known only to stage performers stepping out in front of the footlights and looking out over a packed house on a sellout opening night. The butterflies were still giving some trouble, as I warmed up with a short explanatory introduction prior to dimming the lights and turning on the projector. But then the big rams began to parade across the screen and something about them lent confidence. I forgot about everything except taking the crowd on a guided tour through the mountains – exactly what I had been doing for years, only this depended more on my ability to make the scenes on the screen come alive, giving the audience a feeling of participation rather than just being viewers. The whole performance went so smoothly I surprised myself. The applause that followed was much more than just polite and indicated real enjoyment.

Thanks to my friend Harry Baalim, who was promoting the show, the whole tour was a resounding success. We had a show in a different town six nights a week for three weeks, and by the end of it I felt like I had walked on short rations from one end of the Rockies to the other. Show business proved to be hard work, but it was interesting and gratifying.

That began a branch of my life I have enjoyed ever since. The following winter my trail led me east to Detroit and New York through various bookings at private clubs, sportsmen's meetings, and some new adventures. In Detroit I met Jack Van Coevering, the famous outdoor columnist with the *Detroit Free Press*, who invited me to appear on his television show. This medium of entertainment and communication was then very new, and I had the unique experience of seeing myself on the monitoring screen before I had ever watched a show on a regular television set. Then came an opportunity to make a first appearance in the professional circuits.

Some friends in Minneapolis arranged to have me audition to appear on a scheduled series under the auspices of the Minnesota Natural History Society, where they invite speakers and filmmakers from around the world to participate in an annual program held every winter. I appeared before a board of directors to show them my film, with some secret misgivings. To this day I am somewhat at loss to know why they confirmed the booking, but approve it they did.

In due course I came to the Hall of Arts to put on two shows in one evening, for the series was so popular, the building would not accommodate the crowd in one session. My introduction was given by the president of the association, Dr. Clayton Rudd, and it was the shortest, most pointed one I ever experienced. He stepped forth on the huge lighted platform ahead of me and said, "Ladies and gentlemen, I take pleasure in introducing the only man I ever met with nerve enough to bring the first film he ever made to a place like this! I give you Andy Russell!"

I found myself standing out there in a spotlight in that vast platform big enough to corral forty horses with room to spare wondering how anyone could be so reckless. The footlights were shining up in my face and I was largely blinded by the spotlight coming down from someplace high above. Dimly I could see the hall was packed and right then I would have cheerfully faced a charging grizzly by way of a trade. The welcoming applause did little to still the butterflies. A bit to one side out of the corner of my eye I could see an enormous screen and had a horrifying thought that my little 16-mm film would fade out to nothing on its vast expanse. A microphone reared its head like a cobra ready to strike in front of my nose. Right then I came about as close to complete paralysis as I have ever been. But then remembering there were people out there in the audience I had known and entertained in a different way for many years, I knew it was impossible to let them down. So I lit an imaginary campfire out among the footlights, dreamed up a mountain lifting its craggy head against the stars out back, forgot where I was, and began to talk.

When the old rams came walking beautifully out onto the screen with the sun reflected in their golden eyes, as usual they were an instant hit, and a spontaneous little ripple of applause drifted out across the theatre. Then everything came easier, and before I realized time was passing, the show came to an end. After a fifteen-minute interval I was back for the second session and once more the people loved it. Following almost four continuous hours, I knew what it was to be completely wrung out, utterly exhausted and at the end of my rope. Surrounded by smiling friends, many of them dressed in evening clothes that were a vast contrast to my western garb and boots, I felt like an adventurer who had taken a big chance and somehow survived.

I was staying with people I knew and we were all invited to the house of one of their friends for refreshments. Our hostess was a middle-aged lady of Irish extraction, outspoken and warm-hearted. When she asked what I needed most, a drink or something to eat, I suddenly realized I was ravenous. When I told her I was hungry, she disappeared and in no time came back with a big plate heaped with steaming corned beef and cabbage. How she prepared it so quickly in the middle of the night, I will never know, but never did anything taste so good. Sitting there in her richly appointed house, I polished off that delicious repast with all the enthusiasm of a man half-starved. I do not recall the lady's name, but I will never forget her, for apart from being very attractive, her hospitality was wonderful – something enjoyed and remembered by a mountain man a long way from home.

My photographic work with the bighorns and associated species carried me into many places near and far among thousands of people, and in due course of subsequent events I received an invitation to make a film record of bighorns from birth to death for the historical archives of a wealthy foundation. It was an exciting prospect, even if I had some reservations about accepting it, for the people I was working with knew nothing of the problems involved in such an ambitious undertaking. Too often when you deal with big organizations, creative work gets paralyzed and buried in a jungle of office politics where there is no feeling for, or understanding of, the problems confronting the person responsible for putting the picture together so it can be enjoyed and understood.

But the challenge was irresistible and the problems involved in producing such a film could be surmounted. Had I not been aware of this, I would not have been invited to discuss its various points in the first place, so I signed the contract, and with Dick and Charlie to help me, prepared to launch what turned out to be one of the most interesting and at the same time extremely frustrating efforts of our entire experience.

A Successful Season

Winter was barely over in the mountains when we headed up the trail toward the summit of the Great Divide, west of the ranch. What we found on the pass was enough to make anyone pull up his horse and think about his geography. The snow was still seven feet deep in places and much too soft for pack-train travel. Twice we tried it, and both times we were forced to turn back. On the third attempt we rammed our way through and made a mid-June camp a dozen miles down the west slope along the Kishaneena.

It was a bit like falling out of the frying pan into the fire, for the snow was now melting so fast in the high country that the creeks were all roaring full. Fording the river even with horses was something to be tackled with care in the mornings and sometimes out of reason in the afternoon — if the day was warm.

The grass was lush and green down along the lower reaches of the valley. Deer and elk grazed the park meadows in the evening and at night, sleek as fine new leather in their reddish summer coats. Moose dipped their heads into the beaver ponds and fed on

From *Grizzly Country* (1967)

the new growing shoots in the willow and birch groves. The bucks and bulls went carefully, for their heads were tender, the blunt stubs of new antlers marking the growth of their weapons for that year.

The whole valley was one vast wilderness aviary ringing with birdsong. Golden and ruby-crowned kinglets sang from top twigs of the big spruces and firs. Townsend's solitaires, robins, hermit thrushes, willow thrushes, wrens, and many others were nesting in the trees and banks along the stream. A pair of rufous humming-birds had their tiny nest built on top of a dropping spruce bough overhanging the turbulent rapids twenty yards from the tent.

We travelled far on our horses looking for grizzly sign. We not only searched for grizzlies but also someplace occupied by them where the cameras could be successfully operated. No fleeting glimpses in the timber would do for us. We had to have them in the open. Sometimes we went separately, and sometimes we hunted together. For a couple of weeks, largely due to snow and flood conditions, all we found was tracks, and these were in the heavy timber.

One day I rode several miles downriver and climbed on foot high up along a ridge separating two huge hanging basins. The only fresh signs I found were of goats and black bear, and these were all holed up on the deep shade, for the slopes faced the sun and were as hot as reflector ovens. I came down to my horse in mid-afternoon, tired, discouraged, and suffering from a splitting headache. A plunge in the ice-cold Kishaneena did considerable for my morale, but upon reaching camp I forgot all about my dis-comfort. Dick and Charlie had good news.

They had ridden several miles back toward the divide and then away up onto the top of Lost Cabin Plateau, a part of a height of land dividing the Kishaneena and Sage Creek watersheds. There they had found the high country barely passable for horses, and they were forced to detour around various stretches of deep snow as they crossed the parklands heading northwest. On reaching

Broken Castle — a badly rifted limestone mountain standing out by itself — they tied up their horses and climbed to its craggy top to eat lunch and glass the surrounding country.

Apart from some tracks showing up on the snowdrifts down on a saddle at the head of Sage Creek, there were no other signs of grizzlies. When they finished lunch, for want of something better to do, they pushed a big boulder over the brink of the cliff; it plummeted a thousand feet or more and then went leaping and crashing on down a long avalanche track through second growth toward the bottom of the valley.

To their astonishment the noise of its passing had barely subsided when a grizzly hidden in the timber to one side of the track opened up with some roaring and grumbling at the disturbance. Perhaps this bear blamed another for kicking the rock loose and chose to let him know what he thought of such carelessness. Or maybe he was just startled by the sudden commotion of the falling boulder. The boys did not linger to investigate further but promptly returned to camp.

We rode back up onto the plateau the following day to look over more of the country and find a good location for a bait. It was obvious that some kind of attractor was needed to pull the bears up out of the timber into opener country, where we had a better chance to use the cameras. A mile or so beyond the slide where the boys had startled the grizzly with the rock, we found an ideal spot along a little valley in the midst of a strip of old burn. There by the small stream among scattered clumps of second growth I shot an old horse brought along for this purpose.

There was not enough horse feed on the plateau where we wished to camp, so when we moved up to a suitable site just under a big boulder field at the foot of Broken Castle, we drove all the horses out to the ranch. Loading some necessary odds and ends of food on our packboards the following morning, we headed back across the mountains on foot. When we reached the tent after a long day on the trail, Dick dropped his pack and climbed the half-mile to the lookout back of the camp to check at the bait with his binoculars. He came back on the run just as I was taking supper from the fire and jubilantly announced that a grizzly bear was on the bait.

Next morning after a showery night we hiked over the ridge to the north and down into the valley. A look at the bait through the glasses from an open slope a half-mile away revealed not one, but four grizzlies loafing in its near vicinity – a sight to cheer the heart of the weary hunter.

I remember a childhood experience when I was suddenly confronted with something dreamed about and wanted for a long time. There it was actually within reach – mine at last – but I just stood there enthralled by the sight of it, a little afraid even to move, let alone touch it, for fear the whole thing was just a dream. I felt something the same now as we looked at those grizzlies. Only one who has travelled, frozen, gone hungry, fought fire and flood, and hunted for months on end over thousands of miles of mountains with small success can fully appreciate my feeling. Would they be there when we came within camera range? Or would they vanish?

We slipped like shadows down along the slope through timber and scrub. We tested the wind and found it good. We finally edged up to a low rim of rock on the edge of the little valley for a look. The place seemed full of bears.

A medium-sized, brownish coloured boar was feeding on the bait, while fifty yards above him along the creek a sow and two yearling cubs waited their turn. They were obviously afraid to go anywhere close to the one feeding on the carcass, and they edged around a little meadow looking longingly in its direction. We slipped down under the rim, where some rocks would break our outlines, and proceeded to expose some good footage.

A roaring thunderstorm drove us to cover in the big timber a bit below and behind us about noon, and when we returned to location, it was just in time to see a fifth grizzly coming straight up the slope toward us. He swung past us as he climbed, and when he hit our tracks, he literally exploded into a galloping retreat as though booted in the tail. Another thunderstorm forced us back into cover, and when this one passed, the wind gave our scent to the only bear left in the valley. We returned to camp wet through from a third thunderstorm, but nothing could dampen our feeling of jubilation.

There are camps in wilderness country where things happen so fast that one is hard pressed to find time for sleep. This proved to be one of them. About one o'clock the following morning something invaded the tent. It was not the gumshoeing kind of intrusion wherein one hears a little and imagines a lot. The racket would have done justice to a bull elephant, and when I came straight up in bed clutching a flashlight and reaching for my six-shooter, I was ready to defend the place. But then I remembered the boys asleep by a log out in front of the tent and let the gun lay. When I rose to investigate with a piece of stove wood, the flash revealed the satanic countenance of a pack rat leering out from between two pack boxes, whereupon I stubbed my toe, barked my knuckles on the edge of the stove, and came nowhere near killing the rat. The wily little robber finally left for the outdoors, and I went back to bed feeling the battle had ended in a somewhat less than satisfactory manner. Next to an invading porcupine, nothing is quite so destructive as a pack rat. What they do not chew to rags, they delight in stealing. When one gets into a collection of pots and pans, the resulting uproar would wake the dead.

This one was no exception. I had scarcely slipped back to sleep when again I was jolted awake by the same racket. Again we fought a short, noisy engagement, and again the rat retreated safely to the rock slide. This went on intermittently for about two hours. By the time the rat finally left for good, the eastern sky was getting bright.

I had hardly closed my eyes when Charlie woke me as he rattled the stove and frying pan making breakfast. After we had eaten, we headed back over the ridge toward the bait under a clear sunny sky.

Immediately upon arrival at our shooting location, we spotted the she-grizzly with her cubs up on a ledge on the steep slope directly across from us. She was standing motionless, gazing out across the country. Directly behind her one cub sat on the edge of the drop-off with a hind foot hanging down off the ledge. The other cub was sitting behind him looking innocent and benign. The sow then turned to look at her cubs as though inspecting them. One must have struck her as needing attention, for she went over and gave him a vigorous washing with her tongue. We were fairly drooling, for although we could see plenty of detail through our glasses, this action was far out of camera range.

When they went out to graze on a long, almost perpendicular, open meadow of lush, spring-fed growth, a fourth grizzly – a small male – showed up on the same meadow above them. It was some time before either he or the female became aware of each other, and when they finally did discover that they had company, the smaller one beat a hasty retreat. Circling wide of the sow and coming down the mountain toward us, this grizzly went into a small clump of shintangle and apparently almost fell over the big brown male we had seen the previous day. The big bear immediately gave chase across the mountain slope through alder brush and deadfalls at top speed, but finally he left off the pursuit without coming within striking distance of the intruder.

By this time the smaller bear's nerves were showing signs of fraying; as he turned back toward the bait by a very roundabout route, he shied at imaginary devils all the way down into our little valley. Although he obviously wanted very badly to go to the bait, he could not at first screw up his courage. Charlie and I relayed on him with the cameras while he sashayed back and forth in a welter of indecision before he finally went in to take a fast feed.

Something spooked him, and again he came toward us, walking up a series of logs. We held the cameras on him to a range of seventy feet, where his ears caught the sound of them, and almost simultaneously he got our wind. His expression of sheer, bug-eyed terror was comical. With a great sniff he swapped ends and went tearing away, ripping a hole through the scrub as he went.

Although we waited in the blazing heat all day, there was no further action till evening, when the big boar came back. But he got our wind and left again.

We arrived back at camp just in time to see a big black bear standing in front of the tent as though undecided whether to knock or tear it down. We contrived to give him a frightful scare and saw nothing more of him.

With the coming of darkness my hopes for a good sleep were shattered by the return of the pack rat. This whiskery, sharp-nosed denizen of the boulder field had apparently come to know that I had cold-blooded murder in mind, for this time he made a real running fight of it. Every time he heard a noise from my direction, he left at top speed. Nevertheless, it was an action-packed night, and by morning I felt as though I had travelled for miles. A general inventory of kitchen equipment in daylight revealed the loss of a pot scraper and a bar of soap. The rat had won the battle if not the war, and he was apparently satisfied with the spoils, for he returned no more.

It was shortly after noon before anything showed up on the bait, as we watched in turns from the lookout back of camp. When I spotted the sow and cubs, I headed out alone in a shortcut across the rock slide just under the face of the mountain to try for some pictures. On the way my foot slipped on a round rock, and I took a most spectacular spill with the great good luck of not even getting a scratch.

I arrived in time to get some shots of the two cubs playing on the edge of an elk wallow full of water. Then the sow roused herself from a nap to lead them down the creek toward the bait. They disappeared behind some scrub, and then one cub shot into view on the dead run to be followed a moment later by the other two bears. I was startled by the sudden action and thought they had got my wind. But obviously the sow did not know what to make of it either, for she reared and sniffed and looked all around. Then it was mutually discovered that the first cub was chasing a coyote.

Flying in pursuit of the little grey wolf at astonishing speed, the cub had crossed the creek up onto a flat meadow on a bench beyond. The coyote was surprised and hard-pressed. He scampered like a streak up the steep slope at the foot of the mountain, swung around the top of a clump of shintangle, and headed back down for the meadow. Meanwhile, the second cub had joined in the game. As the coyote shot around a corner of the brush patch, they almost collided. The little grizzly jumped straight at him and missed by a whisker with a lightning-fast wing of his paw. But in the blink of an eye the coyote leaped up and sideways about eight feet into the top of an up-tilted pan of bleached roots, where a big spruce blowdown lay.

The coyote disappeared like a puff of smoke, but the two cubs met face to face, and without a pause or loss of hardly a step they piled into each other in a tail-over-teakettle free-for-all that tumbled them all over the meadow. They boxed, wrestled, tore, and scratched in every direction without let-up for several minutes while their mother sat on her broad rump contemplating their shenanigans with the greatest equanimity.

Meanwhile, the coyote came sneaking around through the scrub toward the carcass to resume its feeding. Then I spotted the little grizzly of the previous day coming cautiously down across the face of the mountain. We had jokingly called him "Casper," after the comic-strip character. Right now Casper was living up to the name, for he was in a fever of uncertainty, stopping, sniffing, listening, and worrying on a hair trigger of apprehension. The

coyote was also upset by his recent adventures, for he kept trotting out of bushes surrounding the bait to make sure no more
grizzlies surprised him. Hearing the approach of the little grizzly,
he immediately ran out for a look; his sudden appearance had the
most comically demoralizing effect on the bear. It was the final
straw that broke the spine of what little dominance he had left.
The coyote undoubtedly shared my astonishment when Casper
stampeded in abject panic without another glance behind him.
The coyote watched him go with sharp curiosity, then he turned
and went trotting up the creek with his tongue hanging out in a
doggy grin. One could almost hear him bragging to his wife and
offspring about putting the run on a grizzly bear.

This grizzly's behaviour was an interesting example of the psy-
chological effect of being the lesser bear in the pecking order of
the valley. Having been repeatedly run off by the larger bears, and
further disorganized by running head-on into us, he had lost his
self-confidence. His terrors had accumulated in his head until now
he ran from everything. In the society of grizzlies there is some
tendency toward social stratification in their dealings with each
other. We had met the lowly Casper. The following morning we
met the Queen.

Following a hard rain that had continued all night into morning,
we did not get an early start. When we reached the lookout shortly
before noon, we saw a complete stranger at the bait – a huge she-
grizzly with twin cubs.

A careful approach into our shooting location revealed a
magnificent specimen in heavy winter pelage with two tiny cubs
new from the den. She was by far the biggest grizzly we had seen
– a bear with the command of royalty. She was dominant but not
obtrusive. There was a strong, quiet dignity about her which no
other bear challenged or ruffled in the slightest. She moved through
the valley around the bait with a quiet sureness. She ignored the
coyote completely and shattered Casper with a single glance. When

the big brown boar came mooching down off the mountain, she stood up about seven and a half feet tall and eyed him coolly. His reaction hinted at some former encounter in which he had learned the folly of argument, for he instantly retreated.

We filmed her walking down across the meandering loops of the creek, reflected here and there with her cubs in mirror pools. We shot the cubs playing in the water and practising walking a slippery, half-submerged log. To appreciate fully the carefree atmosphere surrounding this bear family now in possession of Bear Valley, as we had named it, it was necessary to share it. It was a revealing look into the ways of a grizzly mother. She watched over her family with care but without undue possessiveness. She allowed them freedom, but she obviously meant them to be obedient. There was a quiet, powerful atmosphere of mother love around her that spoke for itself in the very way she moved.

The cubs were small bundles of almost perpetual movement. They examined everything with small inquisitive noses. For every step their big mother took, they took many more. While juvenile and inexperienced, it was very obvious to us that they identified themselves as grizzlies, for they oozed the unmistakable character of their species.

With our cameras we recorded almost every move this grizzly family made. At times we were within a hundred yards of them, and we even shot them while asleep, the big mother lying on her belly with her nose on her paws and one cub sagging back against each burly shoulder.

Finally, the wind took our scent to her nose, and she left on the gallop with her cubs at her heels.

Thereafter the big she-grizzly was extremely suspicious of the place, although she continued to come back at night for feeds of carrion. Once, while waiting, we went down into the bottom of the little valley, trying for a shot at a wolverine. Although we stayed in the open and avoided touching any bushes with our hands or clothes, she came down and immediately picked up our scent fifty yards downwind from the spot where we were waiting. It was a sample of the unbelievable power of a grizzly's nose, for the day was sunny and dry, allowing a minimum of scent to linger.

In a week of continuous activity in Bear Valley we had seen and filmed eight grizzlies. The bait was almost gone. At the same time all the bears were undoubtedly aware of our continuous intrusion, and they were avoiding us by coming when there was no light for photography. We had worn out our welcome here, so we left for home to get the horses, satisfied that we had at last made a start in recording grizzly life but fully aware that we still had a long way to go.

Reviewing our experiences, we had become more and more convinced that carrying arms was not only unnecessary in most grizzly country but was certainly no good for the desired atmosphere and proper protocol in obtaining good film records. If we were to obtain such film and fraternize successfully with the big bears, it would be better to go unarmed in most places. The mere fact of having a gun within reach, cached somewhere in a pack or a hidden holster, causes a man to act with unconscious arrogance and thus maybe to smell different or to transmit some kind of signal objectionable to bears. The armed man does not assume his proper role in association with the wild ones, a fact of which they seem instantly aware at some distance. He, being wilder than they, whether he likes to admit it or not, is instantly under even more suspicion than he would encounter if unarmed.

So we planned to go completely unarmed when we headed north into the wilds of the Central Range of Alaska in the region of Mount McKinley National Park a few days later. Even in the event of a charge, we theorized, a firm stand by a man who neither showed fight nor ran away would serve to throw a grizzly out of gear. Being accustomed to having most everything run from them from the time they are born, when confronted by something that does not move, it is logical to suppose that a charging bear would stop to think it over. But entertaining a good theory and putting it into practice are two vastly different things. This was particularly pertinent when dealing with angry grizzlies, for there would be small chance for second guessing. It was a kind of animal psychology that we had seen at work on occasion with other animals. For a chance to get good pictures we thought it worthwhile to try it out on the big bears.

At the far end of almost a week of dusty driving down the Alaska Highway, we turned south at Big Delta, branched off onto the Denali Highway at Paxton, and finally arrived at McKinley Park Headquarters. This national park, approximately thirty-three hundred square miles in extent, probably holds more big game than any other in the world outside those in Africa. Besides its thousands of caribou, Dall sheep, moose, and smaller game, it has a heavy population of grizzlies. These bears are the mountain type, with a colour trend toward the straw yellow of the tundra grizzly found in the MacKenzie basin, sometimes known as the Toklat grizzly after the river of the same name.

It was afternoon when we arrived, and lead-coloured clouds were hanging low over the country. We could see only the great sweeps of river flats and gravel bars as we drove down the ninety miles of twisting road through the Park. Here and there were scattered small bunches of caribou sifting back from their summering grounds. Away out on the green tundra carpet of the Toklat River valley there was a big lone grizzly busily grazing. With the clouds so low, it was something like wandering past the darkened footlights in a great theatre, peeking under the lowered curtain for brief glimpses, sufficient to make one wonder what the stage setting would be like when the lights came up and the curtain lifted. We were filled with excitement and anticipation as we drove down past the park boundary below Wonder Lake and stopped at Denali Lodge to visit friends and enjoy a most memorable supper.

About 10 p.m. we drove back up the road to make camp. Coming over a rise of ground at Wonder Lake, we were treated to a sight the like of which we have never seen and most likely will never see again. Two huge Alaskan bull moose, with velvet-covered antlers that looked six feet across, were feeding in the shallows a few yards out from shore. In the Arctic twilight they looked like something from the prehistoric past, huge and black, as they dipped their heads under and then lifted them to let the water cascade back into the lake. Then with dramatic suddenness Mount McKinley shrugged off the enveloping shrouds of mist and storm to emerge bathed in golden sunset – a majesty of mountain defying description.

First sight of it under any circumstances is awe-inspiring. It was something to make a man doubt his eyes. It seemed to stand close enough to almost touch, though it was a good thirty miles away. Its huge forty-five mile front was glowing in a light like the reflection of a giant mass of coals, its glittering expanses of eternal ice and snow all purple and rose. From where we stood, looking up from about eighteen hundred feet above sea level to its 20,320-foot crown, it is not only the highest on the continent but, relatively speaking, perhaps the highest in the world. Even Everest viewed from this range is seen from an elevation of fourteen thousand feet and must lose some of its impression of height.

We stood enthralled for a few moments, then suddenly remembering why we were here, burrowed into the Land Rover for cameras. For the first time in many a year I shook with the symptoms of a case of buck fever. Grinding my teeth for control, I fought to screw a movie camera down on a tripod while Dick and Charlie wrestled with another. Somehow we got into action and captured a scene to make a photographer wonder if he was dreaming.

This was our introduction to camera hunting in the grizzly country of Alaska, something to be remembered always as having glimpsed a few moments of beauty not meant for the eyes of men.

Hunting from our camp on the Toklat River was one endless round of excitement. Never were we out of sight of game, and hardly a day went by that we did not see and photograph grizzlies. We worked in ideal surroundings, where vision was practically unlimited, the light excellent for long hours, and backgrounds illuminated like the answer to a photographer's prayer. The weather was largely good, and the atmosphere was the most brilliantly clear we had ever encountered. Mountain peaks sixty miles away showed up on the finders as sharp as the edge of a hunting blade.

Apart from the narrow, winding gravel road and its tourists, the country was much as Charles Sheldon had seen it on his expeditions way back in 1905 and 1906. We were camped within a mile of his old winter cabin site, most of which had been washed away by a change in the river channel. Perhaps we saw even more game than he reported, for the pressure of meat-hungry gold seekers had long since been removed.

The days were long and full of action and interest. For August 11, 1962, my journal reads:

This morning we rose at 4 a.m. After a quick breakfast we packed some lunch and drove up the road about two miles past the Toklat crossing, where we left the Rover. Within a few minutes we spotted a big grizzly away across the valley, where he was apparently grazing in a little draw coming down the slope onto the flats. He was a long way off and nowhere between was there enough cover to hide a fox; so we headed straight for him. By watching his head and moving only when it was down, we reached a spot about fifty yards away from him, where he could be seen feeding in the bottom of the draw amongst some willows. I set my camera up and shot him just as he fed out into the open. Without pausing in his cropping of the grass, he sat down on the slope and scratched his broad bottom back and forth. Dick and Charlie tried to cross a branch of the river a bit below me to get a closer shot, but the grizzly spotted them in the water and ran up over the top of the bank to disappear. We continued on up the valley to eat lunch on a jutting point above the river bars overlooking a vast stretch of rugged mountains. We counted seventy-two Dall sheep, including twelve big rams, on the face of a pinnacle a half mile away. Shortly after we spotted a sow grizzly with a two-year-old cub, as they fed up out of a fold of ground into view. She was located on a bench in a very difficult place to stalk, so we watched and waited for her to move. While we glassed them, they began a really rough game, wherein she appeared to be punishing the cub severely but was actually very gentle. After a few minutes interval of wrestling, mouthing, and chasing back and forth, they left off to feed again. It is at times like this, when grizzlies can be observed living undisturbed in ideal habitat, that a man begins to really appreciate their most attractive characteristics. As they did not seem about to make any kind of move onto more favourable ground, we stalked them. The wind was so shifty, we dared not go closer than about a hundred and fifty yards. By this time the mother and cub were playing again, affording a chance to shoot them as they rolled and tumbled on the tundra. The wind then gave us away and sent the bears away at a tearing run straight up the mountain. She led the way up over the steepest kind of going, climbing almost perpendicular rock in two or three places, and never paused until they were briefly outlined against the sky on the summit. We returned to the car across the great gravel bars where uncounted caribou of all sizes and sex were running back and forth in every direction fighting flies.

This was the first of several times we observed this mother and cub. Any hint of our approach always sent her flying, for she was nervous of human intrusion into her vicinity. Observed while undisturbed, she and her cub were about the happiest, most care-free bears imaginable. Time and again over several days we saw her leave off feeding to play with the young one.

Once I saw them travelling toward some particularly desirable destination across the open flats. The irrepressible cub was feeling so good that he could not contain himself, and he ran up along-side his mother to pass her. But as he passed, he looked at her and continued to do so by twisting his head, until he overbalanced completely and fell in a tumbling heap. Immediately she pounced on him to wool and mouth him savagely, yet hardly ruffling his fur; she then left him to resume her gallop. Instantly the cub leaped up in pursuit, caught up to his big mother, disrespectfully nipped at her flying heels, and once more ran up alongside her to fix her with a stare that pulled his head around until he rolled clear over. Again she leaped on him to maul and play with him before resuming her journey. So they proceeded for about a mile, until they finally reached a huckleberry patch, where they came to a sudden stop and proceeded to fill up.

Never from one moment to the next did we know what we would see or what would happen. We were travelling up along the face of Polychrome Mountain one day when out of the blue a grizzly came barrelling down onto the road right in front of us. In two jumps he was over the bank and heading straight down toward a branch of the East Fork River directly below. I pulled the car to a stop on a turn-out, and in the same motion Charlie grabbed a camera, jerked the door open, and was over the bank in hot pursuit. I started to yell a warning, but it was too late. He was gone at a tearing run down across a steep-pitched little saddle toward a pinnacle overlooking the river. The grizzly had been heading in a parallel course, but he had changed direction. The bear and Charlie met almost head-on in the saddle.

In a split second things were in a high state of tension. The bear, a small, precocious, bad-mannered three-year-old, just recently turned loose on his own in the world and afraid something or somebody would find out just how little he knew, was fighting mad. From a few short yards he took a stiff-legged lunge at Charlie with his back hair on end and his mouth wide open. Charlie stood his ground, and for a few interminable moments they argued. Then it became apparent that the grizzly wanted to find a way out of this unheard-of predicament – but without losing face, as is the inherent way of grizzlies. He solved his problem in a unique way by beginning to feed. It was a most interesting example of what might be termed "displacement activity." To cover his discomfiture and fright, he wanted us to think – and probably wanted even more himself to think – that he had come to this place to feed, and, by the little red gods, he was damned well going to feed! While we filmed him, he ate about every kind of plant that grew on that dry slope, including some unpalatable heather.

Needless to say, we were impressed and grateful, but we were also delighted when he, in a subtle sort of way, leaked out of the immediate scenery down a brush-choked chimney toward the river.

Almost immediately we spotted a big, beautiful, light-coloured female with two handsome yearling cubs in a little pocket behind us. All of us were completely engrossed in shooting her when a stick popped behind us, and lo and behold! There was our erstwhile friend back again. But this time he did not linger or pass any cheeky comments; he had apparently spotted the she-grizzly, and for some reason he wanted no further part of the vicinity. The last we saw him, he was going over the mountain the way he had come.

The country fairly teemed with game. At the same time that we were filming these bears, there were two more in sight out on the flats across the river. Thirty-odd head of Dall sheep ewes and lambs were feeding on a shoulder about a half-mile back of us, while uncounted caribou grazed and moved for as far as we could see with our powerful glasses. A few feet away a big fat marmot looked us over from the top of his home boulder, all the while keeping an eye peeled on a lazily wheeling golden eagle. Everywhere in all directions the parka squirrels barked and chirped.

The entire region was like a vast multi-ring circus with a program that continued unbroken for twenty-four hours a day under the usually bland skies of the Arctic summer. And photographers wanted to discover the reason why they were so exhausted. It was because they hated to quit long enough to sleep. Sometimes we just dropped into the green carpet of tundra to sleep awhile. We ate prodigiously, and we stopped travelling only when the weather made it impractical. We became as lean and hard as rawhide from the long hours afoot under packs. There seemed to be no beginning and no end to opportunity here, and as long as there was light and the film held out, there was always something to stalk and shoot.

Later that day, having played out the opportunities with grizzlies, Charlie and I spotted an eagle sitting on the ground high on a shoulder of Polychrome Mountain. It appeared to be dozing, so we started up to try for some pictures. This sort of thing is usually the longest kind of gambling odds in favour of getting nothing but plenty of exercise, but our luck was running gilt-edged that day. After a long climb we crept up to within twenty-five yards and got some spectacular footage of the big bird taking off and wheeling out over the darkening valley far below us.

The ever-present caribou were a constant source of interest and amusement. While travelling through the mountains we were encountering them every day in about every conceivable kind of surroundings except the sheer rock faces. At best the caribou is a somewhat pixilated beast liable to do most anything. Sometimes, especially when the nose flies are bad, they go almost insane.

Dick was watching a big old grizzly digging in a squirrel hole along the low bank of a creek one day. Suddenly out of nowhere a young bull caribou came bounding up the creek, splashing water in every direction, and passed the bear so close that he almost splashed water all over him. The bear never even lifted his head but continued with the digging as though caribou did not exist. A few minutes later the caribou came tearing back down the creek and again passed close to the bear with a great clatter. The bull was hardly out of sight before he came back again. Each time neither animal gave the slightest sign of recognizing the other. Finally, whatever interest was holding the bear played out, and he moved off.

We saw and once filmed grizzlies and caribou passing within feet of each other with no reaction other than a casual glance on the part of either animal. This was long past the calving season, and the grizzlies knew that they had no chance in any kind of foot race with a caribou.

The caribous' reaction to us was ever erratic. Sometimes they would give us little more than a glance as we passed. At other times and for no apparent reason they would ogle us with utter horror, elevate their ridiculous tails, and race away as though pursued by devils. On occasion they confused their motives and made us laugh by tearing away for several hundred yards, then stopping and looking, then racing back to look at us some more at close range.

One afternoon we were coming back after a long hike, and we had stopped for a rest. Up on a peak about a mile away against the blue sky was a magnificent caribou bull with a rack of antlers like two small trees. Photographically speaking, we did not usually go out of our way to film caribou; but there was something about this one that we couldn't resist. My ambition was dampened a bit by tired feet, but I could see that the sight of the bull standing up there against the sky was bothering Dick and Charlie. Soon they took off through a long dip to stalk him.

After several minutes, when they were well out of sight of him, the bull took off at a mad gallop straight down into a deep canyon. In a little while he came dashing up the other side and ensconced himself once more against the sky on the tiptop of a pyramid-shaped mountain. The boys spotted him there and sat down to watch.

Several minutes later the bull once more launched himself at top speed back down into the canyon. The next thing I knew, he was coming over a saddle straight at me. Caught by surprise, I barely had my camera ready when he came to a rigid stop with his head buried in a willow bush right in front of me.

I had the lens on him, watching for some movement, when I saw an ear flicker. Then the other one twitched. Gradually, bit by bit, various parts of his anatomy joined in until he was vibrating from end to end in a sort of ecstasy of discomfort – a kind of nose-fly ballet. He brought it to a sudden, jerky climax by throwing up his head, kicking up a great clod of tundra with a hind foot, and stampeding away for parts unknown.

Regardless of the numbers of hoofed game we encountered almost daily, there was no evidence of predation by grizzlies among them. The bears did capture ground squirrels when the opportunity afforded itself, a part of their activity which seemed more of a lark in getting a tasty morsel than a serious part of their feeding. We were attempting to get a shot of a grizzly with some Dall sheep in the background one morning when an unexpected eddy of wind gave us away. Immediately our film subject took off up the mountain at a gallop. He apparently surprised a parka squirrel away from its hole, for he veered a bit and scooped it up in his mouth without losing a stride. The last we saw of him on the skyline, he was still on the high run with the squirrel dangling from his jaws.

Another afternoon I was watching a big, lone grizzly feeding out on a green island of tundra in the midst of the East Fork River gravel bars. The bear suddenly quit his grazing and chased after a parka squirrel. The little animal ran into a strip of scrub brush, and when the bear plunged after the fleeing morsel, a covey of willow ptarmigan exploded into flight all around him. The grizzly momentarily checked his stride, and the delay probably saved the squirrel's life. To see the grizzly in action amid flashing wings all lit brilliantly was an almost cruelly tantalizing thing to a photographer, one of those nuggets of film material missed due to excess range or sudden occurrence that gives no chance to get the camera into action. But even if no record was captured on film, I will always be able to see on my private mental movie screen the picture of a great, straw-coloured grizzly rough-locking to a skidding stop with his head high and his ears cocked in the midst of rocketing ptarmigan, all backdropped by the snowy, ice-clad Alaskan peaks.

All of us had our memorable moments while wandering among the Alaskan mountains. Charlie's twenty-first birthday came at the Toklat River camp, a milestone he proposed to celebrate by climbing a mountain alone. As it turned out, the mountain-climbing plan got sidetracked, but in a way that lacked little in adventure.

He headed out early in the morning toward an impressive set of peaks lifting their summits above the head of the river. He left the valley on the far side and angled up the slope of a ridge toward a high saddle. While passing a steep-sided gully, he looked down and saw a grizzly busily turning over rocks in search of bugs and grubs. It seemed that Charlie was fated to encounter precocious three-year-olds, for this was another of the uncertain-tempered youngsters.

The bear left off his rock-turning upon seeing the man and headed up the slope straight toward him as though intending to treat him in the same way as the rocks. Charlie stood his ground, coolly shooting with his camera, until it was barely fifty feet away. When he yelled, the bear stopped, hesitated, and growled before turning to head back down into the gully. When Charlie resumed his climb, the young grizzly walked along parallel to him at a range of a few yards, growling and rumbling to himself. A quarter of a mile up the mountain the unpleasant animal discovered some squirrel holes that captured his attention. Charlie was not sorry to see the last of him.

From the summit of the saddle he spotted the same twelve rams we had seen before on several occasions. They were feeding and loafing on a steep slope a half-mile ahead, so he took the opportunity to try for some pictures. But the rams were spooky and proceeded to lead him on a merry chase over rock slides and cliffs, always tantalizingly close but keeping just out of good camera range. Under lowering clouds with rain spitting down intermittently, Charlie persisted and finally, just as a storm broke, he obtained his first good shots. As the rain came pouring down, he took shelter in a shallow cave with a sloping floor under an overhang at the top of a talus fan, where he ate lunch and then fell asleep. He woke with a great start rolling down the rock slide in the rain – a somewhat strange and unusual place to fall out of bed. Again he stalked the rams, and now they were more co-operative, allowing him to obtain some grand photos with spectacular backgrounds.

Late that night Dick and I looked out from the tent door through the stormy gloom and saw Charlie coming away out across bleak, cold flats. It was blowing and raining hard in scudding gusts of icy water that penetrated everything. By the time Charlie arrived in the cheery warmth of our tent, I had the soup pot steaming hot and fresh tea brewed. He was soaked to the hide, famished, and tired; but he was wearing a grin that spoke of rare sport and grand hunting among the crags.

The pattern of adventure is never constant. When one hunts grizzlies with a camera, it is not necessary to court it, and at the same time there is no point in being brash. We gambled a bit on occasion, but the risks were calculated; the successful gambler does not ignore the odds or step too far beyond the bounds of safety. To invite trouble was not our way, for it would have been unfair to the big animals we studied. We had no wish to cloud further their history by becoming unpleasant statistics. But careful as we were, there were times when we slipped a bit, and then things could go wrong lightning fast.

Dick had occasion one day to give our theory about charging grizzlies a really thorough testing. He and I spent part of a morning scouting up a fork of the Toklat above camp; but when a storm began rolling in over the mountains, I headed back. Dick proposed to do some exploring by climbing over a rugged spur range toward Sheldon's old winter cabin and returning from there to camp. It was a long tough climb and late afternoon when he showed up, somewhat shaken, still looking a bit grim after a hair-raising experience.

He had been coming down a long, steep tundra slope above the river, tired, hungry, and perhaps thinking more of camp than where he was heading. Ahead of him a pile of rocks stood up, and instead of swinging to look behind it, he thoughtlessly walked right up on top of it and thereby broke a rule.

Not more than twenty feet beyond, a grizzly was feeding in the midst of some berries. He was just as scared, astonished, and embarrassed as Dick; but he recovered first and charged with a bawl of anger straight up the rock pile. Dick was carrying a sheep horn he had picked up on the mountain. He stood his ground, lifted the horn overhead, and told the grizzly in strong language that if he came one step farther, he would brain him. It was a desperate bluff, but the grizzly stopped eight feet away. Then for about thirty seconds – perhaps the longest half-minute Dick will ever live – he and the bear faced each other and argued in angry tones.

The bear finally broke off the exchange by backing slowly down off the rocks, then sidling away for several yards, grumbling and growling steadily about the bad manners of those who surprise grizzly bears at close range. Finally he quieted down and began to feed again in a berry patch about two hundred yards away.

Dick sat down and shook for a while before resuming his journey to camp. It had been a frightening experience, but as is usually the case, it could not be blamed on the bear.

Right here I may as well confess that in telling of various incidents involving grizzlies, my references to their sex are largely guesswork when dealing with single bears. When speaking of a grizzly with cubs, it is correct and accurate to describe her as a sow or a female. But when speaking of a single bear, my reference to gender is more convenience than proven fact. Except for size – and this is not always a reliable way to separate the sexes – one lone grizzly bear looks just like another in general outline. Aside from feeling of them – an understandably unthinkable liberty – I know of no sure way to tell a sow from a boar in the field.

Dick's close-quarters argument with the grizzly did not deter him in his avid pursuit of good bear pictures. One morning not long afterward we were travelling up toward the summit of what we called Jaeger Pass when we spotted a big old grizzly busily feeding on berries out on the edge of the open gravel beyond some strips of willows. Dick got his camera ready first and eased down into a rocky gully to stalk the bear. I was coming about a hundred yards behind him, when he came out in the open about that same distance from the bear. The grizzly saw him, stood up briefly to look him over, and then proceeded at a fast walk straight toward the camera. Obviously the bear did not recognize what he was looking at, for curiosity stood out all over him. But the closer he got, the more uncertain and angry he became. The hair rose all along his back till it stood up like a badly trimmed hedge, and his expression became belligerent. At about forty feet he swung sideways and veered off a bit downwind. When Dick's scent struck his nose, he registered surprise and plainly did not enjoy it. With obvious intent he swung back around to the sweet side of the wind, decided the whole business was beneath further notice, and began to feed on berries again.

Meanwhile, crouched behind his camera and making no motion whatever except for a slight swing to track the bear, Dick never stopped taking footage. In this one long sequence he obtained some of the most dramatic material we collected. It was rare film in that it showed a grizzly coming at close range, displaying uncertainty and anger; but all aspects of the incident were in control, and this makes it rarer still. It is an outstanding example of the possible association between a grizzly and men, a significance that will likely be missed by most who see the film. Dick's pictures of this bear were the result of cool nerve and determination, a characteristic that I failed to emulate on this occasion.

Turning to me as I came up to him, Dick asked, "Did you get that?"

"No," I confessed. "I was paralyzed!"

For exploration of the unknown this kind of association with the big bears could not be surpassed. It was purely fascinating. Never could it become boring drudgery. No two encounters were ever alike for the simple reason that no two bears were alike, and even individuals react to their mood of the moment. Even though we had all grown up in the wilds and worked with animals all our lives, the grizzlies tossed us the greatest challenge we have ever faced. It was not enough just to be able to get the best possible pictures with the cameras; we perforce had to study each individual to some extent in order to portray it successfully on film. We came to know some individuals by sight and, generally speaking, what reaction to expect of them at our approach.

For our convenience in identifying them we even gave them names. There was Blondie, the playful one with the two-year-old cub, and Toklat Joe, the big bear of amiable disposition that Dick filmed successfully. There was Nitchie, the big, light-coloured female with the twin yearlings, and another bear we called Grumpy, with a temper like a buzz saw – a bear I did not trust as far as I could have thrown him by a hind foot.

These bears were the ones we saw most often, and likely they came to know us, a condition of minor importance, but one that may have helped create the more neutral atmosphere desired for photographic work.

One morning when Charlie was away up toward Igloo Creek investigating a wolf kill, our friend Charlie Travers, the Park Ranger located at the Toklat Station, came in from patrol and reported seeing a grizzly with cubs just a little way from camp. Dick and I loaded the movie cameras and went to investigate.

Up along the Toklat on a bench below a steep twenty-foot terrace we found Nitchie and her cubs feeding on berries among some low willows and birches. For perhaps half an hour we moved along very slowly above her, shooting film of the family activities through various lengths of lenses. Then another big bear came out of the willows across the river straight toward Nitchie's berry patch.

This was a definite breach of grizzly ethics, which Nitchie frowned upon decidedly. The cubs were obviously schooled not to trust other grizzlies, for they showed consternation at the approach of the outsider, none other than old Toklat Joe. The she-grizzly was in something of a dilemma, for she was caught between us and the intruder from across the river. We were somewhat surprised to see her move closer to us, until she was directly below.

We were treated to a rare opportunity to film a series of sequences recording this unusual and largely unacceptable competition for the same berry patch. Nitchie did not at first make any hostile moves toward her ursine visitor, but she carefully kept herself between him and the cubs while she continued to feed. As he fed, he moved towards her, pushing her up closer and closer to us. The cubs were in a fever of excitement and worry. They paid us not the slightest attention but alternately reared to look at the visiting bear. Once I saw one flatten out behind a bush with its nose pressed on its front paws, obviously trying to hide. Sometimes they tried to walk on their hind feet and inevitably fell to all fours.

While the mother did not appear to be watching us, Dick triggered her into a rush on two occasions by winding his camera too fast. These short charges were little but a bid for more room, for she returned instantly to the cubs.

Then, as I expected, she ran out of patience. Like a flash of light she suddenly pivoted on her heels and charged the old boar. About seventy-five yards separated them, and she covered it at top speed. Through the camera lens I could see him bracing himself and setting his hind feet in a solid toe hold to meet a horrific collision. But at the last instant the angry sow checked, and though she refrained from hitting him, she put her nose up close to his and cussed him out in tones that dripped of impending violence. It was one of those times when all living things within earshot paused to listen and to feel the vibrations of tension. Toklat Joe wisely rode out the crisis by not moving a muscle or making a sound. But when she finally backed off and returned to her cubs, he turned away grumbling and mumbling to himself, as though saving face by muttering threats of murder and mayhem had she made one more sound.

We were much impressed by her obvious desire to go to almost any length to avoid a fight. She had been subjected to a most unusual and worrying situation in which she had every excuse either to tangle with the intruding grizzly or to put the run on us. But she had contrived to solve her problem without violence in consideration of the safety of her cubs – a definite tribute to her intelligence and a grizzly characteristic we came to admire more and more.

Dick and I returned to camp with some excellent film exposed. As most of our film and time was used up, it was time for us to leave on the long road home. We had enjoyed some views into the secret places of grizzly life, perhaps most impressive for what they showed that remained to be seen. We knew by the width of the vista opened to us the great scope of exploration still to be done. We were determined to return.

Return to the Toklat

It was early June the following spring when we pulled off the trail in the cold, blue twilight of the northern evening and rolled out our beds under some gaunt cottonwoods on the edge of the tundra hills of Alaska. Here and there new green leaves were just beginning to break from the buds of the willows and cottonwoods, as though reluctant to brave the cold winds and lowering clouds. Winter had only taken a step or two in retreat, and it still showed its gleaming teeth among the high hills ahead of us as though of half a mind to come back.

There were 2,250 miles and six days of dust, frost heaves, mud, and hard driving behind us. There were still 300 miles to go before we could set our tent once more on the Toklat River, and by the look of the high country they were going to be tough miles. We were bone tired as we eased down into the warm, feathery softness of our sleeping robes.

After we broke camp early next morning, we drove straight into winter. The lakes on the high tundra were still frozen solid. The whole country above timberline was one vast waste of deep

From *Grizzly Country* (1967)

snow. The newly ploughed highway was little more than a rock-and ice-strewn track winding through freezing slush, water, and chuckholes, which slowed our sturdy Land Rover down to a grinding crawl. Sometimes we could not see a quarter-mile through the blizzard of blowing snow that felt as though it came straight from the polar ice cap.

Finally dropping down into lower ground near McKinley Park headquarters, we were cheered to leave the snow behind and come into country beginning to green up. When we reached the Toklat River campsite after ten hours of hard driving, we found ourselves back on the edge of winter again; but we were happy, for it was like coming home.

While putting the finishing touches on setting up camp the following morning, I saw something dark-coloured moving in the brush away out on the tundra flats across the river. The binoculars revealed a big female grizzly with two yearling cubs. A light-coloured spot high on the shoulder of a mountain beyond was another mother grizzly with two small first-year cubs. Even at extreme range their long, luxuriant coats were evident and shone like silver in the sun.

The whole country was moving with game. The big alluvial flats and lower slopes of the mountains were alive with caribou restlessly grazing and moving from place to place, then lying down to chew their cuds. There were hundreds of these animals in sight – the leading ranks of the coming migration, as yet not fixed in its purpose or direction. Contrasting sharply with the caribou and mixed with them here and there on the mountain slopes were bunches of snow-white Dall sheep, the rams magnificent in their unshed winter coats. Through this gathering of the cloven-hoofed ones the grizzlies moved, a powerful, dramatic facet of life in this subarctic land.

Their relationship with the caribou was not altogether peaceful at this time of year, for the cows were just moving off the calving grounds up on the Teklanika River. The easy pickings among newborn calves were past, for they were growing fast and were now active enough to outrun a bear; but some of the grizzlies did not know it yet.

One morning shortly after our arrival on the dripping tail of a nightlong downpour of rain we woke to find it capped by a blizzard whose big sticky flakes threatened to flatten our tent with their weight. Permafrost was still so close to the surface that we had done little more than make slight dents in our efforts to dig drainage canals, which were now plugged with snow and running over. A two-foot-wide stream was running through the middle of the tent past our beds. We made breakfast with our boots scrunching in three inches of wet black muck. While Charlie and I set about putting the camp in some order not quite so reminiscent of a beaver lodge, Dick took advantage of a slight lifting of the storm to go up onto Jaeger Pass with the cameras.

At a point about a half-mile from the summit he was standing just under a solid overcast obscuring the mountains and the top of the pass. Away down a big twisted draw toward the Toklat he suddenly spotted three caribou – a cow, a yearling, and a calf – running up toward him at top speed. Then around a bend of the creek a hundred yards behind them came a grizzly in hot pursuit. Obviously he had caribou calf in mind for breakfast but was having a hard time even getting a good smell of it.

When the caribou passed along the slope under Dick, they were running easily with a lengthening lead. Then the grizzly went by at top speed in long bounds. Every jump was punctuated by a great breath – *whoosh* – *whoosh* – *whoosh* – and every few jumps the bear dropped his head to scoop up a flying mouthful of cooling snow. He was persistent even though far behind and going by scent. The last Dick saw of him as he disappeared into the clouds, he was still running hard, although all he was likely to get was an even keener appetite and sore feet.

The grizzlies, as usual, were almost continuously on the move. They seemed particularly restless, probably due to the breeding season combined with sharp appetites after the long winter of fasting. They followed their noses from one interesting smell to another, spending most of their time grazing or digging roots. We recognized individuals moving from Sable Pass to Thoroughfare Pass, a distance of ten or twelve miles, in three or four days. As they moved, we also moved back and forth through this great studio, forty miles long and ten miles wide.

Although their long winter coats changed their looks a bit, we were able to recognize some bears known the previous summer. I was sitting on a bench overlooking the wide gravel bars of the East Fork River one day when out from behind the projecting snout of a bank strolled a big sow with twin two-year-old cubs. It was old Nitchie and her family. Within an hour of this spot we found Toklat Joe, looking bigger and more whiskery than ever, with his chewed-up ears now well camouflaged by fur. Blondie's cub was a three-year-old this year, and he had been turned loose to fare for himself. Several times we saw a bear closely resembling the playful one of the previous summer; but now that she had joined the fraternity of childless females and was ranging alone, it was difficult to be sure, for wheat straw-coloured coats are not uncommon in that country. Dick suspected that the optimistic one seen chasing the caribou was her cub.

Wandering the country watching these and other bears was like being among old friends, although the grizzlies showed little inclination to join us in that thought. We were still intruders, tolerated in part but allowed few liberties. We conducted ourselves accordingly. However, we moved with more confidence among them now, for we had learned something of their ways, as well as having acquired a smattering of the manners expected of us in grizzly society. We had come to have a real liking for the big bears, and our fascination with their ways was even keener.

It is necessary to like an animal subject if one is going to collect good picture records of it and look into its life with a true perspective. Although it is still impossible to prove or disprove at this point, I am convinced that animals have extrasensory perception – a kind of sixth sense also known to humans, but latent in us because of lack of use except in some primitives. Living season after season with grizzlies and bighorn sheep, as we have done, there were times when a certain subtle communication seemed to exist wherein we were granted certain liberties and a measure of trust far beyond ordinary human–wild animal relationship. As a result we gained opportunities to know them better and work at close range. These were the rewards for going a fumbling, uncertain step or two past the timeworn beliefs and prejudices and overcoming some fear of the grizzly. Sometimes I stood and marvelled at how I could have lived so long in wilderness country and learned so little.

For a long time it was thought that all grizzlies weaned their cubs at two years and that these did not den with their mothers again. Adolph Murie, the famed naturalist and writer, did not agree, and from evidence we encountered there was good reason to think this wrong, at least in northern latitudes. Now old Nitchie proceeded to show us the fact.

We were watching her one morning up near the foot of Polychrome Mountain as she and her family were poking around a bench meadow feeding on grass. The cubs were busy a few yards to one side when some signal seemed to pass from the mother; for they went to her immediately, and she squatted for them to nurse. The weight of their enthusiasm bowled her over flat on her back, where she looked a bit overwhelmed and outnumbered under an enthusiastic mound of young grizzlies weighing close to one hundred and fifty pounds apiece. On several other occasions thereafter we saw them nurse, and although we made no record of the time lapses between feeds, she undoubtedly fed them several times each day.

We were able to compare three different ages of cubs following their mothers and nursing regularly. There seems to be good
reason to believe that the cubs suckle all winter. What else would
prevent the mammary glands from drying up? How the mother
succeeds in making up for the consequent dehydration without
drinking is truly a mystery. It will likely remain such, for grizzly
bears are light sleepers and undoubtedly would take exception to
anyone prying into their dens.

This was June, the mating season for grizzlies, and we were particularly keen to record as much of this little-known phase of their
lives as possible. We had heard that grizzlies return periodically to
the same locality for their love-making ritual, which lasts day after
day for a week or more, and that we would have little difficulty
seeing them if we could locate such a trysting place. Perhaps we
dealt with particularly restless non-conformists, or maybe the cool
weather had something to do with it, but this did not prove to be
the case.

Our first sight of a mating pair was up on Sable Pass, where
we watched a light-coloured female being escorted by a big
rusty-coloured male for some time one afternoon. Perhaps their
courtship was on one side or the other of the peak of ardour, for
their activity was limited to keeping company, at least as long as
we were able to watch them.

This male is worthy of mention, for he was a rarity, a cripple
with a totally stiffened front leg. The bear carried this leg bowed
out at the elbow with the toes turned in, and the whole lower leg
below the shoulder blade seemed to be solidified in the joints.
Adolph Murie told me that he had observed this lame bear for
several seasons and thought that he had originally been injured by
a very heavy dose of porcupine quills. Whatever caused the injury,
this was a tough, unprepossessing-looking grizzly, but he did not
seem to suffer much discomfort from his bad leg.

The weather was cold and wet during most of the mating season, allowing for limited observation. No doubt if it had been warm and dry, the pursuits across the valley flats would have been much shorter because of heavy winter coats and a resulting shortness of breath.

Charlie and I watched one mating pair running and walking aimlessly in great loops and tangents for over an hour one day on the naked gravel of the Toklat bottoms. In that time they must have travelled at least five miles, and when they finally disappeared away upriver, they were still going at a good clip with the female in the lead as usual, just as coy and hard to catch as she was at the beginning.

The following morning we spotted this same pair about a mile above our camp. Shortly after we focused our binoculars on them, the boar reared and coupled with the female without any preamble or ceremony. The copulation lasted for over twenty minutes, and then both bears disappeared into a wash full of willows – no doubt suffering from tender feet.

When we were trying to come within camera range of courting bears, we were very much aware of their ground-eating stride and complete disregard of the kind of country ahead. When a grizzly appears to be just strolling along, a man has to go almost at a long trot to keep up unless his crotch is a long way from the ground. Even Charlie and Dick, who went like greyhounds trying to keep the mating pairs in sight, had small success unless their quarry chose to stop. I found myself wishing for a horse.

When in top bear country looking for bears and striving for those unusual and significant shots so necessary to illustrate the beauty and drama of the subject in the film story, anything can happen and sometimes does with amazing suddenness. One evening we were standing in front of the tent after supper, and I spotted a big light-coloured grizzly out on the bars.

"Here comes a bear," I announced, "and it looks like Blondie."

"Two bears," corrected Dick. "The boyfriend looks like old Grumpy."

Sure enough, a big, dark-coloured animal had just appeared from behind a stringer of brush fifty yards to the rear, and he did have the look of our erstwhile bad-tempered acquaintance of the previous summer.

The bears were about a half-mile out on the open bars across the braided channels of the Toklat. The sky was breaking in the west after a cold, miserable day of wind and rain, and the light was strong enough for pictures. I had just finished cleaning and checking out one of the cameras, which was mounted on a cradle supporting the big 500-mm lens, now screwed down solidly on a tripod. So I grabbed it and headed out in the hope of getting a shot or two of this mating pair.

The big lens is a heavy, cranky combination only used on occasions like this, and it is not blithely shouldered for a day's climbing on speculation of finding use for it. Its twenty-power magnification on a 16-mm camera has its good points, but these include no kind of magic. The most effective range is somewhere inside three hundred yards, depending on the nature of the subject involved. So I headed out at a trot for a mount of gravel at about this range from where I hoped to intercept the grizzlies.

It seemed I had barely got under way when the bears crossed in front of me; but they pulled up to investigate some old bear diggings on the far edge of the gravel bars. Blondie was still in the lead, and when she came close to a nesting colony of short-billed gulls, they set up a great crying and began swooping and diving at her. This was just the beginning of a chain of the most maddening frustrations.

With the low sun backlighting their brilliant white wings, the gulls took turns wheeling high and then peeling off in sizzling dives ending in a zoom right over the bear's head. I was gritting my teeth at missing this tremendous shot, when Blondie chose to heap more frustration on my head by rearing and swatting at the birds with her enormous paws. Grinding my teeth in utter despair and muttering imprecations at the size of the cannon I was carrying, I plunged ahead, hoping to get some pictures before the show was over. The footing out there did not help; it was something like trying to run across a field of loose bowling balls.

In the meantime Grumpy became extremely busy with something in the low brush on the edge of the tundra, and when he picked it up in his mouth, I saw that it was a dead caribou calf. At this point Blondie apparently decided there was no future in trying to play badminton with flying sea gulls, and she began circling back toward her mate. The wind must have given his selfish activities away, for she suddenly stiffened, threw up her head, and then went straight to him. Without a bit of ceremony and notwithstanding the fact that he was bigger, she immediately challenged him for the dead calf.

Grumpy may have been in love. He might have backed off a bit, even if reluctantly. He could have at least offered to share the deadfall with her. But he did nothing of the kind. He reared up and swore at her in tones that carried clear to camp, where Dick and Charlie were watching through a spotting scope. The unimpressed Blondie also reared and roared right back and promptly clamped her teeth over the end of his lower jaw; whereupon they proceeded to flail each other unmercifully with their big front paws. Their roaring rang off the mountains, and the great wads of hair flew in every direction. It was a fight to scare the little animals into hunting their holes and the big ones into attention. It was truly awful.

By sheer weight Grumpy forced his opponent over on her back, but this only multiplied his difficulties, for now he was up against four raking paws instead of two. They rolled and swore and bit and clawed, while I ran desperately trying to get into range.

Grumpy did his best to trade more than he got, but his best was not good enough. Blondie still had her hold on his lower jaw. The punishment was too much for him, and he suddenly broke free with a torn ear dripping blood, more gore running from a foot-long slash down one shoulder, and a cant to his lower jaw as though it might be broken. Throwing a glowering glance after her departing suitor, Blondie proceeded to clean up the remains of the calf.

My efforts had gone for nothing; things had happened too fast for me to get anything but a short shot of her feeding on the prize after I came into camera range. If those two grizzlies had taken lessons on how best to frustrate a photographer, they could not have done a better job.

Happily, not all our efforts ended so dismally. One of the preferred shots on our list was a series of close-ups of a bear or bears. Up on the slopes of the East Fork, Dick and I got our chance one day. We spotted Nitchie and her cubs grazing on a patch of lush grass, and again we made a stalk with the Big Bertha lens rigged on camera and tripod.

Old Nitchie was in a mood to ignore us. By moving slow and easy, we came down from above across the green velvet carpet of tundra to within seventy-five feet of her and the cubs. What intrigued us was her control over the cubs. We could see their eyes roll as they watched us, yet because their mother chose to ignore us, they followed her lead.

Through the big lens Nitchie's profile more than filled the view-finder. I could identify the herbage she was eating, and I could clearly see the flash of yellow tusks. Completely engrossed with the operation of the cameras, we failed to notice some danger signals.

At first the grizzlies were feeding on a particularly desirable patch of grass, paying us no attention as they worked around a spot about seventy-five feet away. Old Nitchie's desire to ignore us during this stage of the game went so far that she lay down with her nose on her paws and her tail toward us as though for a nap. One cub came to her and lay with its head on her side, using her for a cushion. Then they worked around us till they were about fifty feet downslope from Dick and about twenty-five yards aslant from me. Dick was swiftly and smoothly operating the still camera when Nitchie's feeding began to slow up. Several times she stood broadside and lifted her head up and gazed away off at nothing in particular. Why we failed to note these danger signals along with the almost imperceptible flattening of her ears can only be because of our complete absorption in getting some rare material.

With a snort she suddenly whirled and rushed Dick with both big cubs flanking her. We barked at her in one voice to stop, which she did, but she was of no mind to turn. For a few long moments she and Dick faced each other, and she was the picture of thinly controlled menace with fire burning in her eyes.

"Back this way slow and easy," I said softly. "Give her room to go up the mountain."

Dick eased away from in front of her and, as is usually the way, she took the opportunity to break off the argument in a face-saving manner. With no further show of belligerence she and the cubs moved up the mountain, where they again fed, paying us no more attention. We left her there, perfectly happy to let well enough alone. Later, when we viewed the films taken of this episode, we were astonished to see how obvious her danger signals had been. She had given us plenty of time to move out before she finally charged. Keen interest and concentration can be a danger in themselves when getting pictures of a grizzly mother and cubs.

There was another grizzly mother using the Toklat flats. She had two yearling cubs, beautiful little bears with fur so long and silky it could be seen blowing and rippling in the wind. She was a stranger. Because she was so typical of the colour of the northern type, we called her Tananna.

One afternoon, following a hard shower, Dick and Charlie got the chance to try for some pictures of her as she and her family were digging roots on the big flat directly across from camp. Dick was busy rigging the big lens on one camera, while Charlie took the other and went ahead to try some medium-range shots with the 150-mm telephoto.

There was a steady crosswind blowing. The bears were feeding among some waist-high willows and birches when Charlie reached a spot about 120 yards from them and shot what remained of a roll of film in the camera. Using his rain parka as an improvised shade, he proceeded to reload. While he was thus occupied, Tananna spotted a parka sleeve flapping in the wind and reared to inspect it. Her eyes told her very little except that this strange-looking apparition had not been there before, so she began to circle downwind of it for a reading with her nose.

Meanwhile, Charlie finished reloading, and when he pulled the parka aside, she was striding around him with the cubs trailing at her heels. Seeing an opportunity to record her reaction when she got his scent, he lined up the lens on a spot directly downwind and waited for her to walk into the view-finder.

The camera hid her from his sight as he stood hunched over it with a finger cocked on the trigger. When she failed to appear in the lens, he lifted his head to look just in time to see her coming like the wind with her mouth wide open and her ears flattened out against her head. The fishtailing wind had given his scent away sooner than expected, and instead of running, as most grizzlies do upon striking man smell, she charged.

There is no more lonely place on earth than out on a breezy tundra flat with a grizzly coming in a wide-open, flat-out charge. Charlie did what we had done on such occasions before. He anchored his feet, facing her, until she was only about twenty yards away and close enough to hear him. Then he stepped toward her.

"Ho!" He snapped out the command as though on military parade.

Tananna did not check her stride, but she swerved and led the cubs away up the slope of the mountain.

Tananna was as handsome as she was disconcerting. She wore a golden, honey-coloured mantle over her shoulders and flanks that blended into the dark brown of her legs and feet. She was in magnificent condition, gleaming in the sun like pale, burnished gold. She was very possessive about her cubs and very much afraid of us – a most dangerous combination that caused her to show fight almost invariably when we approached. We respected her from the profoundness of a certain fear of our own. We admired her, for she was a beautiful bear and a brave and admirable mother who put her cubs' safety before everything.

One day we caught her and the cubs in a striking sequence as they crossed the Toklat, quartering past us. To enhance the picture the bears passed a yearling caribou going the other way so close that all four animals were in the finder at once. The caribou gave them a curious look, but the bears did not spare it a glance. They came up the bank downstream a hundred yards below and headed for the broken slope of rock behind a band of cottonwoods and willows just back of us. Dick and Charlie moved fast to circle behind this screen, where they could shoot more pictures of the grizzlies climbing the rocks. While in the brush they could not see the bears, but I noticed the trio change direction toward the boys. Consequently they came out on the far side much closer to the cameras than anticipated. Immediately the hair rose over Tananna's shoulders, but for once she did not charge. One of the cubs overrode this bit of tolerance by spotting the photographers and going curiously toward them. Tananna changed her mind in a twinkling and charged. A sharp yell from one of the boys did not stop her. She kept coming until she reached the cub, whereupon she shouldered it to turn it back, slapped it on its way, and then followed — looking back over a shoulder and whuffing angrily as she went. Tananna was explosive.

It is utterly impossible to study and work with grizzlies in the wilderness without being aware of the life patterns in the intricate and often mysterious ecological tapestry.

We saw the long-tailed jaeger dive in a spectacular display of aerial acrobatics at a passing golden eagle flying over the alpine basin where the black and white predatory gulls were nesting. Like Tananna, these birds entertain a feeling of fierce possession, which they even vented on her when she chose to travel too close to their nesting site. They dove at us, too, when we moved in to film them, even going so far as to rap Dick smartly on the head with their feet.

It would be hard to find species more diametrically opposed in habit than bears, men, eagles, and long-tailed jaegers; yet the jaegers chose to tie us all together. While the association was not always one of tolerance, who could say for certain that we were not sometimes dependent on each other in some inconspicuous ways? We were all a part of the pattern in those mountains, joining at the moment in making a film record that might serve in some small way to add to men's knowledge, thus serving to bring possible mutual benefit to all.

We were being continually reminded of the throbbing power of the life surrounding us day and night. One morning we woke to find the Toklat flats swarming with caribou, all heading toward the McKinley River and the summer grounds beyond, walking, trotting, and sometimes even galloping in a steady, mile-eating gait. The great migration accompanied itself with the clicking of hoofs across the gravel and tundra. This exodus was not a solid river of animals but rather a flowing chain of herds numbering from a few dozen to hundreds. They moved along the bottoms, climbed over incredibly rough summits, and traversed the slopes in between.

Away up on a shoulder of a steep mountain above Thorough-fare Pass we saw a bunch of about five hundred young bulls stand-ing in a solid swarm on the forty-five-degree pitch of a big snowdrift fighting flies. They stood stoically enduring with their heads down close to the cool snow, and it seemed nothing could stir them from their weariness. Then over the ridge back of them came a lone bull at a wild gallop trying to escape the stinging flies. He panicked the whole herd, and they went rushing off with a great clatter of hoofs across the snow and down the serpentine spine of a ridge to the valley floor. Out on the broad flats they mingled with another herd and swept away down the Thoroughfare River to the McKinley.

On the two-mile-wide gravel bars of the upper McKinley, above the snout of the Muldrow Glacier, we caught up to them again, now joined with the main herd, and filmed acres of caribou standing so thick in places that the gravel did not show through between. On one occasion I estimated roughly over a thousand head showing in my camera view-finder at one time.

This is one of nature's great spectacles, reminding us of his-torical descriptions of the great herds of buffalo on the plains in the old days. Within a few days we saw between six and nine thousand head of caribou. Through these herds, as they had among the buffalo, the grizzlies moved; but here the species were on easier terms.

Old age and accident caused deaths among the caribou, and the grizzlies laid claim to these with their usual relish for carrion. At no time did we see the smallest evidence of a grizzly killing caribou, although they often hijacked the wolf kills. With their uncanny noses they could find a wolf kill while it was still warm.

Through the long daylight hours of the northern summer, among islands of sunshine and storm, we wandered like carefree boys through this great natural circus, sometimes laughing at sheer comedy and again catching our breaths at the beauty and the stark drama that sometimes unfolded before us. We did not know from one minute to the next what we would encounter. It was a real wilderness kaleidoscope of colour and action.

One bright morning we were lying prone in the warm sun looking down from a ridge crest over the broad reaches of the upper Moose Creek valley. Overhead the white clouds ran, tossing their manes, like wild horses at play in the blue pastures of sky. In front of us, scattered in bunches across the huge basin, were caribou feeding and loafing, enjoying a breeze that kept flies and mosquitoes inactive.

Suddenly, I was startled to see a big white animal moving in some brush a couple of miles away across the valley. At first I thought it was an albino bull moose that we had seen lower down near the mouth of Moose Creek the previous year; but when it finally moved out into a clearing, it proved to be a grizzly. We watched this unusual animal for over an hour as it climbed and fed its way straight up and over the mountain range beyond.

For several days we prowled this part of the country trying to find this grizzly again, but apparently it had disappeared among the peaks beyond our reach.

Then one morning when I was sitting on a promontory along the banks flanking the McKinley River, a slight flicker of something on the move caught my eye about two miles downstream. I swung the binoculars to it, and there was the white grizzly coming my way along the foot of the bank on which I was sitting. But then to my chagrin the bear turned out across the river's multi-channelled bed toward the snowy peaks of the Alaska Range. He practically walked through several bunches of caribou, and I could almost taste the disappointment of missing another chance to shoot him with the camera. As though reading my mind and relenting, the bear suddenly turned again and came straight toward me. Apparently he was out for an aimless stroll this morning, just following his questing nose.

He finally disappeared into the mouth of a steep ravine about halfway to the Muldrow Glacier, whereupon I picked up my camera and headed out to try for some footage of him. It was an optimistic jaunt, well larded with footwork, millions of mosquitoes, and sweat. For two hot hours that bear and I went like sin at a church warden's convention. We never quite lost each other, but somehow we never came any closer to getting acquainted. At the start the bear was about a mile ahead of me, and when I finally gave up the pursuit for want of leg muscle to keep up the fierce pace, the bear was still about a mile away – and we were both not far from where we started.

I took up a position on the breezy end of a low ridge near the mouth of a little valley emptying out onto the flats, and sat down to watch him.

If ever there was an absolutely aimless and completely carefree bear, this was the animal. He poked his nose into countless bushes without seeming to pause to investigate whatever he found. Several times he started what looked like the beginning of a nonstop marathon to the Arctic coast, but soon he turned back. He jumped nesting ptarmigan and chased ground squirrels in a most light-hearted fashion, but he caught none. Finally, as I had been hoping, he came straight toward me and turned up a little creek about one hundred and fifty yards below my stand.

Through the nine-power glasses I examined him closely. The pelt was not pure white but a pale cream. This was no albino, as we first thought, for the eyes were dark. Somehow I got the impression that it was a male, although as usual I confess to more than considerable guesswork.

The camera was just trained on him with the focus screwed down to razor sharpness, when suddenly he came to a rigid stop with one front paw uplifted, like a pointer dog fastened on a covey of birds. Thinking he had located a ground squirrel, I waited with trigger finger cocked for instant action. The bear remained frozen, moving not a whisker, for an interminable half-minute or so while a thousand mosquitoes took advantage of a lull in the breeze to bore into my back as I was hunched over the camera. I endured their drilling for as long as possible, and then I straightened up slightly to throw some slack into my shirt. At that instant the grizzly banged the ground smartly with his paw and whirled away in the same motion. To my utter amazement a fine, fully grown caribou bull exploded out of the willow clump that had been just under the bear's nose and galloped up the creek. The grizzly turned to watch the caribou go, and as though delighted with his own joke, reared back against a low bank and playfully waved his paws. Meanwhile, the surprised bull turned to look at the bear. Then with his ridiculous tail hoisted at a jaunty angle, he came prancing back down the creek and stopped, facing the bear at about twenty yards. There they stood for a few moments, gazing at each other in an amiable fashion, until the caribou suddenly jumped away to the side and headed for the river. Without another glance after him the grizzly came up into the draw below me to feed and loaf among some little meadows.

This was a revealing experience. Here was a grizzly, likely weighing in the vicinity of six hundred pounds, that had spent a good half-minute within ten feet of a sleeping bull caribou. He could have leaped on the animal and killed it with the same ease that a wolf would kill a rabbit, yet he had chosen deliberately to spook the caribou and let it go. More than ever I was convinced that some grizzlies never learn to kill anything bigger than a caribou calf.

Making a new grizzly acquaintance and studying its individual characteristics was always an intensely interesting experience full of unknowns; they are as individualistic as people. One does not just walk up to a strange grizzly and introduce oneself. Unless you enjoy living dangerously, the introduction is subtle and patient, and even then one is never sure what the reception will be. Unlike meeting humans, it is better and far more rewarding to be loftily ignored in grizzly society.

We will never forget Sultana. We named her after the original Indian name for Mount Foraker, a seventeen-thousand-foot peak close by Mount McKinley. Foraker was known as Sultana in the old days, meaning "The Woman" or "The Wife," the mate to Denali, the Indian name for Mount McKinley that means "The Great One." The white man's arrogance and egotism in changing these names is not admirable; for no man, not even a president of the United States, deserves such a mountain to carry his name. It is in very bad taste, but this is apart from my story.

I first met the bear Sultana up along a little tributary of the East Fork River across from Polychrome Mountain. She was a huge, old, chocolate-coloured grizzly with a tiny, almost black cub gambolling at her heels. I took plenty of time working in close enough to her for pictures, for mother grizzlies with new cubs are particularly touchy.

Keeping the wind in my favour, I eased closer and closer. I probably took at least an hour to go a hundred yards. I was encouraged, for several times when I was sure she could see me, she paid me not the slightest heed.

I was wearing a waterproof nylon rain parka and pants instead of the usual soft cotton jeans and buckskin jacket, for it had rained earlier and the brush was soaking wet. My sons inelegantly called these pants "whistle britches," and would sooner go wet than wear them. Right now I was heartily agreeing and wishing I had left them in camp, for at almost every step the brush scraped the cloth with enough noise to alert her. Finally she became so restive that she took the cub up across the bars onto a dry wash coming off the slope. It was puzzling, for she had paid practically no attention to the sight of me.

She was now in a much better position for me to stalk. Keeping the wind in my favour, I made a wide circle and came down the rocky wash from above. Free of the brush, it was not easy to go quietly, and I finally reached a spot about fifty yards from her when a rock rolled a bit under a boot sole. This tiny noise instantly galvanized her into hair-trigger annoyance. But even though my clothing was in sharp contrast to the background, she still failed to locate me exactly. However, she was angry and upset enough to go stalking away with her hair standing on end into a patch of head-high willows, where I had no inclination to follow.

The next day we located her again farther up the valley and spent considerable time watching her. Again, she was sensitive to noise but failed to bristle up when we were in plain sight. We finally realized that she was almost totally blind. Once we were aware of this, it was necessary only to be very careful with the wind and equally quiet to obtain good film records of her.

Again and again we went to watch this great bear, and somehow she became one of the most fascinating grizzlies we knew. Perhaps it was her size and the fact that she was a blind mother with the responsibility of a tiny cub not much bigger than one of her massive paws. Maybe it was because she was so devoted to her offspring, around which her world revolved. To be sure, she shed more light on the admirable character of the grizzly.

Several times we saw her suckle the cub. The gentle loving motions she displayed during this procedure, the hallmark of mother love among most all warm-blooded creatures, was enough to make a man swear never to kill another grizzly. At intervals of about one and a half hours, Sultana would leave off whatever she was doing and half-rear and spin on her heels to go over backward on the ground. She would hardly be flattened out before the cub would land ecstatically on the vast expanse of hairy bosom and grab a teat while she caressed it with gentle muzzle and paws. The cub would move from one dug to another until all were sucked dry; then they would play awhile, with the young one galloping and bucking up and down her belly, smelling noses, and playfully swatting with paws. Sometimes she would cut this off by abruptly standing up and spilling the cub to the ground. Sometimes they would drop into a short sleep. Once I found them dead to the world, the mother lying on her back with all four paws outstretched and the cub lying on his belly sound asleep on the middle of hers.

One of the desired sequences on our preferred-shot list was of a grizzly mother suckling her cubs. We recorded this scene at long range and now hoped to get a close-up. The chance came one afternoon while we were watching Sultana in some fairly heavy brush at the foot of a mountain slope. Suddenly she moved off, heading up behind a knoll. Instantly Charlie was on the move, swinging his camera up onto his shoulder.

"She's going to feed the cub up in that hollow behind that point," Charlie said. "I'm going to make a try for it."

"She might hear the camera," I cautioned, for he was going to be very close.

"There's enough wind to blank it out," he assured me as he headed out.

There are moments in a musician's life when the notes leap from his instrument as pure and perfect as music can be. The artist knows times when his brush seems to guide his hand into painting better than he knows. There are also moments in a nature photographer's life when he is at one with his subject and the whole country. The light of the sun is his magic, the film is his canvas, and the camera is his instrument – golden inspiration stirs his heart. Then he can do no wrong and is truly the artist. To watch him in action in such an enchanted moment is something to remember. This was such a time for Charlie.

He went alone. Somehow, through willows as thick as fur, he worked his way soundlessly up the back of the knoll. It was a grand piece of stalking, and when he reached the top, I saw him spread the tripod legs and plant the camera in one smooth motion.

No sooner was the camera trained than Sultana appeared on the edge of a little marshy clearing fifty feet below. Almost immediately she sagged back and spun on her heels, going over on her back, whereupon the cub proceeded with a single-handed riot. If bears can smile, Sultana grinned from ear to ear with pure joy – a sort of bearish beam of pleasure and indulgence. The cub pulled and tugged, leaped from one dug to another, and left wet spots in her fur to mark the trail of his passing.

Just as he finished, the wind died and the whirring of the camera caught her ears. Instantly she leaped to her feet, the picture of vibrant explosive menace. For a long, long moment it seemed as though even the mountains held their breaths. Then she was gone.

Sultana was blind, but it is doubtful that she missed her eyes very much, for her ears and nose were as sharp as razors and told her most everything she wanted to know.

Inevitably the time came when we had to tear ourselves away from these idyllic mountains. It was our last night on the Toklat, and we were sleeping under the spruces in order to get an early start in the morning. Something woke me from a deep sleep, and when I looked at my watch I saw the hands pointing to midnight. The whole country was enveloped in that great northern stillness so profound.

Through a gap in the trees over the mountains to the north the Great Bear, or Big Dipper, swung with its pointers zeroed on the Pole Star. I lay there snug in my robe, caught in the spell of the quiet, contemplating this group of stars and its related constellation, the Little Bear, and wondering at these ancient ties between bears and men.

PART FIVE

UNDERSTANDING
THE WILD

Although not a trained professional biologist, Andy Russell is a keen and thoughtful observer of nature. At a time when most ranchers saw grizzlies as unrepentant cattle killers, Andy went against the tide of public opinion by challenging that notion. His magazine article "Can Animals Think?" roused the ire of an academic who criticized him for being so presumptuous as to talk about animal intelligence without benefit of formal academic credentials and rigorous laboratory experiments. But Andy stuck to his guns and continued to report what he saw and what he learned about Rocky Mountain wildlife.

White Sheep of the Arctic

T he most beautiful wild sheep of North America has its home among the mountains of Alaska and the Yukon Territory. This is the Dall sheep (*Ovis canadensis dalli*), whose fleece, white as snow, stands out in brilliant contrast to the bare mountain slopes on which it lives, while the horns of the ram range in colour from pale gold to deep bronze.

In habits the Dall varies little from the bighorn, of which it is a subspecies. But the horns of the ram, unlike those of the bighorn, sweep out and away from its head in a graceful, flaring curve. As the horns do not affect its vision (as do those of the bighorn, which are close-curling and massive), the Dall does not possess the bighorn's habit of rubbing off its horn tips. The Dall is also less boisterous in the breeding season and is seldom seen with chipped horn base or bent fighter's nose.

My first expedition in search of Dalls had a memorable beginning. Scheduled to assist at the live capture of some Dall lambs for a game farm in Alberta, I was motoring with my son Dick and a friend along the Alaska Highway west of Whitehorse. It was a

From *Animals* (1964)

warm afternoon in early May, and we were coming off the pass toward Kluane Lake, when across Slim's River on a mountain slope I spotted a curious-looking whitish smear of considerable size. It looked as if a giant snowball had been shattered against the rocks. Could it be sheep? We stopped the station wagon and had a look through our binoculars. The white smear resolved itself into a herd of about 150 feeding sheep. Never in a lifetime of roaming the Canadian Rockies had I seen so many wild sheep in one bunch. It was a thrilling sight, but one which to us would become commonplace – for later we grew accustomed to the sight of several hundred sheep in a good day's climb through the mountains.

Previous to this expedition, I had spent almost seventeen months making a film study of the life and habits of the bighorn. With my sons I had learned how to approach the sheep without cover or subterfuge to a distance of only a few feet. The bighorns accepted us into their community as friends – and now we were curious to see what would happen with the Arctic sheep. Within four days of our arrival in the mountains around Kluane Lake, we were photographing Dalls at a range of fifty feet or less.

During the lambing season, the most interesting time for observations, the animals congregate low on the mountain slopes in search of new spring greenery, and rams can be seen together with yearlings, ewes, and lambs. The lambs are born on certain favourite spots, invariably in extremely steep and rugged country that is apparently used for this purpose year after year. It is amazing that more lambs do not fall off the cliffs to their death.

I once observed the birth of a lamb. The ewe was standing on a narrow ledge on the face of a high broken cliff. With few preliminaries she lay down in a little hollow in the three-foot-wide ledge and gave birth. The whole procedure took only a few minutes. The lamb struggled to its feet and tottered precariously on the edge of nothing, while its mother licked it dry. Then, without glancing back, the ewe blithely set out along the ledge, with the lamb staggering along behind on untried legs. The ledge grew absurdly narrow, and I held my breath as the lamb appeared to defy the laws of gravity. Only sheer luck seemed to prevent the wobbly-kneed, awkward creature from plunging to destruction. When she reached a wider place, the ewe stopped and allowed the lamb to suckle. The warm milk had a magical effect, for when they continued their journey, the lamb skipped and gambolled as actively as a mountain sprite.

Like bighorns, Dalls are playful and intelligent animals. The lambs are especially fond of frolics and indulge in some wild games on the precipitous mountain slopes. In Alaska last year we had our camp opposite a slope on which there was a bunch of twenty-five ewes with their lambs. We saw this bunch every day over a long period. Two or three times a week their tour of the mountain brought them on to a low shoulder directly opposite our tent. Here they grazed on a steeply sloping meadow on the rim of a broken cliff face. Quite often one or more of the older ewes acted as baby-sitters for a large number of the lambs while their mothers fed. For a long time the lambs would remain quietly with their ewe-nurses waiting for their mothers to fill themselves up with food. Then, as if at a signal, the lambs would leap to their feet and scamper off with bleats of anticipation in search of their mothers to enjoy a feed of warm milk. If the day was fine, the lambs would often conclude their meal with a game of follow-my-leader or a slide down a steep snowdrift. Once I saw a lamb leap exuberantly into the air and land, with all four feet bunched together, on top of its mother as she lay chewing the cud.

At the foot of this slope there was a fox's den, where a pair of prolific red foxes had seven cubs. These, too, were often observed playfully rolling and tumbling around the mouth of their den. One sunny afternoon the fox cubs were gambolling boisterously among the flowers while the vixen watched, sometimes showing her teeth and pink tongue in a little smile. A hundred yards up the slope from the fox's den, the band of ewes and lambs were standing watching the foxes with intense curiosity. Then an old ewe decided she must have a closer look. She came marching down the hill in a matronly fashion, with her lamb at her heels. Not far from the den they drew up on a little terrace to watch the fun. The lamb was fascinated by the cubs and could not resist going nearer. Ears pricked forward and head held high, the youngster edged closer and closer. One of the cubs noticed the lamb and grew curious too. Step by step they crept up to each other and, extending their small frames forward to the absolute limit, they shyly sniffed noses. Then both of them wheeled round and fled back to their own kind. Neither of the parents showed much concern at the proximity of the young to one another.

At this time we were working on a film of the life of the grizzly bear, and we were very interested in its relationship with the Dall. Several times we observed sheep and grizzlies feeding on the same slope. The sheep paid very little attention to the bears and moved only casually away when they came too close for comfort. For their part the grizzlies showed no recognition of the sheep. Although it is not unknown for grizzlies to attack sheep, this happens only very rarely and in the most unusual circumstances.

On this and three subsequent expeditions into Alaska and Yukon Territory, we travelled many days through Dall sheep country but found only scattered evidence of predation. Wolverine take some toll, especially during the winter months. The big northern variety of the Canada lynx also preys on the sheep during the hard months of the northern night. Timber wolves kill them, but only under the most favourable conditions, for on steep slopes they are normally no match for the agile sheep.

The sheep cover different ranges for summer and winter grazing. In summer they move on to higher ground above the level of flies and mosquitoes. In some places these short migrations take them across wide river flats. It is startling to see a bunch of these animals, normally associated with steep slopes, way out on the tundra flats, miles from the nearest mountain. In June 1963, I observed some twenty-six sheep crossing the wide flats along the Sanctuary River in Mount McKinley Park. They looked nervous as they walked or trotted in a long line through low birches and willows. In such country they are certainly vulnerable to preying wolves, which also tend to intercept them in narrow defiles and mountain passes.

Hundreds of Dall sheep used to be killed by hunters who supplied the northern mining camps, but this practice has been stopped. The future of the species looks bright. Climate and geography conspire against the intrusion of agriculture into Dall territory, and there is practically no commercial timber to lure the timber industry. Mining and oil developments have affected some small sections of the range, but not enough to cause concern. Perhaps the substitution of the airplane for the sled dog as the chief means of transport in the north has been the most important factor in reducing human predation. Thirty years ago, every man in the north owned a team of five to seven dogs. These were fed by every possible means, and in certain places Dall sheep contributed heavily. One trapper told me that twenty-five years ago he used to kill forty to sixty Dall sheep a year for his family and his dogs. Dall sheep are still hunted during the annual open season, but the effects of this are insignificant, owing to the vast extent of their range.

Golden eagles kill fewer lambs than is often supposed. We spent hours watching eagles circling above groups of sheep, but never did any of them attack one. The eagles seemed to prey almost exclusively on the numerous ptarmigan and ground squirrels, but if one did fly close over the sheep, the lambs promptly skipped under their mothers' bellies for shelter.

Fortunately also, Dall sheep have no contact with domestic sheep, as the bighorns do farther south, and therefore catch none of the domestic-sheep diseases which occasionally play havoc with the bighorns. (Wild sheep are as vulnerable to these diseases as the Inuit and the Indian to the diseases of the white man.) All in all, hard winters and deep snow appear to be the chief causes of mortality.

To sit, on a summer's day, on a high slope in the Dall sheep mountains is an experience to cherish. Flanking the wide valleys, the mountain peaks run chain on chain toward the horizon. Above six thousand feet the mountains are draped with tumbling blue glaciers and glittering snow. The air is normally as clear as crystal, so that peaks as much as fifty miles away are visible in sharp outline against the bright blue of the sky.

Here and there on the flanks of the lower valleys, white dots move against the colourful carpet of the tundra. These are scattered bands of Dall sheep. A motionless white dot is visible on the point of a rock, and great golden horns are outlined against the sky as an old herd patriarch swings his head. He is at the end of his life, with the years marked by twelve deeply indented rings on his horns. He has fed well throughout the summer, but now the front teeth of his lower jaw are almost gone, and he is doomed. Next spring his bleaching skull and those great sweeping horns will lie among the new-blooming alpine flowers, a reminder of a generation past.

The Otters

From its headwaters in British Columbia, the Flathead River flows down into Montana, finally emptying into Flathead Lake. It is a wild and magnificent wilderness river at its upper end, lying couched between the high crags of the Rockies and a secondary range to the west. Both the river and its feeder lakes, hidden away among the flanking mountains, teem with fish, making it an otter heaven. It was in this wilderness paradise that Proo and Kim grew to adulthood.

Proo and Kim were river otters, young adults from families that lived and foraged along the North Fork of the Flathead River and its many tributaries. They mated in late winter, and the following summer they came up a creek flowing west out of Bowman Lake, to play and feed along its wild shores. Sleek, muscular animals of incredible grace, their movements were one long aquatic ballet as they pursued fish and played in the clear mountain waters.

They had Bowman Lake to themselves, for there were no other otters there, and what prompted them to move there is no way to tell. But one September evening Kim led the way up another creek

From *Andy Russell's Adventures With Wild Animals* (1977)

flowing out of a twisted canyon at the east end of the lake. They had explored this creek several times, but had always turned back at a bubble-strewn pool that lay at the foot of a high waterfall. This time, however, Kim led the way up the side of the canyon, along a series of ledges, through ferns and shrubbery to the top of the falls. There, they travelled steadily on up the stream toward its head, sometimes leaving it to detour around other falls, but generally staying with the water.

Almost as much at home on land as they are in water, the otters went at their flowing lope, so smooth it is deceptive in its speed, a gait that eats up the distance without seeming to be fast. Their route took them through heavy timber to timberline, where the larches were all gold in autumn dress, and where the creek flowed under overhanging canopies of alders and willows, rattling and rushing swiftly amongst boulders. At the first hint of dawn, the otters were on top of the pass straddling the Continental Divide, and here the creek was reduced to a trickle by remnants of melting snowdrifts that still lingered in the hollows.

They followed a well-marked trail until the black bulk of a big grizzly hove in sight over a rise in the pale light, prompting them to slip away to the side among some big, jagged rocks with the breeze in their favour. The travelling bear was unaware of them till he came to the musky scent of their tracks, when he paused, curiously sniffing, then uninterestedly continued on his way. The otters, meanwhile, had moved on over the crest of the pass to the head of another creek flowing northeast.

This was the headwaters of the Kootenay River, and Kim and Proo greeted the stream with enthusiastic splashing, though it was too small for anything but a swimming stroke or two in its deepest places. They loped through the shallows, slithered down steep little runs like wet silk ribbons, sometimes rolling in spiral twists, as fluid as the water in which they travelled. Side creeks fed the stream, and within a mile it was deep enough for swimming. They revelled in it, powerful sweeps of their muscular bodies shooting them through the pools like two big fish.

The stream was barren of fish, as nearly all high streams are, because trout are cut off from the headwaters by impassable falls in mountain country, so the fishing was bad, and the otters kept moving. They came to a water-worn chute, where the creek sluiced at a steep angle over smooth rock into a frothy pool effervescing with bubbles, and they shot happily down its length to arrive with scarcely a splash. Kim surfaced, snorting softly to clear his nose, and headed for shore, intending to climb back to the top and slide again.

He was still in the water, only his head showing on the surface, when his nose picked up a scent – a sweet, warm smell arresting his motion so that he drifted around behind a rock pointing like a weathervane into the current. Proo came alongside him, and they both lifted their heads cautiously to look over a fringe of grass and other plants rimming a tiny meadow by the pool. Both otters sank and swam to the riffle downstream, coming to shore behind a screening clump of willows. Circling wide through a patch of alders, they came to the higher side of the little meadow, over-looking a covey of spruce grouse warming themselves and feeding in the first rays of the rising sun. The otters were among them before the birds were aware of their presence, and quick as light they pounced on two, killing them so fast there was scarcely a movement apart from the fluttering of wings as the survivors flew up into the small scrubby trees circling the place.

When the otters had fed, there was nothing left but some feathers stirring a bit in the thermal breezes wafting up the slope. Proo and Kim touched noses briefly and then began rolling over and over, mouthing each other gently and wrestling in play, before stretching out in the sun among the greenery for a brief rest. They soon took to the water again, rolling and twisting around the pool in graceful undulations. Then, without any sign seeming to pass between the two, Kim suddenly pointed his nose downstream and shot away. Again they were travelling.

The creek rapidly grew into a small river, a fast mountain flow roaring and leaping over the falls and down whitewater rapids, where the otters did not have to drive themselves but could drift with the stream. When they came to a falls that wasn't too high, they simply went over it in a long smooth dive; the higher ones were detoured in brief overland excursions through the dense forest that now crowded against the water. At one particularly high falls, a big driftwood log was standing on end, with the spray playing over its protruding snags of broken branches. The otters climbed down along its slippery, slanting trunk as though they had done it twenty times before, though it was completely new to them. Sure-footed as cats and complete masters of their sur-roundings, they dove off it into the pool, hugging bottom till they surfaced in the shallow riffle below.

It was evening, and high peaks were still rosy in the setting sun, when the otters reached the spot where the river empties into the Kootenay lakes cradled in the valley between ranks of giant spruce and ancient cottonwoods. They had been travelling nearly twenty-four hours, and both were hungry and ready for a period of rela-tive inactivity. Proo climbed up onto a driftwood log to groom herself, while Kim investigated a log jam out where the ripples of the stream lost themselves on the mirror surface of the first lake. His ears caught the sound of branches snapping, and he reared up on a log to look at a giant bull moose browsing among the willows at the foot of an avalanche track. Paying it no further attention, he humped slowly along the log to a sand spit sticking out into the lake. Here he rolled, and scrubbed his coat for a while before entering the water to dive under a floating pad of driftwood.

The flickering movement of a trout caught his eyes as it darted away, and a powerful twist of his body instantly sent him in pursuit.

The fish turned, twisted and dodged, frantic to escape, but the otter followed its every move, slowly closing in until his teeth snapped shut on its back. Then he returned to the sand spit, climbed up on the log, and proceeded to eat his catch.

Proo came to investigate, but was greeted by an ominous growl, which sent her back across the sand to the water. Her fishing trip took her a bit longer, but she was soon back on shore with another fat trout.

When they finished feeding, the otters travelled a short distance to a tangled heap of logs left by winter avalanches, and there in a dark, dry cavern under the pile, they found a comfortable nest and slept.

In the morning they were off again, making a long circuit of the shoreline of the two lakes and the short swift section of river that joined them. It was a pristine, lovely place, teeming with fish and many other kinds of life. A family of fully grown harlequin ducks in drab juvenile and female plumage floated on the surface of the first lake, but the otters paid them scant attention. On the second lake, near the end where the river exited, there was a small beaver house built on the edge of a semi-floating island made of tangled grass braided into dwarf willow roots. The otters climbed up on its dome-shaped roof, examining its freshly plastered coating of mud and sniffing the musky-sweet smell of beavers before sliding back into the water.

Along the shore of the lake, Proo came to a place where a little spring flowed out of a wet carpet of moss growing at the feet of some big spruce. This miniature delta was fringed with emerald-green watercress, which she sampled with relish before beginning to dig into the wet muck, hauling up gobs of it with her front paws and rooting around in the blackened water with her nose. A movement under her paws triggered a quick plunge, and her teeth closed on a squirming frog that had buried itself in the silt under the little flow for the winter. She ate it and started digging for another. Behind her, Kim came out of the lake with a small trout in his jaws. The hunting was good in this place.

The Indian summer days were warm with a gentle chinook wind blowing down the valley off the Divide. The tops of the high peaks had a light frosting of new snow that was a silvery contrast to the golden larches just below timberline. The few cottonwoods along the lake shores were a brilliant yellow against the deep green of the conifers. Sometimes alone, more often together, the otters wandered the lakes, and up and down the river, exploring, feeding, and frolicking. They were fat under their shining coats of rich brown.

One evening a thick, clammy fog settled down from the peaks, and the north wind came cold with snowflakes drifting on it. By morning the whole country was transformed into a snow-draped wilderness, and the lake surfaces were covered in lead-coloured slush. Somewhere up toward the summit of the Divide, a flock of Canada geese, trying to cross over the pass, lost their direction in the storm. They dropped lower, circling and honking. When they found themselves over the river, they doubled back along it to the lakes, where they landed near the island. Not long afterward a flock of several hundred mallards came flying low up the river and joined the geese. The place was suddenly alive with bird sounds.

Otters are naturally curious animals with a penchant for investigating everything around them, and Kim and Proo swam out for a look. Travelling underwater, they surfaced here and there, sniffing and peering toward the raft of ducks till they were within a few yards of them. Then Kim dove and slid up under a fat drake. He grabbed it by a foot and pulled it under so suddenly that it had time for no more than a short lifting of its wings and a cut-off squawk. Kim took it deep, released it, shifting his grip to its neck before it could move, and killed it with a swift crunch of his teeth. He surfaced to get air about fifty feet from shore, and towed it the rest of the way to the snowy beach.

Proo was not hungry, for she had just killed and eaten a trout, but she was feeling playful. Diving under the ducks, and looking up, she could see the outlines of them clustered on the surface, and she came up to nip one lightly. The hen mallard quacked in panicky alarm at this shocking attack by something from the depths, and jumped into the air to land with head held high a few feet away. Her sudden leap caused a slight ripple of concern among the ducks in her immediate vicinity, making a hole in the tightly crowded bottoms visible to Proo. She surfaced very briefly in the middle of the gap thus created and dived to repeat the manoeuvre. Again the duck of her choice leaped up in consternation, with an accompanying clatter of other wings. This sudden vanishing of outlines excited the otter so that she continued to nip and bump bottoms till the whole flock took to the air.

Proo surfaced to find herself surrounded by a broken tracery of slush where ducks had been. Only the geese remained in a close bunch by the edge of the island, so she turned her attention to them. Their reaction was more ponderous, but just as satisfying. After a couple of submarine sallies, however, sharp eyes quickly spotted her head as she came up for a look, and the geese climbed up onto the island, spoiling Proo's game. The ducks landed again after a couple of circles of the lakes, but Proo had lost interest. She swam away toward the outlet of the river, where she was shortly joined by Kim.

There the otters climbed up to the top of a steep slanting slab of rock below a low waterfall to slide down, making a trough in the snow and ending in a plunge into the tumbling cauldron of a deep pool. Again and again they climbed, to repeat the tobogganing until their track was slick with ice from the water on their fur.

A big lynx crouched watching them, a few yards away under the wide-spreading branches of a spruce, but the smell and the size of them, coupled with their strangeness, cooled his first inclination to attack. His muscles relaxed as he watched curiously until they left their game to disappear back upstream. Then he faded into the snowy forest in search of something more familiar to satisfy his hunger. A smart move – had he attacked them, the otters would have ganged up and drowned him.

The storm had been short, but the snow was a foot deep when the sun came out to light up the wintry wilderness. This transition between warm fall days and the first breaths of winter is a restless time of year among wild animals. On the few remaining bright, golden days the sun seems to kiss the earth with a cooling fervour, as though saying goodbye before the arrival of cold and deep snow.

There are deep valleys in the mountains running parallel to the daily passage of the sun. In these valleys the high flanking peaks hide the sunlight from December to March. Most of the bigger animals, particularly the cloven-hoofed ones, shun these places.

The bears escape winter's grip by going into dens for the cold months, and living off their fat in semi-hibernation. The beavers take refuge in their dome-shaped houses, feeding on the bark of willows, aspens and cottonwoods stored in submerged piles under the ice. The winter birds, well insulated by thick plumage, endure the cold as they forage over wide areas. The pine squirrels build bulky nests of dry moss in the trees and live off caches of pine nuts, spruce, and fir seeds and carefully dried mushrooms, sleeping during the sharp cold spells. The pine martens live by hunting the squirrels, just as the otters hunt and eat the aquatic life found under the armour of ice that covers the frozen lakes, ponds, and streams.

Kim and Proo found an old abandoned beaver run dug into the bank of the river between the lakes and moved into it. Its mouth was deep under water, so they had quick access to the lakes and good fishing. Sometimes they swam up to the open water where the river came down swiftly into the lake. Occasionally, they made short journeys through the snow under the timber along the edge of the lakes, but as the loose fluffy blanket piled up, these trips were abandoned. Swimming under the ice was easier.

By February there were twelve feet of snow on the level, and because the sun had never shone during the cold months, it had remained a loose blanket. Now the sun was back, growing higher and stronger every day, and the snow began to settle. The otters could travel easily from one open hole in the river to another, but still there was small inducement for them to wander very far.

As warmer weather began to open the river, Proo was heavy with young, her usually sleek outline bulky and her temper short. One day her tolerance of Kim broke and, in a snarling fit of rage, she drove him out of the den so vigorously that he did not return. He burrowed down among the logs to take up residence in their old nest.

It was just pure luck that he was out fishing the day an avalanche cut loose high on the mountain slope above the lakes and came roaring down, smashing into the log jam and tearing it apart, finally coming to rest with a great pile of snow extending halfway out into the upper lake. Its plunging weight broke the ice, and the snow mass displaced thousands of tons of water, the resulting wave inundating Proo's den and driving her out, where she found that the water level was up into the timber. When the flood subsided, the snow was dirty with forest flotsam, and the ice of the lower lake was covered with water.

Kim swam around the snout of the snow pile, inspecting this sudden change of landscape, and climbed up onto the great mound for a brief reconnaissance before taking to the water again. He swam through the lower lake into the river, heading for new country, leaving the place to Proo.

When she went back to it, her den was damp and cold, so unattractive that she abandoned it to search for better surroundings. There was an urgency to her looking as she travelled along the shoreline of the lower lake, poking her nose into every nook and cranny along the edge of the timber. Most of the land was still deep in snow, but on top of a steep-sided little gravel ridge near the river outlet, she came on a big, bleached-out cottonwood log lying in the midst of a thick growth of willows. It was forked at one end, and in the middle of the fork there was a round hole big enough to accommodate her. She found the interior of the hollow log, lined with bits of rotten wood, dry and ideal for a hide.

When she came back to it from a fishing trip late that evening, she did not enter the log until she had made a circle all around it, sniffing and examining everything, to satisfy herself that nothing had intruded upon her new territory. Then she slipped through the hole, but even in the security of the hide she was restless, and came out again to poke aimlessly around as though in search of something. Finally she found a small patch of old dry grass along the rim of a bank, and proceeded to collect mouthfuls of it to carry back to her log. After several trips, her nest was arranged to her satisfaction, and she stretched out on her grassy bed.

That night her kits were born — four tiny, helpless little mites with eyes sealed shut. They squeaked and nuzzled as she licked them dry, until one by one they fastened on to a dug to nurse.

During these first hours after their birth, Proo was by turns keenly on edge and alert to the slightest noise outside the log, and gently — even ecstatically — preoccupied with her new family. She licked them with soft caresses while they cuddled up close to her belly, secure and content in her warmth.

No longer was she a carefree wandering animal, for she spent no more time away from her hide than it took to feed. She did not play any more, but pursued fish with a swift, fierce concentration of purpose, anxious to be back with her family.

The kits developed quickly, and by warm weather they were trailing their mother to the lake, where they took to the water without hesitation, soon as much at home in it as she was. By June, the family was taking longer and longer expeditions away from the hide. Proo would lead and the kits would bring up the rear, the first one with its nose even with the end of Proo's tail, and the rest single-filing behind in close formation. As they followed undulations of the ground – up and over logs and rocks and around trees – they were an unbroken chain, moving in formation like a long brown ribbon.

In the lake, when Proo dived in pursuit of fish, they dipped under in an attempt to follow but their dives were very shallow.

When she reappeared, she usually had a trout crosswise in her mouth. After reaching shore and locating some suitable cover, she ate the head off her catch, leaving the kits to maul the rest of it while she dived back into the water after another.

One evening, when she took them back to the hide, she heard something moving and crackling among the willows near it. Rearing behind a patch of green fireweed to her full height, she found that the log had been rolled to one side. Behind it, a big grizzly was sniffing around in the brush. With a low growl of warning, she quickly led the kits back to the lake and they swam up toward its head. She took them into a big eddy in the river, close by the mouth of her old den, and dived. Quickly exploring the den, she came back out to the young ones, who were milling around, fighting to hold their position in the swirling current. Grasping a kit in her mouth, she dived back into the tunnel with a powerful twist of her muscular body, and deposited it inside, above the waterline. Not wasting a motion, she repeated the manoeuvre until her family was all safely inside, then she took them up the tunnel to the small chamber hollowed out at the top. This place was not as dry as the log, but it was a good hide, located under the spreading roots of a giant spruce, and safe from any intrusion.

For a while, the kits required her help in the dive to and from the river, but it was not long before they learned to make it by themselves. The young otters grew fast, and by late summer they were swift, powerful swimmers. Now the family was continually ranging and playing together, welded into a solid unit. Their lives seemed to be an unending game of follow-the-leader, with Proo as the leader. As closely as possible, the young ones copied her every move. They were diving now in pursuit of fish, though their enthusiasm surpassed their success. Even so, they came close enough to whet their zeal for more trying, and they revelled in the excitement.

One day in mid-July something new appeared by the lake – a tent pitched on the meadow by the beach at the lower end where the river exited. It was the camp of a doctor and his wife on their annual wilderness-fishing trip into the Rockies. They were accompanied by their fox terrier.

The lady was not as keen as her husband about fishing, and spent a good deal of her time wandering about, watching birds and photographing flowers.

Proo became aware of them when the sounds of supper preparation and the smell of campfire smoke alerted her, but she was not unduly alarmed, as she had encountered people and camps before. Like all wild mothers she was always cautious, and for a while she kept the kits close to the hide. They were a restless brood, their energy and enthusiasm difficult to contain for very long at a time. One morning they were causing Proo considerable anxiety by diving out of the tunnel one at a time, and finally she took them out to the upper lake.

On a sandbar by the log jam at the foot of the avalanche track, she began to dive for a trout, while the kits played on the sand among some big bleached logs. Proo had just surfaced a few feet from the shore with a fish in her jaws when the lady and her dog came out of the timber fifty yards downwind from the otters, and immediately the dog caught their scent. He gave a sharp bark of excitement and streaked away, arriving among the kits before his mistress comprehended what was going on.

The fact that he suddenly found himself confronted by several small animals, instead of one, confused him for an instant, which probably saved a life. His open jaws were just reaching for one of the kits when Proo smashed into his hide, and instantly the quiet was convulsed into a scene of utter bedlam, accompanied by snarls and hair-raising screeches, chilling in their utter savagery. Proo was attacking with a red-eyed intent to kill, sparked to burning intensity by her mother instinct to protect her young. The dog, though he was in excellent condition, young and strong, found himself up against a terror, bound in muscles like steel springs and with the speed of lightning.

They rolled and spun, locked together in a death battle. The otter's hide was tough and loose, so that no matter how or where the terrier grabbed her, she turned in her skin and nailed him with her teeth. Although wild with anger, she was fighting with a pattern; she was working him toward the water where she would have an overwhelming advantage.

But before they reached it, the lady arrived, screaming at the top of her lungs and waving a stick. With no thought of possible consequences, she waded into the mix-up, breaking her stick over the otter's back. Although mad with rage, the otter realized she was now outnumbered, and broke away to plunge into the lake and disappear. Her kits had long since gone, but she sensed that they were ahead of her, and she turned toward the hide.

Meanwhile, the lady had gathered up her dog, and, with blood running over her clothes from a deep gash on its shoulder and a badly torn face and ear, she headed for camp. The good doctor had some sewing to do.

Proo gathered up her family and took them back into the hide. For a while there would be no problem keeping them there, for they were shaking with fright. As for her, she tingled with the pain of bites, but apart from a few punctures in her tough hide she was unhurt. Just the same, for a while she growled at every sound that came through thin spots on the tunnel's roof, and even at the kits when they jostled her as they nursed.

Next day the tent on the lake shore had vanished, along with the people using it, but a few days later another appeared, and again Proo found herself sharing the lake with people – a condition that made her nervous – and her discipline of the carefree kits became stricter.

She was restless, and one morning during a rainstorm she led the kits down into the river. This time, she did not turn back at the first falls, but continued downstream for several miles until the river emptied into Waterton lakes.

The tourist season was at its height and there seemed to be people everywhere; the noise of power boats, large and small, assailed her ears during daylight hours, prompting her to hide with her family in any kind of available cover. At night, it was comparatively peaceful, a time for her to catch fish as she explored. The creeks coming down the steep mountain flanks into the main body of water were short, swift, and small, for the most part offering no attraction. For a couple of days she explored a larger creek, fishing at its mouth and living in a log jam upstream near a waterfall, but even here, it was a constant worry, for people came and went along a trail close to the water.

At last, in the dark of night, her restlessness drove her to lead her family along the west shore of the main lake until she suddenly found herself on the edge of a well-lit town. Here the air was full of even more noise and strange smells, so she retreated back along the beach for a ways and then struck out, swimming across the lake to the far side. She followed this shoreline, but before she had gone very far, it began to pinch in closer and closer to the town, where the shore was rocky and offered no cover, so she pointed her nose inland, climbing along the side of a rocky ridge.

Now, for the first time in her life, she was being driven hard in her search for cover – any kind of cover. As dawn paled the eastern sky, she came to the edge of a little marshy slough trapped among scrub aspens in a fold of the slope. Among some small trees she found a hide. After nursing the kits, she went foraging in the shallow water, but apart from a few frogs and snails, the place was barren.

That night she was on the move again, leading the kits up onto a height of land that jutted from the base of a mountain looming dark and high against the stars. An updraft of wind brought the welcome smell of much water to her nose, and she speeded up her descent toward it, with the kits in close formation at her heels. As they were crossing a bare rock rib in the starlight, the last young otter in the line was lagging a bit. Suddenly, on silent wings, a great horned owl dropped from the top of a snag to strike. The big bird would have been successful if its intended victim had not taken that moment to close the gap ahead of it. The owl found itself looking at what appeared to be a much bigger target, and checked itself momentarily, the flash of its wings alerting Proo. Instantly she presented the owl with a snarling target – open-jawed and formidable, with teeth bared – turning it away to find something easier to kill.

The scent of water turned out to be a lake along the base of a low, broken cliff, and Proo immediately went fishing, but with no success, for here the water dropped sheer away to great, gloomy depths. After a couple of fruitless dives, she continued down the lake shore at a steady pace. Dawn was just breaking when she led her family into the top of a river.

At the first big pool below the lake, she dived and found it teeming with fish. She quickly killed a heavy whitefish, which was torn apart and eaten ravenously. Then they all rolled and scrubbed themselves on the damp shingle of fine gravel and sand, before setting out again downriver. As they passed through some grass on the edge of a stagnant back-water pool, Proo came on a garter snake. Hardly breaking her stride, she grabbed it by the head, killed it with one crunch, then, trailing its body to one side like a bit of rope, proceeded to eat it by jerking it into her mouth in munching gulps accompanied by gusty growls as the kits took turns trying to fasten on to the trailing end. They got no part of this delicacy, and shortly the still-wiggling tail disappeared down her throat.

A quarter-mile below, they were under a giant old ruin of a cottonwood. It had once been forked twenty feet from the ground, but a windstorm had broken off one fork, leaving a splintered blaze on the trunk. A hole showed in the scar. The tree was still alive, with the top of the remaining portion covered with green leaves. At its base it looked like any other big cottonwood, but between the forking bosses of two heavy roots, among a tangle of greenery, Proo poked her nose into a hole. She slid into it, and found herself in a perfect hide inside the hollow trunk, with a little patch of blue sky showing through the scar high overhead.

But the day had scarcely started when she became aware of people, for this stretch of the river was a favourite place for fishermen. Proo had no way of knowing that they posed no threat inside the park. Her experience with the dog had left its imprint, so she remained in a constant state of nervousness all day, hearing voices, sniffing the alien smell of humans, and aware of the crunching vibrations of footsteps.

As soon as it was dark, she returned to the river with her family, continuing her search for a haven of peace and quiet, a quest that had taken on an aura of urgency. Her way was tortuous, following the shore of the stream and two adjoining lakes, although it did not take them far across the country. During the second night after she had entered this river, she came to a muddy-bottomed creek flowing from the south into one of the lakes, and followed it up through a heavy growth of willows and aspens to where a big beaver dam blocked the stream. This dam was the first of many built like a series of steps, each one with a pond above it.

Some were old construction surrounded by bleached stumps and snags amidst tangles of deadfall, the ponds dotted with water-killed trees, still standing, bleached out by weather, white as bone. In the newer ones some of the trees were still green. It was a wilderness of water, tangled timber, and brush engineered with incredible ingenuity to stop water from running downhill. There was no obvious pattern to the dams and ponds, yet it was effective, for the stream was under almost complete control. No flood could wash out this marvellous series of mud-and-stick constructions; high water merely widened the ponds, spreading them out into the surrounding timber, to search out hollows and lie there till the excess water slowly drained off.

It was a beaver city laced with a network of canals, underground tunnels, and dams, with ponds surrounding the domes of their houses. The ponds teemed with life: fish, mainly suckers; wild ducks, geese, and other wildfowl which used the acres of water and the diversity of ideal cover; mink and muskrats which had joined the beaver hosts. The warm water was full of vegetation that supported masses of aquatic insect larvae and crustaceans, all part of an intricate and abundant food chain. The trees and brush along the perimeters were alive with birds, large and small, from eagles to hummingbirds. For Proo and her family it was like discovering heaven.

The otters' arrival made hardly a ripple on the surface of this complex life system of water and forest, yet they wrote a paragraph of history, for no other otters had made tracks along this stream for more than half a century.

Almost instantly, Proo's brood became avid fishermen. When they came up over the top of the first dam at dawn and dived into the pond, they found themselves in the middle of a school of suckers darting hither and yon like a cloud of blunt-nosed projectiles. Proo immediately fastened her teeth in one, swam back to the dam and proceeded to eat; but her kits excitedly milled around as though unable to believe what they were seeing. They dived again and again, and although they were anything but skilful, there was no way they could miss. In a short while, all five otters were lined up along the top of the dam, busily chewing on their catches, the kits occasionally declaring their territorial rights by glaring at each other and growling fiercely in comical threats. As they finished their fish, they dived back to catch more, eating till they bulged, and then catching even more for the sheer excitement of it. Proo sat hunched in the warmth of the rising sun, grooming herself, and one by one the kits left their sport to join her.

Again she led the way upstream over one dam after another, cruising among flooded trees, exploring. There were a thousand hides to choose from here: leafy bowers deep with shade, caverns under tangled logs, and various holes and hollows under over-hanging banks. It was a jungle – green and intertwined with lush growth – where the otters blended and lost themselves in the tangled wilderness of water and timber. The maze of beaver waterways offered a host of diversions for the curious otters, to say nothing of an abundance of feed. Here they could move freely without encountering humans, for although this place was within a few miles of busy highways leading into the park, no people ventured into this tangle in the middle of a trackless aspen forest. It was truly wild, but not always so quiet.

One evening, on the tail of an oppressively hot, close after-noon, Proo and her family emerged from under some tall leafy cow cabbage plants to play and dive among some half-submerged logs. A great towering cloud rolled in over the western mountains, its undulating rim looking as white and hard as carved ivory, backlit by the sun it had blotted out. It was moving fast, and the deepening gloom was suddenly torn by jagged shafts of lightning. Thunder rolled like giant drums, shattering the quiet, echoing and banging off the mountain slopes.

A splattering of raindrops dotted the surface of the pond where the otters played. The steady undertone of a rushing roar that accompanied the storm rose to a sudden climax as hailstones suddenly descended with a thunderous pelting that drowned out all but the loudest blasts of thunder.

Proo immediately led her family in search of shelter, the arrival of the hail giving her little time for choice. Some of the stones were as big as duck eggs, and most were over half an inch in diameter, so the danger of injury to the kits was very real. Although she had never experienced anything like this, she sensed the peril and took the first shelter she found. It was a wedge-shaped cavity under the rotten butt of a big dead log lying on the bank.

She led the way into it in a rush, followed closely by the kits, each one crowding up and overlapping the one in front till the whole family was stuffed into the hole – all except the rump and tail of the last one in line. This shelter, which would easily have held all five otters a month before, could now contain only four and a half. The protruding one got a big hailstone squarely on the root of its tail, which made it squeal and claw its way desperately ahead to dislodge the otter in front of it. It in turn clawed its way forward to dislodge another, which in turn found its rear exposed, and in short order the process was repeated. So it was only a matter of time before Proo found herself at the rear of her brood with her hindquarters exposed to the elements. She growled and grumbled about it, but endured.

The hailstorm ended as quickly as it had begun, revealing the pond grey with floating ice, the trees half denuded of their leaves, and the ground herbage pounded flat. The surface of the earth was white with a four-inch coating of hailstones. The otters took to the water again, unmindful of its sudden chill, to swim upstream.

Here and there dead ducks floated on the surface; it was their moulting season, so the storm had caught them without the usual protection of thick plumage. A bull moose lay inert, half submerged in the water, killed by lightning as he had waded across looking for shelter. A crippled red-tailed hawk clung to its perch on a branch on a cottonwood, a drooping wing proclaiming a broken bone that condemned it to a slow death. A great horned owl shook itself, trying to dry its bedraggled feathers, squeaking querulously as it looked down from a more sheltered perch on another big tree. The storm had been cruel to the wild ones. Only the beavers, muskrats, mink, and otters escaped unscathed in the corridor cut by the hail, and as darkness came down these were out swimming and feeding as always.

Through late summer and early fall, the otter family, the only ones of their kind living there, revelled in the wild abundance of the valley hidden away among the forested hills. But one morning, as they played on a slide over the water sluiceway of a big dam, Proo discovered the scent of another otter. She was instantly alert and watchful, as if the scent stirred old memories. Suddenly she saw the head and neck of a big otter thrust up out of the water of the pond below, as it watched the kits tobogganing down the slide. With a fluid motion, quick as a flicker of light, Proo launched herself in a long splash to go streaking out toward the visitor. Surfacing, she lifted her head and forequarters high to look, just as the other otter did the same, and they hissed at each other as they began to circle.

It was Kim, recently arrived over a height of land separating this creek from another, a tributary of the Belly River, where he had spent the summer. After some preliminary skirmishing and introduction, both otters began to play – a beautiful, powerfully smooth water ballet, trading the roles of pursuer and pursued, ecstatic after a long separation.

But there were limits to Proo's permissiveness with Kim, for she would not allow him to approach the kits too closely. They, in turn, were shy, never having known another adult otter but their mother. However, otters are naturally very sociable animals, and a kind of loose family association developed between Kim, Proo, and the kits. While he obviously welcomed the fraternization with his own kind, he was much more restless than they were, often disappearing for days on some trip beyond the drainage of the creek.

By winter the young otters were almost totally self-sufficient, pursuing their own prey, but still maintaining their close ties with their mother, following at her heels wherever she went.

Except where the ponds were kept open by big springs or fast water, the ice and snow that covered them was marked by the distinctive trails of the otters. This was not like the deep snow country of their birth; it was much more subject to strong, warm chinook winds blowing from the mountains. Cold spells and snowstorms were interspersed with periods of wild wind that stirred up ground blizzards so thick that the air seemed to be a moving river of the white stuff in unsheltered places. Tracks would be wiped out within minutes, then a new fall would offer a clean page on which all the animals could write the stories of their passing – repetitious, yet often dramatic in detail.

The otters fed mainly on fish, sometimes eating their catches in caverns under the ice caused by a lowering of the water level, but more often sitting on the ice by an open hole. For the most part their scats glistened with fish scales; occasionally they showed fur from muskrats; and sometimes they were green with vegetation picked up as they foraged among underwater aquatic gardens for the swarms of fresh-water shrimp found there.

Late one evening in February, as a three-quarter moon flashed periodically through fast-drifting clouds, Proo led the way down the creek and past the lowest dam for the first time since the otters had arrived in the valley. When she reached the broad expanse of frozen lake at the creek, she led the way out across the wind-polished ice. Here the young otters revelled, at first in a thoroughly disorganized mix-up of rolling and sliding, but then following her lead in a rhythmic pattern of two loping jumps and a long slide.

In their usual close-coupled line they went in step, a routine that carried them rapidly across the slippery surface.

Proo led them thus across the lake to the spot where the river flowed out of it, and there they plunged into an open hole at the top of a swift riffle, and, taking advantage of air pockets under the ice to breathe, they continued on downstream. The fast water of a rapids was exciting but not the least frightening, for the otters were in their element, ecstatic with the exhilaration of the buffeting water adding to their speed.

They came to the mouth of a creek that ran down a little valley from the north and into the river, and Proo pointed her nose up it. This slowed down their travelling some, though they continued at a steady pace, sometimes on top of the ice and sometimes under it.

Late the next afternoon I found otter tracks far from the haven of the park, in the midst of a wilderness of beaver dams built below a series of big artesian springs – the headwaters of the creek. As I stood among some willows, examining the unusual trail on a skiff of new snow covering the ice over a frozen channel, a flicker of movement on top of a spillway on a dam a few yards upstream caught my eye. Five otters appeared and slid down the half-frozen chute to disappear under the ice. About a minute later, they appeared again on top of the dam below, obviously heading down the creek.

The lives of all animals are fraught with risk from the moment they are born, regardless of where they live, but when furbearers like otters leave the shelter of a national park to come into a settled area, they are exposed to far greater dangers. For otters have a bounty on them: not a price on their heads, but on the rich coats they wear. Even though otters are extremely rare, they enjoyed no protection in regulation – perhaps because they were thought to be non-existent in this region. As I stood looking after them, I wondered what their fate would be, for there were trappers working this part of the country.

Perhaps it was pure luck, maybe it was because their visits to the various creeks were so irregular, or possibly they spent most of their time in the park, but somehow they missed getting into trouble that year.

One spring morning, after the ice had gone out and the creek was boiling with melt-water, I stood on the edge of a bank behind a fringe of willows and looked down into a swirling pool flecked with foam and bubbles eddying in the current. The otter family was playing there with a chunk of old dry horse manure one of them had apparently rolled down from the bank. It floated as buoyantly as a cork, and they were taking turns swimming under it and flipping it into the air, pushing it under and passing it back and forth like players in a game of water polo. It was a fascinating and very rare opportunity to observe an exhibition of otters' innate love of play, an inborn characteristic which sometimes leads them to astonishing innovations. As they are very shy, lovers of seclusion, and tremendous travellers fond of heavy cover, their games are not often witnessed except in the tracks they leave. My privilege was something to cherish, and I watched till their improvised ball got so wet it disintegrated, and the otters disappeared, still unaware of their audience.

Several times that summer, while fishing for trout along the creeks and the river both in and out of the park, I found their tracks. Because they were still travelling as a family unit, their trail was easy to see. Only the male travelled alone, though on occasion he joined them.

By fall, the young otters were almost fully grown, and every time I saw their sign I wondered again what was in store for them. What fate would be their lot as they led this idyllic life along the waterways at the foot of the Rockies? As it turned out, there was to be a drastic change.

When winter came again, the moccasin telegraph carried the news of a trapper getting a big otter in one of his sets. His friends came from all around to see this marvellous pelt, all of five feet long from the nose to the tip of the tail. He kept it hung in a conspicuous place in a lean-to adjoining his cabin, where he often stood to gaze at it in admiration.

He was something of a romantic, and was heard to say as he showed it to a friend, "There you hang, all glistenin' and gleamin'! You'll look mighty handsome hung around some fine lady's shoulders."

His first success prompted further efforts, and Proo's family fell victim to his artfully set traps, one by one. It is unlikely she experienced grief, only a sense of loss and loneliness, but for certain she developed cunning where traps were concerned. When greening-up time came again and her fur was sunburnt and worthless, I found her tracks once more, where I had first encountered them the year before, along the upper reaches of the creek outside the park. It was a fleeting contact I would not often experience again.

All that following summer and fall I watched for her tracks, but her sign was scarce, appearing at long intervals over a very wide area.

Now there was little sign of play along her trails, for her life seemed to be an endless, restless searching for another of her kind. Near the end of the tourist season, the captain of the big launch that plied the upper Waterton saw an otter on a driftwood log on shore near the mouth of the Kootenay River. It was likely Proo retracing her old trail back up to Kootenay lakes.

Where did she go? Who knows? No sign of any otter has ever been reported again along the foot of the mountains. Perhaps when the larches were turning gold once more she retraced her old trail back up over the pass across the spine of the Rockies and down into the country where she was born. Maybe there she was joined by another otter to mate again and raise other families along the wild upper reaches of the Flathead River.

She did not know it, but she had contributed something very special to my life. Sometimes I recall with nostalgia those months of reading track stories in snow and silty mud, and I cannot help wondering what became of her.

Much-Maligned Wolverine

N ot long ago, in the mountains of Oregon, a hunter killed a wolverine, an animal long thought to be extinct in that state. No doubt the hunter did not realize he was shooting an animal that had not been seen in Oregon for fifty-four years. He may not even have known what sort of creature it was. At any rate, the wolverine was killed, which was unfortunate; and then the misfortune was compounded by publicity across the continent.

The usual highly misleading and untrue remarks about wolverine character were published in newspaper stories and broadcast by radio and television. A report in a trade publication is typical: "Capable of terrorizing and ravaging every other animal," the article stated, "its plundering tactics make it dreaded even by burly woodsmen. . . . This fellow apparently fears nothing. Without hesitation it attacks with a bloody-lusty viciousness that usually is a fight to the death. . . . Incapable of significant speed," the article continued, "it relies on the kills of other animals, whom [it] drives away – even the bear and mountain lion will relinquish prey to

From *Field and Stream* (November 1966)

[it]. The wolverine will stalk hunters and trappers, lurking in the background to rob supplies and traps. And if this is not enough, it will ruin everything in sight with an extremely foul-smelling fluid that is discharged from the anal glands. Truly a most obnoxious creature."

All other reports of the incident followed similar lines of nonsense and fractured fact, the same sort of unjust maligning the wolverine has been subjected to for decades. It's time the record was set straight.

The wolverine *can* be very cunning, but this attribute is usually developed to its keenest edge by association with men. In the days when I was a professional trapper, wolverine stories were rampant wherever trappers met. To hear their tales, one would be inclined to suppose this animal was the devil in clever disguise. There was good reason for the exaggeration.

Wolverine country is wild country, where the trapper makes his sets for the valuable furs of mink, marten, fisher, fox, and ermine. These small traps are set out in lines for miles, each baited with a piece of bloody rabbit flesh or an attractive scent lure. The trapper makes his rounds as often as possible to pick up the trapped animals, and reset the traps with fresh bait. The wolverine, being just an overgrown weasel with a predominant curiosity and a great appetite for meat, does not take long to become aware of the trapper's activities. He is normally acutely shy, but as time passes this begins to wear thin. In due course, the wolverine starts following dogsled or snowshoe trails, leaving tracks for the trapper to see on his next round.

Naturally, the wolverine is attracted by the baits. Just as surely as he tries to take them, he proceeds to get his nose or paws pinched in traps too small to cause him anything but momentary surprise and discomfort. Very soon, being highly intelligent, he learns to avoid the traps in getting the baits, and before very much longer he is also stealing furbearers from the traps.

This development can be a financial disaster for the trapper, unless he succeeds in trapping the wolverine – no easy task at this point. Wolverine, being great travellers, can cover a lot of trapline in a single night, caching what meat isn't eaten at once. Trappers tend to think of the wolverine as almost supernatural, and as a result many of them approach the task of getting rid of one with so little self-confidence that they are clumsy and crude in their attempts. Each marauding wolverine, having come to know a good deal of the man with whom he is associated, must in turn be studied as an individual, and destroyed by discovery of some weakness in his make-up. Very few trappers have this sort of guile.

I knew one man who was run completely off a lucrative trapline in the Alberta Rockies by a persistent and highly developed wolverine. I knew another trapper over among the mountains rimming the Okanagan Valley in British Columbia who found four of these animals visiting his trapline one winter. He was intrigued by the challenge, and methodically set about trapping them, one by one. The fourth proved to be the hardest of all to catch, but he finally managed to trap her – a very handsome female. By this time the trapper was coming to know and admire wolverine, so much so that he hated to kill her; he proceeded to muzzle her, tie her feet, put her in a packsack, and snowshoe out to civilization with her on his back. He then built a stout cage of welded steel and shipped her to the Stanley Park Zoo in Vancouver, where, as far as I know, she still lives.

Most trappers never realize that they themselves are largely responsible for the development and cultivation of the real master thieves among wolverines. All across the wilds of western and northern Canada are cabins built by trappers and prospectors. Nearly always such a cabin has a grub cache built nearby, where supplies, fresh meat, and furs can be placed out of reach of husky dogs, bears, and wolverines.

Such a cache usually is built in four trees growing close together in the form of a natural square. A small log cabin is constructed on sills, fastened to these trees — a kind of tree house far enough from the ground to be out of reach of dogs and the tallest grizzly. However, wolverine and black bear are agile climbers, and to foil them, smooth tin is nailed around the trunk of each tree a few feet from the ground to keep the animals' claws from getting a purchase. To further discourage the acrobatic and enterprising wolverine, some cache builders nail several dozen large fishhooks, barb up, just above the tin. Occasionally porcupine skins are used instead of the hooks. In spite of all such precautions, however, the wolverine sometimes finds a way to circumvent the hazards.

Every once in a while, a wolverine breaks into a trapper's or prospector's cabin. The resulting uproar and destruction are sufficient to make a strong man weep and do nothing whatever to enhance the wolverine's reputation.

Here again, curiosity, prodded perhaps by the smell of meat or skins carelessly cached in the cabin, is the most likely factor starting the animal toward a life of crime. After considerable preliminary reconnaissance, the wolverine finally grows bold enough to gain entrance by tearing a hole in the roof, digging under a wall, or climbing down the chimney or through a broken window.

Once inside, the animal suddenly finds himself beset by a flood of strange smells and surrounded by four walls. In such claustrophobic surroundings, he may suffer a momentary panic, whereupon things begin to happen. Ordinarily, the scent carried in the pouches of the anal glands is used sparingly as a calling card, a boundary marker establishing territorial claims, or identification in breeding season; but when excited, angry, or frightened to a high degree, the wolverine's muscular control is spasmodic, and the scent is discharged copiously all over the place. A little bit of wolverine scent is not too bad, but in large doses it is awful, although not nearly so blinding or lasting as the essence dispensed by his near cousin, the common skunk. Just the same, a cabin broken into by a wolverine can be unfit for human occupation for a while – depending, of course, on the sensitivity of the nose involved or how cold it is outside.

We humans are poor losers. When a wolverine proceeds to make us look like fools, we are inclined to patch up our bruised egos either by stretching a point here and there or by telling outright lies. If we tell them long enough, we start to believe them ourselves and they become more or less established as fact. So the wolverine has acquired a reputation as the scourge of the wilds, terrorizing and ravaging other forms of life – dreaded even by burly woodsmen.

Now, I've known burly-looking woodsmen who would sleep on a pile of sharp rocks before they'd consent to camp near a grave. Many are highly superstitious, which is good reason to question some of the things they have to say about wolverine. Consider the supposed mean and ferocious characteristics of this animal. Such terminology is relative to the user. There is nothing ignoble about the wolverine. True, he is a killer, but he has no patents on this characteristic. He is a thief by the standards of men, but unless conditioned to thievery by association with mankind, he is normally very shy. Certainly no wolverine has been known to make a full-time living exploiting his own species. He is a magnificent fighter with a high courage. Cornered, he will undoubtedly jump a man or even a mighty grizzly; but given any kind of chance, he will retreat, for wolverines are far from being fools.

He has been known to go through an entire team of huskies like a runaway meat grinder, leaving it a bloody, ragged shambles; but the dogs declared war first. Like his cousin the dirt-digging badger, he can fight well anywhere, but he's twice as good at the bottom of the pile and does not pause to give much thought to odds. He is a superb warrior that always follows the rules of nature in his battling. Man could take some lessons from him.

Known to science as *Gulo luscus* and to trappers as carcajou, the wolverine is one of nature's most mysterious and interesting animals. A close counterpart of the North American species is found in Norway, Sweden, Finland, and Russia. One Swedish naturalist kept several wolverine as pets, finding them clean, intelligent, and entertaining – a sharp contrast to the picture ordinarily painted here.

The wolverine is often found in zoos and zoological gardens, but he has never adapted sufficiently to captivity to reproduce under artificial conditions. Al Oeming, western Canada's famous owner and operator of a zoological garden, has kept several pairs in spacious enclosures for years, but so far none has reproduced.

Oeming is a great admirer of the wolverine, and he scoffs at talk of their savagery. He even feeds his captives from his bare hands. I have seen him stand with a forty-five-pound male wolverine reared against his thigh while it takes a piece of raw meat from his hand. This was a fully mature animal that had been trapped in the wilds only a few months previously.

The jaws and teeth of the wolverine are formidable, capable of crushing bone and tearing the toughest flesh. His heavy claw-armed paws can also be used with devastating effect. He is low-slung, with heavily muscled shoulders, loin, and haunches, making him look squat and somewhat ungainly. The fur, a deep brown colour with an orange-shaded stripe like an elongated horseshoe lying along the back, is heavy, glowing with a rich sheen. This pelage is a great insulator, resistant to collecting frost, and Inuit and northern Indians use it to trim their parka hoods.

Mature wolverine will weigh from twenty-five to nearly fifty pounds, and relative to their gross weight they are prodigiously strong, as are all the weasel species.

My son Charlie once saw a tiny short-tailed bush weasel catch and kill a cottontail rabbit. The little animal found himself in an undesirably exposed condition with his kill, so he grasped the rabbit by the side of the head with his teeth, got under the carcass, and slid it along the crusted snow surface to a little overhanging cornice of a drift, where it was soon hidden. Such a weasel would not weigh more than three or four ounces. His prey outweighed him many times.

Relatively speaking, a wolverine is probably just as strong. I once saw where a big wolverine had hijacked a quarter of venison weighing about forty pounds. The fresh snow on the ground told how the freebooter had climbed the tree to get the meat down. It was an awkward load for such a low-slung animal to handle, but the wolverine grasped it by one end with his teeth, apparently slid the load over his back until perfectly balanced, and then walked away with it down over a rough rock slide. I followed for a quarter of a mile down the steep-pitched slope. What amazed me most was the lack of any sign of dragging. In only one or two places had the meat made a mark on the snow. I trailed this wolverine down past timberline for another quarter of a mile until the tracks were lost on bare ground. The meat was never recovered.

Upon claiming a kill made by another animal, the wolverine drops a little scent. It has often been said that a grizzly or a cougar will relinquish the kill when he smells this; but there is good reason to question such a folk tale.

I once saw a wolverine feeding on the carcass of a big buck mule deer that had slipped on an icy trail and fallen off a cliff in the mountains. That night a grizzly claimed the dead deer and, after feeding from it, buried the remainder under a great heap of loose rock and debris. Next morning, my two eldest sons and I saw and filmed the wolverine returning to the carcass. We watched him dig out a piece of venison and carry it to a small stream where the meat was washed free of dirt and fly blows before it was eaten. Along with this interesting and new discovery of wolverine fastidiousness we observed that the grizzly came back again that night for another feed. As far as we could tell, both animals continued to feed on the carcass in turns till it was consumed.

Some years later my sons and I observed a wolverine near a horse carcass being fed upon in turns by eight grizzlies. Although we could not see this wolverine feeding on the dead horse because of low intervening brush, there was no doubt he was slipping in for a snack when the chance was afforded. Just as obviously, the grizzlies could not have cared less – so long as they didn't catch him at it.

In both of these instances the wolverine concerned was extremely careful and very nervous at the proximity of grizzlies, and took no chances on being surprised.

Another time, my son John found a place where a cougar had killed a cow elk on the frozen surface of a small stream in mid-winter. A wolverine had found this kill too and had been feeding from it when the cougar returned. The big cat jumped the intruder from the bank of the creek. The ensuing fight was short, though the wolverine was a large one. John picked up the body, which was undamaged except for two tooth punctures on each side of the head. The skull was crushed. The cougar had made no attempt to eat the meat for, like most flesh-eaters, she would have to be starved into eating weasel. John trailed the cougar in the deep snow and eventually succeeded in treeing her – a fairly large female showing no marks of the fight. We still have the skin and skull of the wolverine.

The wolverine is a most specialized predator and also a part-time scavenger that ranges widely over his territory. He readily takes advantage of any lucky windfalls, such as the remains of kills made by hunters or those of cougar and wolves. But when conditions are right, he readily kills animals much larger than himself, such as young caribou and even full-grown deer and mountain sheep. Because he is not a particularly fleet animal, he must have deep, crusted snow or the opportunity for a close stalk. His living largely depends on small game – birds, mice, and rabbits. Such game is easier to catch and kill. Like all animals, including man, the wolverine works no harder for a living than necessary.

I was once sitting on the rimrock of a mountain ridge overlooking a steep-sided cirque, where a little lake lay cradled among alpine meadows. Just under me, on a green bench, several cow elk were lying contentedly chewing their cuds, with their calves sprawled around them among the flowers in the sun. One old dry cow, the likely leader of the bunch, threw up her head to gaze intently down across the lake at something. My glasses followed in the direction her nose was pointed, and I saw what looked like a small black bear moving among a screen of brush and dead logs. But when the animal came into sight on an open meadow I realized he was a large, handsome wolverine.

For perhaps twenty minutes I watched him industriously investigating every log, bush, and tuft of grass on the clearing. Once I would have sworn he was hunting frogs in a marshy spot by the lake. Later I saw him dig furiously under the butt of a fallen log. Later investigation showed the wreckage of a mouse nest. Although fresh elk sign littered the place, and their smell was noticeable even to my nose, the wolverine showed not the slightest interest. Although he would not hesitate to kill a young calf if the opportunity arose, the highly possible prospect of six hundred pounds of angry mother descending on piledriver hoofs was not to be taken lightly. A wolverine does not get to be this big and old by being so brash.

Like all the weasel clan, the wolverine has a temper like a buzz saw, and when his blood is up he can be completely blind to pain and consequence. These animals have been known to tangle with phlegmatic porcupine and, upon being stung, to fly into a blind rage, scattering porcupine in all directions, but dying themselves from an overdose of quills as a result.

How old they get, how often they breed, and many other facts of their lives are largely unknown. No man has been privileged to observe numbers of them in the wilds, no matter how many years he has spent wandering wilderness country. My sons Dick and Charlie and I spent most of two summers travelling through the rugged mountains of central Alaska in the region of Mount McKinley making a study of grizzlies and their associated species. This is reputed to be amongst the finest wolverine range in the world, yet we saw not a single one there in that time. And because the big weasel does not prosper in captivity, many of the secrets of his way of life will probably remain hidden for a long time.

From what little I have seen of this animal, I admire him very much. He is truly beautiful — a very specialized product of his environment, fashioned by evolution to live well in the austere and often forbidding climate of his range. His strength is phenomenal, his ways not unattractive, and he is among the most active and acrobatic of animals. To suggest that he is so stupid that he will attack anything at any time is laughable, for he is highly intelligent. To describe him as obnoxious is complete ignorance. The wolverine has been maligned too long.

Can Animals Think?

S howing clear and sharp against a background of craggy, snow-covered peaks, the big bull elk made a fine picture in the field of my binoculars as he lay bedded deep in the snow on the slope of an alpine meadow at timberline. Although the sun was shining, it was a snappy ten below. Hunkered down in the lee of a wind-blown pine, I watched through my glasses, shivering in the biting wind. Up on the meadow, a thousand yards away, the big bull seemed comfortable enough, well insulated by his heavy coat of hollow hair.

Through my twelve-power Zeiss glasses, I could see every detail as he lay peacefully chewing his cud. When he tipped his head a little, all twelve points of his mighty antlers were cleanly outlined against the white slope.

After half an hour had passed, he stood up in his bed, looking down over the country below as though trying to decide where he would go for his afternoon feed. Apparently he saw nothing more attractive than the meadow where he stood, for, stepping

From *Natural History* (December 1946)

out of his bed, he began pawing down through fourteen inches of snow for the tasty bunch grass beneath.

After watching him feed for fifty yards along the meadow, I caught a flash of movement on the edge of a stunted clump of balsams two hundred yards farther up the mountain beyond. A second later a big grey coyote stepped into view. After looking down the slope for a minute at the elk, the brush wolf trotted down into the meadow in a business-like way. There he poked through the tufts of grass sticking up out of the elk's tracks, looking for mice. Although I watched him carefully, I did not see him catch a mouse. Slowly he investigated each of the pawed-out places, until he came up within a few yards of the bull's rear. There he stood for a few moments sizing up the situation. Obviously his technique was wrong. Apparently deciding to change his tactics, he trotted casually around the bull, until he was directly in front of the big animal. Stopping again, he looked up into the elk's face from a range of only a few feet.

If the old bull saw him, he did not show it. To say he ignored the saucy coyote would be an understatement. He was the royal rajah suddenly confronted by one of the untouchables. He didn't look at the little wolf – he looked right through him, and went on feeding as though he didn't exist. As for the coyote, he seemed to think this lack of recognition was just what he wanted. After a moment or two of close study, he dodged around to one side of the bull and stood practically in his shadow. The elk still ignored him, so he moved even closer. Then, as the bull lifted a forefoot to paw away the snow from the grass, the coyote stood poised to pounce on any mouse that might be kicked out of his cover. Almost unable to believe what I saw, I watched that smart little wolf use the proud old bull for a sort of unsuspecting mouse digger for the better part of half an hour. Several times I saw him duck right under the elk's belly and snatch a mouse from under his feet. Finally, the old bull lay down again, and the coyote went happily on his way, much benefited by the use of his smart, well-developed brain.

There are people who explain the many curious actions of animals by the use of one word – instinct. To my way of thinking, the word instinct covers a very small part of animal behaviour. Anyone who doubts this need only go afield with a pair of good binoculars and all the patience he has. To see wild game meet the everyday emergencies of their lives and solve the ever-changing problems of their existence is the surest way to be convinced that animals use more than instinct to stay alive.

Different species of animals have highly developed senses to suit their particular needs. Some have sharp eyesight, others depend upon their ears, while a keen nose is the outstanding organ of protection used by many. The Indian has a way of explaining this.

He says, "A needle fell from the pine in the forest. The bear smelled it as it fell. The deer heard it. The eagle saw it fall."

In the Rockies of the far West we could exchange the mountain sheep for the eagle in that quotation, for the sheep has marvellously keen eyes.

In addition to highly developed organs of sound, sight, and smell, or combinations of the three, most animals have a well-developed brain. Furthermore, they can use that brain to good advantage.

A number of years ago, a small colony of beaver established itself on our ranch. At first there was only one pair in a small dam on the headwaters of the creek that wanders down through a muskeg before coming out on some flats, where our hay meadows are located. Under careful protection, the beavers increased and spread out, until their dams were actually flooding a good part of our meadows. Then they energetically began to build a dam that threatened to flood a bridge crossing the creek, and we began to realize that something would have to be done.

Optimistically we pulled out the offending dam in hope of scaring the beavers into another part of the creek. It wasn't as easy as that, for in a couple of days the dam was as good as ever. Then began a contest to see who was the most stubborn. Every night after work we pulled out the dam. Every morning it would be as good as new. We tried scarecrows. They worked for one night. The next night the beavers ignored them, and built up the dam. It soon became quite plain we weren't getting anywhere, for the beavers got so tame that they often swam down to repair the breach, while we were in the act of making it. In spite of our failure, it was amusing to see a big beaver come paddling downstream with a huge moustache of weeds and mud sticking up from his face. If we were too close, he would slap the water indignantly with his broad tail and dive. But just as soon as we retreated a little, the dam would be once more under repair.

Finally, when we were about ready to give up, our hired man had a brilliant idea. Taking a few old boards and nails he fashioned a water wheel with bright tin cans for paddles. Then tearing out the dam, he placed the wheel on uprights so that it would turn in the strong current. Then with an added touch of genius, he hung a huge cowbell on an overhanging limb so that the paddles of the water wheel would clatter on it as it revolved. We all rubbed our hands together with satisfaction. At last we had those persistent animals beaten.

The morning after the wheel was installed, everything was as it should be. The creek gushed through the breach in the dam merrily turning the wheel, which made an ungodly racket on the bell. We had visions of beavers scrambling madly upstream to get away from that devilish contraption down by the bridge. The second morning we investigated to find a surprising sight, which caused the hired man to swear mightily, and made us realize we were dealing with some very smart animals.

Although none of us was there to see what happened in the night, the signs were plain to read. Sometime in the night a big beaver had come out on the bank upstream to think over this new threat to the peace and well-being of his colony. A few feet farther up the bank a six-foot chunk of half-dry, peeled poplar pole lay where it had been discarded the season before. The beaver went up to it, and in less time than it takes to tell it, rolled it over and pushed it down into the water. There the current picked it up and carried it downstream. In a few minutes it floated into the breach of the dam, jamming the wheel solidly, and like magic the silence of the night was restored. In a matter of minutes the whole colony was at work repairing the dam. When we arrived next morning the pond was brimming full again and, to add insult to injury, the cheeky beavers had used the water wheel for reinforcement.

Today, we don't use that bridge any more. It is under about two feet of water. At the moment we have about 150 beaver dams on the ranch. As a matter of fact, there is some doubt as to who owns the ranch – we or the beavers.

To most of us the skunk is just a smallish black animal with white marks on his back, a touchy disposition, and armed with a gun that is always "loaded for bear," or anything else that threatens him. We don't particularly dislike him. We respect him. When we do think of him at all, it is with our noses wrinkled, and our thoughts may wander to prominent newspaper advertisements featuring pink soap. When threatened, he has the habit of "shooting first and asking questions afterwards," but aside from that we don't give him a great deal of credit for having much sense.

One fine April morning three years ago I had reason to revise my opinion. I was out riding, looking for strayed horses, when I spotted a skunk feeding out in the middle of a hundred-acre flat. He wasn't much out of my way, so I rode over for a closer look. When I was still well out of range of his scent gun, he suddenly saw me and flagged his tail up in warning. Keeping at a discreet distance I stopped my horse, waiting to see what he would do. After a few minutes' hesitation he decided to move, making off at a shambling gallop for the nearest timber, a quarter of a mile away. Keeping back at a safe distance I followed. Then I rode off to one side trying to turn him away from the trees. To my surprise he responded perfectly, heading away at a new angle and apparently satisfied just to travel. After a little more experimenting I discovered I could drive him anywhere. If I had had a bucket, I am sure I could have corralled him in it. Just for fun I decided to try to drive him home – a distance of two miles.

Heading him across the big flat, I chased him toward a chain of meadows leading to the buildings. He drove better than most domestic animals, and we made good time for the first half-mile. But he was short-winded, and his gallop soon fell off to a shuffle. Then, while crossing from one meadow to another through a narrow strip of brush, he came close to a willow brush, and, seeing his chance, dove into it.

Stopping my horse, I cautiously approached him on foot from the windward side. I had given up all hope of getting him home, but was curious to see what he would do if I stayed awhile. When he showed signs of uneasiness, I squatted on my heels and just watched. Facing me, he stamped his front feet threateningly a few times at first, but after a few minutes he settled down, and began to dig and eat the fresh green shoots of new grass growing at the base of the willow. Cautiously I moved closer. Several times he lifted his head, giving me a long look, and I could almost see the mental cogwheels turning through those bright black eyes. After considerable thought he seemed to decide that I meant no harm, for he allowed me to come up almost within reach. After a reasonable length of time, I carefully picked up a six-inch twig from the ground and held it toward him. Stretching out his neck he sniffed it, and then he went back to his grass.

Moving very slowly, I reached over with the twig and gently touched him on the ear. Other than to twitch his head, he paid no attention. Then I scratched him a little just back of the jaw. That was his weak spot. He must have been itchy there for a long time, for he stretched out his neck and, with his eyes half-closed, enjoyed my scratching as much as any dog or cat ever did. After a few minutes I discarded the twig and offered my bare hand. He would allow me to reach him, but just as soon as my fingers touched his fur, he would ruff up his tail in alarm.

Being too close to take chances, I didn't press our acquaintance. If I had only had the time and a few tidbits in my pocket, I am sure I could have handled that skunk in a comparatively short time. What interested me most was the way he seemed to know that I meant no harm. Most wild animals are extremely shy of man and take a great deal of persuasion before they will allow any familiarities.

Of all the big game of the North American continent, the bighorn ram is considered by most hunters to be the most difficult to stalk. In the first place, nature has given him a marvellous pair of eyes — eyes equal, I believe, to a man's aided with a fine pair of six-power glasses. Then, too, his native range, the high, rugged peaks of the Rockies, offer him protection on their craggy flanks, helping him to put distance between himself and his enemies. Mountain sheep are not only masters at making fools out of their enemies and finding a living in a country noted for its hardships, but they actually play organized games. The young of most animals enjoy a good frolic, but this play is usually just an aimless scuffling or scampering. The young and old of the mountain sheep family play organized games startlingly similar to those played by schoolboys.

One summer, my partner Bert Riggall, noted authority on wildlife, was camped with a party of trout fishermen near the British Columbia border in southwestern Alberta. It was a warm evening in early July when Bert stepped out of his tent with his glasses for a look at the mountain face back of the camp. A quarter of a mile to the west the sheer cliffs of the Continental Divide rose three thousand feet to the skyline. Bert played his glasses back and forth over the mountain looking for game, and was not surprised to see a lone mountain sheep ewe standing silhouetted on the summit against the sky. In a few minutes, the old ewe was joined by nine other sheep — all ewes, lambs, and small rams.

Directly under the sheep, a steep, hard snowdrift ran down a hundred yards to the top of the main cliff, which dropped off sheer, overhanging hundreds of feet into airy space. To Bert's great surprise the old lead ewe suddenly stepped over the edge and shot down the snowdrift with her feet set, straight for the cliff below. Ploughing down over the crust at high speed with the snow squirting up from her hoofs in showers, she seemed bent on suicide. When only a matter of feet from the lip of the cliff and a terrible plunge to a sure death, that astonishingly active old grandmother made a sort of four-legged Christi turn and galloped merrily off the snow onto a dry, rocky rib to one side. Then she began climbing as fast as she could leg it to the summit. One after another the rest of the band followed her glissade, each making that hair-raising, nonchalant turn on the edge of disaster and climbing back for another turn. Down in camp the whole party sat breathless with glasses glued to their eyes watching every move of that daredevil game, played so expertly by those masters of the crags. The sheep went on with their play with no let-up until it was too dark to see.

At another time, Bert and a party of mountain climbers watched for two hours while five young rams played "I'm the King of the Castle" on a small conical pile of loose rock left by a receding glacier. One ram would take his place on top of the mound and stand off repeated attacks by the other four, until he was dislodged. Then the winner took his turn, and so on.

One autumn we were out camera hunting with a party in sheep territory. Climbing up the side of a high dividing ridge one morning, we cautiously poked our eyebrows over the skyline to glass the basin beyond for game. In spite of a careful combing, we could see nothing, so we got to our feet and walked boldly out onto the summit and headed up the crest of the ridge toward another basin higher up. We had not gone fifty yards before Bert spotted a bunch of fine big rams. Bedded deep in a boulder field, they were so well camouflaged that we missed them completely on our first look. One thing was quite plain. They all had their eyes fastened on us as we stood outlined against the sky a thousand yards above them. There were five of us in the party, and we held a hurried council of war before moving on. We decided to continue on along the skyline as though we hadn't seen the rams, until we came to a huge boulder a couple of hundred yards farther up. There, while momentarily hidden, two of us would drop under the ridge to try a stalk for some pictures, while the other three continued on in plain sight to draw the rams' attention.

At first, things went as we hoped. We arrived at the boulder and, while briefly screened, two of us doubled back, keeping out of sight. When Bert and the rest of the party stepped out into the open, the rams were still bedded down and apparently not alarmed. But before they got much farther the big sheep jumped up and hit the rocks running. When last seen they were stringing out over a pass a mile away and still going strong. I won't say that mountain sheep can count, but they acted as if they knew that three plus two makes five. This is a good example of the keen intelligence of the bighorn, and a good sample of what the sheep hunter is up against.

Ever since I was able to walk, I have been observing animals, both wild and domestic. The longer I live, the more astonished I am at the limited scope of my knowledge of their ways. Although I have spent a good deal more time than most people watching them, I still see but a fraction of their lives. What are they doing in their dens and way up in the fastnesses of the peaks, where I cannot follow? Can they converse in languages of their own? These are some of the questions that puzzle me. Of one thing I am sure. For the most part they have keen brains and know how to use them. Give them a fair chance, and they will survive to be enjoyed by countless generations to come.

PART SIX

NATURE'S ADVOCATE

The construction of the Oldman River dam in southern Alberta raised a vocal outcry from conservationists, environmentalists, and aboriginal groups. Andy joined with other celebrities, such as singer-songwriter Ian Tyson, to protest the construction of the dam. But this was not his first stint as an advocate for conservation and the preservation of wilderness. Throughout his life he has championed the rights of wildlife and the wild, in newspapers, magazine articles, in his films, on the lecture circuit, and in his books.

Why Man Needs Wilderness

S ince man first punched the ecological time clock and checked in on his world of technology by making use of fire, it has only been moments in biological time. But in that short period he has contrived to become the dominating force, the climax competitor in the world of nature, able and carelessly willing to deprive other creatures of their means of life. He has been too often a destroyer instead of a benefactor, and his carelessness has now come to a point where he endangers his own continuance.

In spite of his intelligence and his great technical developments which have given him the dominance even allowing passage to the moon, he is displaying some dangerous blind spots. For apart from the fact that he may contrive to blast himself out of existence by his fascination with war and weapons, he is now confronted with the possibility of extinction by the more subtle but just as final means through loss of environment via pollution and overpopulation.

He is a child of the wilderness, but largely ignores the importance and significance of his source, seeking to compromise real

From *BC Outdoors* (February 1971)

values of life by exploiting and wasting his environment in the name of fast profits and what he likes to call "progress."

He can read in his own history the records of the fall of various civilizations, all directly caused by ignorance of environmental requirements, qualities, and conditions insuring continuance. The tracks are there for him to read how the island of Crete lost from nine to eleven feet of its topsoil and a flourishing people lost their empire; how Libya turned from a fertile land – the granary of North Africa – into a parched desert. The history of ancient and modern China is a chronicle of what happens when people mine and overpopulate the land without thought for environment. Yet man is persisting in doing those very things that have been the undoing of his predecessors, but now because of numbers and technical power, the danger is global.

What is most amazing and disturbing to the onlooking naturalist is the complacency and calm of people in general – largely intelligent people directly affected or due for destruction of their way of life if the present trend goes on. Particularly here in Canada, where our literacy is high, where our communication system is amongst the finest in the world, and where we have one of the best informed populations extant, we continue to stand in comparative quiet not insisting with near enough vehemence for government to take immediate steps to control a most dangerous situation.

Canada possesses a great portion of the remaining wilderness of the world with its yet untapped abundance of resources. Of this British Columbia has the biggest part of choice wild country – natural real estate of great beauty and wonderful ecological pattern owned by the people. Indeed, the ecosystems of this province include those ranging from the semi-desert country of south-central areas to the verdant green jungles of the rain forest on the west coast and thence to the sub-arctic mountains and plateaus of the north. This great triangle of life patterns is unique in the world and very valuable, not only because of its natural resources, but also because of its great variety of climate and scenic features. But in spite of the obvious, the people do not seem to care what happens to their beautiful land.

It has been explained as a condition brought about by affluence and the artificial environment wrought by man. For example, scores of thousands of people in Vancouver alone earn their living from some aspect of the forest. They can look up any time the sun shines – and smog permits – to see the mountains on which the trees grow. They can see the mighty Fraser River, rolling down from the vastness of interior B.C. They can look out over the big blue ocean where log booms float in tow of busy little tugs, where great ships head for distant horizons carrying rich cargoes. This, unfortunately, is as close as many of these people ever come to appreciating the wilderness that ensures their existence. To them, the pollution of air and water, the abuse of land by bad logging practices, the ever-increasing environmental damage to the ocean is simply an unavoidable part of the "good life," the chrome-plated, neon-lit, artificial atmosphere of prosperity. Few ask what happens when the wilderness that brings this wealth is all gone.

Even those who enjoy the outdoors and make their living from the fast-growing tourist industry are complacently watching wilderness country being torn open and trampled underfoot. Their living is being threatened before their eyes and they are remarkably quiet. Surely they must care!

Last August, I was one of a party of five hunters on a pack-train trip out of a fly-in wilderness camp in the wilds of the Liard River watershed in northern British Columbia. The various members of this party had flown in from as far away as Florida, Mexico, New York, and Alaska. For two weeks we rode and climbed through some magnificent mountain country teeming with big game. Three of the hunters took big stone rams for trophies – our total bag. I was hunting with my camera and the sportsman from Mexico took nothing since he saw no ram that met the high standard he set for himself.

If one must put dollar values on things, the average stone ram trophy of this region nets the province about $2,500. What other king of livestock sells for these prices? Yet the government of British Columbia plans to set up a whole development of this region from power dams to mining, apparently writing off the vast long-range recreational potential as unimportant. The outfitters and guides are aware and they are worried, but are making remarkably little noise in defence of their way of life. Nor do they seem to be aware of the potential power they and others in the tourist industry can wield.

My trip through that northern hunting country was taken in an atmosphere of nostalgia for me because only ten years ago I was an outfitter operating a forty-five-horse wilderness pack outfit in southwestern Alberta. Almost overnight, after fifty years of continuous operation in our family, this pack-train business was wiped out by intrusion of the oil industry. If the trade had been a fair one, it would not have been so bad, but for every quarter-acre actually used by the petroleum industry, hundreds more were broken open and left wasted. So the problems involved are familiar.

The people of British Columbia wishing to preserve some natural environment and wilderness must organize and demand action to ensure proper long-range environmental management if they are to retain some natural features unique to their province and vital to happy continuance. It is a matter of making best use of communication, of pointing out some basic facts of the overall dangers of letting such a land become defaced and ugly to the point of destruction. It is to know that wilderness and the species of living things it supports can get along without man, but that man cannot get along without them. If he tries he will have destroyed his own environment and be faced with ultimate extinction.

Every interested individual, old and young, can assist with this preservation of environment by writing to political representatives. These people should not just ask but insist that the necessary protective measures be taken to preserve our environment. Politicians, after all, are the servants of the people. They are very sensitive of public opinion, and bound to move in the right direction if enough pressure is exerted. Neither politicians nor industrialists have any valid argument against this request. In the long haul it is as much to their benefit as it is for all others – a simple matter of mutual survival through recognition of the necessities of tomorrow. It can be ensured by placing a few necessary rules for the game on the table, a game where the chips are ultimately life itself.

Signs indicate that young people are aware of and dissatisfied with conditions as they stand, but are too often confused by side issues to make best uses of their opportunity to help. It is not nearly enough just to protest. Some well-illustrated, concrete kinds of projects under cool, well-informed leadership are necessary to bring the dangers of environmental waste into public focus.

For example, a biology class at the Winston Churchill High School in Lethbridge, Alberta, decided to do something about the pollution of the Oldman River there. They embarked on a project and interviewed various officials, industrialists, and politicians. They organized and went on field trips gathering information and evidence needed for a paper titled "The Dirty Old Man." They produced one of the best works of its kind – a paper that has received wide circulation in the press and on the air. It has become a milestone in western Canadian history.

They followed up this publication by organizing and setting up a sort of pollution-of-environment exhibition in which part of their fine school was used for displays and various illustrations pertinent to the subject. This in turn became the focal point of a five-day educational symposium attended by educators, naturalists, scientists, agriculturalists, and others. Here ideas were exchanged, necessary recommendations discussed, and material broadcast over radio and television.

It is in this way that a nucleus of a program can be welded together which is the only hope for a world beset by problems of overpopulation and the absolutely vital necessity of environmental control and management.

A crash educational program of the public as well as students of every grade is of paramount importance fulfil this end. For if the young and the mature can combine their enthusiasm, drive, and experience toward solving this problem, then man and nature can learn to live together in harmony to ensure not only the preservation of wilderness and all remaining forms of life but also the preservation of man himself.

Grizzly Country | A Vanishing Heritage

G rizzly country is the rain-forest jungles of British
Columbia's west coast, where the rainfall can reach as
much as 180 inches a year. In this dripping climate the
timber grows to enormous size and the undergrowth of vicious
devil's club and tangled brush is all but impenetrable. Here one
sees the dramatic spectacle of the Pacific salmon following their
destinies back from the rich ocean pastures to cast their spawn in
the rivers where they were hatched four years before. They return,
not just to the same river, or the same bend of that river, but, if
possible, to the same gravel-bottomed riffle where they emerged
from the egg.

Driftwood washed down from clear-cutting logging operations
sometimes chokes the streams to a point of no passage. Chemical
effluents from industry poison the water. Even if the salmon get
through and around these man-made barriers, they are prey to
many things, part of the food chain natural to the rivers. Seals,
eagles, gulls, and great blue herons gorge on them. Sometimes
even wolverines, cougars, and wolves take their toll of the silvery

From *Nature Canada* (April/June 1975)

hordes. Where the mighty grizzly still survives, he turns into an avid fisherman during the migration of spawning salmon.

Grizzly country is also the boreal valley and high timberline alplands of the Rockies and interior mountains of British Columbia. This is a region of great variation in climate, from near-desert conditions to deep-snow country where annual snowfall sometimes reaches as much as sixty feet. The grizzlies have largely disappeared from the regions of mild dry climate. In the deep-snow country they are still found in some numbers, though they are far from abundant. In such areas the only big game that can survive, apart from a scattering of moose, caribou, and mountain goats, are the bears, for they snooze the deep-snow months away snug in dens beneath the heavy white blanket covering the mountains.

Grizzly country is also the vast, rolling, multi-hued sweep of tundra lying like a Persian rug along the wide valleys winding between snow-capped ranges of the north, and all along the Arctic coast from Alaska to the Coppermine River. Here the grizzly enjoys a vast range folded into the caribou prairies of the Arctic – not so dissimilar from the Great Plains region it once knew as it fed and roamed among uncounted millions of bison.

Grizzly country is still the beautiful foothills of Alberta, sloping down to the parklands and prairies along the east slope of the Rockies. There one sees clear mountain streams taking their first fast run on the long journey eastward to the sea. Here in spring the lush glacier lilies carpet slopes recently covered with snow. When they first come out of their dens, the grizzlies feed on the lilies, stripping the plants from the ground with gusto. If I were asked to illustrate a scene of utter serenity and peace, I would choose a picture of a mother grizzly wandering across such flower-covered slopes with two small cubs gambolling at her heels. This is truly a part of the deep tranquillity that is the wilderness hallmark.

Here on our ranch adjacent to Waterton Lakes National Park in southwest Alberta, we still play host to the occasional grizzly bear during spring, summer, and fall. At one time they wintered here, as one or two old caved-in dens attest. We are on friendly terms with our silvertip visitors. Not once over the seventy years since the ranch was originally homesteaded has anyone been hurt or any property been damaged by the bears. Indeed, my wife, Kay, and I raised four sons and a daughter in a playground shared by the bears. From the time they could walk, our children were schooled to be unafraid of the big animals, and "never run from a bear" has always been the unbending rule. However, we have also been careful to exercise the utmost respect for the bears and never to put ourselves in the position of being an aggravation if it could be helped. We and the bears each mind our own business without undue conflict. I once saw four grizzlies feeding on new spring growth in the same field as 120 grazing yearling steers. Neither bears nor cattle seemed interested or alarmed at the close proximity. Occasionally a grizzly will learn how easy it is to kill cattle, but for the most part leaves them alone.

Bears of any kind are extremely intelligent animals. Grizzlies are also innately curious, a characteristic that sometimes brings them close to us.

Last spring the snow conditions in the mountains were still heavy when the big bears came out of their dens. They were forced down to lower ground and we found ourselves host to three grizzlies feeding close by our buildings in the aspen groves. Late one evening Kay was home alone when the dog set up a fierce barking that woke her, so she got up and let the dog into the house. She was wakened again in the small hours of the morning by the dog raising bedlam in the front room. She went out to investigate the uproar and found herself face to face with a big grizzly standing on the veranda looking curiously through the glass front door. When the bear saw her, it reared for a better look, but when it did it could no longer see through the seven-foot door. Again it came down onto all four feet, peered curiously through the door and then ambled away to lose itself in the shadows of early dawn.

Our ranch is still much as it was when the Indians hunted buffalo on its meadows. There are likely as many beaver along the creeks as when the first settlers came. The ranch's ecosystem is shared by elk, moose, mule deer, whitetails, and black bear, along with a teeming population of smaller animals and birds. Apart from the wire fences and grazing cattle, it is wilderness – what amounts to an extension of the national park. Hence it is also grizzly country.

Because the park has been careful and efficient in handling its garbage, there has been very little grizzly-human conflict there. Park grizzly population is probably just the same as it was when white men first saw it.

Indeed, if one examines a map showing present grizzly populations, it is clear that most grizzlies still range where the country is as yet unspoiled wilderness. Where wilderness has deteriorated or disappeared and wildlife management has been geared to outdated harvest principles, the grizzlies have dwindled or disappeared. And while management has improved considerably in most places, it is still hampered by low priorities and competition with branches of government promoting industry. Largely speaking, government policy has shown small appreciation of wilderness values, with consequent disastrous impact on the big bears.

Thousands of miles of access roads allegedly built for fire protection and mineral and oil prospecting, with little or no attention paid to watershed damages, have resulted in such an increase of human intrusion that the grizzly has largely disappeared from what was prime range comparatively few years ago.

The grizzly has suffered more than any other big game where cattle graze in publicly owned forest reserves in British Columbia and Alberta. The bears are all fond of carrion. When a cow that has died from any cause is found with signs that a grizzly has been feeding on it, the onus of the responsibility for the death of the cow is too often hung on the bear. Even an expert can't always tell if a grizzly is really the culprit. Cattle owners too frequently have arranged for bear removal when it is not justified.

Access roads, in conjunction with harvest-type management, have also allowed for overkill by hunters. When large numbers of hunters can reach into almost every valley, they are a threat to the big bear. Even if they do not shoot him, the noise and continued disturbance often causes him to move to another area far less favourably disposed to hold him. This is what is meant by habitat destruction.

Alberta has given some added protection to the grizzly by limiting licences and closing the country south of the Bow River to hunters. However, it is questionable if this move came in time. No real effort has been made to make a count of the grizzlies left in Alberta outside the national parks, a necessity of good management.

Very recently British Columbia has launched a dramatic new program in forest and wildlife management. For the first time these two departments are beginning to work together. (This should be something for Alberta to contemplate, for there has been little or no co-operation or communication between these two branches of government in this province.) B.C.'s program now includes comprehensive research on the grizzly. While the province is still allowing some hunting of the big animal, this is being carefully watched.

Even in most of the western national parks, the big bears have suffered due to poor garbage-disposal methods. Although techniques are better than they were, there is still plenty of room for improvement. Of course, the immensely increased tourist visitation is the underlying cause of the problem. Priorities have changed, but consequent administrative responses have not kept up.

One of the management practices used in the parks, and open to question, is the application of paralyzing drugs to garbage-eating bears, so they can be loaded in a cargo net and transported to remote areas by helicopter. Some grizzlies "home" back to the source of easy pickings in a short time, and again have to be moved. Grizzlies have long memories of such indignities, and although paralyzed during the operation, they are still very conscious. It is understandable that their normally short-fused tempers are not improved by this experience, and for an innocent and unsuspecting hiker to meet such a bear can be a traumatic experience. In the Yukon Territory's Kluane National Park, some hair-raising grizzly-human encounters have occurred in an area where an intensive research program was carried out with the help of these gun-impelled drugs. While research is needed, perhaps science should be considering other methods less likely to create rogue bears.

Overall successful management and preservation of the grizzly are directly bound with the recognition of true wilderness values. Grizzlies and wilderness go together like bumblebees and flowers; without one, the other will perish.

Better long-range planning is a major requirement for bear management and wilderness preservation. Government has always been glacier-slow to adopt things that go against old policy and far too quick in the promotion of things that appear politically advantageous at the moment. Good environmental policy is not contradictory to human and industrial welfare. It is a matter of moving more quickly to make the best use of already available knowledge. The environment comes in for much political lip service, but too little positive action in practice.

To me and to many others, the grizzly bear is a vital living symbol of Canada, of its magnificently rich natural endowments and history. The great bear could be the icon of far-seeing wisdom and careful management of our wonderfully alive and beautiful surroundings — a signal of our deep concern for the heritage of our children's children.

What good is easy living and wealth for this generation if it robs those we sire and profess to love? Where does the responsibility lie for the fostering of a deep appreciation for other kinds of life?

These are questions more people must answer promptly, honestly, and intelligently, for time is rapidly running out.

The Death of the River?

It soon became very evident that the rumour was fact. In 1976 the government announced that it was planning to dam the Oldman just a few miles below the confluence of the three forks of the river where it ran through a canyon. The lake thus formed would flood all three valleys and drown thirty-one ranches to a greater or lesser extent, making all of them uneconomic, and completely destroying the home sites of nearly every one of the parcels of land involved. Some of the old homes date back to before the turn of the century, qualifying them as historic sites in the early settlement of the country by the old-time cattle-ranchers.

To those of us who know something of the impact of dams, culturally, environmentally, and ecologically, the announcement of the planned dam was a catastrophe. We knew that these features of the issue would likely be totally ignored in the rush to provide big construction contracts, lots of (temporary) construction jobs, and irrigation water to relatively few farmers. We were aware that the economics of the proposal would include as costs only the actual construction of the dam and the expenses involved with

From *The Life of a River* (1987)

the appropriation of the lands due to be inundated. For the history of such projects here or anywhere else on the continent, or in the world, shows that the cost estimates never include all the damage done to the people who really own the rivers – and pay for their destruction, in every way.

I wondered what the Peigan people living on their reserve a few miles further downstream would think of such a development, which not only would interfere with the holy river of the Blackfoot tribes but would also affect their lands. For if water was to be used to irrigate farmlands to the east, it had to be taken by canal down through the property granted to the Peigans by long-standing treaty rights. They had been hosts to water diversion for irrigation use north of the river from a weir and a canal located on their land since 1910. How would they react to this additional intrusion? The government proposal, which involved hundreds of pages of information (and what turned out to be considerable dis-information), made no mention of how much land would be needed for this canal, or what arrangements had been made with the Peigans for its use.

No part of the report made any mention of whether the formations of the land and the underlying bedrock would, literally, hold water. Those of us who had been interested enough to look at it over the years knew that the bedrock was extremely porous sandstone with overlying beds of gravel, sand, and what appeared to be some layers of volcanic ash here and there. All of this is about as waterproof as a sponge. When the dam-site surveyors had drilled down into the formations on both sides of the river several years before, the porous nature of the sandstone had forced them to use compressed air to keep the drilling bits clear; when water was injected under normal procedures it just kept right on going into the rock.

All of this made it unlikely that the proposed holding-basin could even be filled with water unless its whole bottom was lined with concrete. With canyons running in from both sides, over-hanging cliffs here and there all along the river on its tributaries, and the generally steep topography of most of the slopes, this would be an astronomically expensive undertaking, if not totally impossible. To make matters worse, the slopes of the valley are prone to sluffing – and such massive landslides into the water would be accentuated by flooding. Not only is sluffing very dam-aging to the holding potential of water in such a lake, but it can be downright dangerous to a dam, drastically altering its topo-graphy, or its level.

I had travelled back and forth across this land on foot, on horse-back, and by automobile for years, and the memory of seeing it from the ground made me wonder about something. So I char-tered a light plane and flew over it. From a height of three thou-sand feet, the whole area was laid out like a map – every detail of the rivers I had fished so often, every home site and their relation to the land in sharp detail. In a few minutes we could travel across country that had once taken me all day on saddle horse. We winged out over the lower stretch of the Castle, banked north to the Crowsnest, and followed it up to where we could see it come out at the mountains like a silver rope cast in sinuous curves along its valley between the hills. Then we swung north, flying parallel to the front of the long ridge of the Livingstone Range, across the Todd Creek valley, and over onto the north fork of the Oldman a few miles downriver from the gap. It was a crystal-clear day as we winged back down the Oldman with the great grassy basin of the Waldron Ranch off our larboard wing, the front of the Porcupine Hills dead ahead, and the sweep of farming and ranching land to starboard. Following the river we could see every fold of the ground as we flew back to the dam site, and I knew that what I had suspected was true. In all of that great expanse of country there was not one lake or slough, apart from some beaver ponds along Todd Creek. Unlike the country a few miles to the south, which is dotted with lakes and sloughs, this area was like blotting-paper: its porous, sandy soil soaked up the run-off water and would not hold it.

I wondered if the minister of lands and forests or any of his immediate advisors had ever flown over it, or, if they had, if they could understand what they had seen.

Another pass with the plane took us high up along the east front of the Continental Divide, from Waterton Park in the south, following the main range of the Rockies north. From the head-waters of the south branch of the Castle River on the park border through to the head of Oyster Creek, we flew over country that I had travelled for twenty-five years with the pack train, when it was so wild that the only trails were those we had cut or that had been blazed through virgin forests by the Stoney Indians. This was the core of the Oldman, the area where its many branches flowed down off the roof-tree of the continent through twisted canyons and across flower-strewn green meadows. I had often seen animals there – elk, deer, moose, bighorn sheep, mountain goats, bears, and others – thousands of them over the years, but it had never occurred to me that the most powerful and numerous of them all could possibly do as much damage in so short a time.

The tracks of man showed here now. The heavy scars of roads – for logging and for oil and gas exploration – were traced along every river and almost every creek on the east slope of the Rockies. And, what was much worse, the timber at the headwaters among the high timberline basins was being clear-cut, leaving thousands of acres of naked slopes criss-crossed with the tracks of heavy machines and the smashed remnants of shattered trees wasted in the rush for profit where there really was none. With all cover ruthlessly ripped away, the topsoil, the vital and precious resource that had been slowly accumulating for ten thousand years since the Ice Age had melted off these mountains, was now being washed away downhill in spring run-offs that carried it in brown floods down the river.

What was incongruous and contradictory about this was that if the dam was being built to control floods – as we had been told by government news releases to the press – why was this problem being exacerbated by cutting timber in the river basin that was its natural control, and why did the government continue to hand out clear-cutting licences?

I had flown down the length of the Mediterranean over country where people first realized the power and fertility of the soil many thousands of years ago. They had multiplied there, built great cities, and known enormous wealth. They had cleared the forests then flourishing in North Africa and turned the country along the lower stretches of the Nile and in Libya into a vast granary. They had cut the cedars and other trees on the beautiful areas of Lebanon and Crete for timber and masts for their ships to carry them afar on voyages of conquest and trade. When the timber was gone, they had turned loose flocks of sheep and goats to eat the grass that grew to take its place. In time there was nothing to hold the rich topsoil, nine to eleven feet deep, and wind and rain had moved it down into the sea, leaving little but sand and bare rock. As a result, many of their cities had been left abandoned, while the farmlands in North Africa were claimed by encroaching desert – the Sahara – all except a narrow strip along the Nile River.

The Nile itself tells us a further instructive story. Every year floods came down this great river bringing millions of tons of natural fertilizer from up along its tropical headwaters, to inundate and enrich its valley and estuary and help sustain a great fishery off the coast. The people flourished. But then, following the Second World War, the Egyptian government saw an opportunity to harness the Nile for electrical power and irrigation, and in due course negotiated a contract with Russian engineers to construct a dam. So the great Aswan Dam was built, and for a little while it seemed to be a marvellous thing.

But, as is the way with dams, nothing has worked out the way the planners expected. Now that the natural fertilizers no longer come downstream, it is necessary to use artificial fertilizer and chemical insecticides, and this, along with the salinization that accompanies irrigation, is poisoning the soil more and more every year. The Nile no longer deposits vast quantities of fertile silt on surrounding land, which for thousands of years afforded good growing conditions for plants. With no replacing silt, the bed of the Nile is eroding and the banks are crumbling, while the sea relentlessly chews away at the coastline, thus reducing the estuary. Large numbers of big buildings are in danger of collapsing through instability caused by the rising water-table, while the proliferation of weeds in the irrigation canals and in the river itself is much greater than expected. As for the commercial fishing at the mouth of the Nile, that has almost disappeared.

The dam that sounded so wonderful has proved to be such a total disaster that the president of the Egyptian Republic recently appealed to scientists to put their wisdom and knowledge at the disposal of the state to solve that country's present difficulties. He pleaded, "You must help us achieve a victory over the major challenges that Egypt will have to face between now and the year 2000. What is required is a serious scientific study of all aspects of our problems, both present and future. Among these, *the secondary effects of the building of the Aswan Dam require your special attention. To overcome them is, in effect, one of the main challenges Egypt has to face.*" (My italics.)

Dams are a relatively new development in the industrial and agricultural worlds. Here in Alberta we have been aware of some of their implications since the 1960s, when the government came up with a grandiose scheme to move water south from the Mackenzie

River drainage system through a complicated series of dams, diversions, and canals involving every river south to the international border. It was called the Prime Plan, and folders expounding its advantages were circulated by mail to every taxpayer in the province. The cost of the scheme ran into billions of dollars, but the dollars then flowing into the government coffers from oil and gas development left the politicians unconcerned about the price tag. But those of us who were aware of the ecological and social impacts of moving water from one river system to another, and of the enormous amount of good land that was being flooded – and of the obvious, though unmentioned, intention of eventually exporting it over the border into the United States – were deeply concerned. We knew that, as the Americans ran out of water, pressure would increase on Canadians to send their water south. As Michael Keating wrote in his book *To the Last Drop: Canada and the World's Water Crisis*, this would mean "turning the prairie rivers into a gigantic plumbing system."

We had plenty to be concerned about, for we had seen how brutally oil and gas exploration had been carried out on the east slope of the Rockies, and had seen the roughshod manner in which private landowners with surface rights were treated. It was perfectly obvious we were all up against a get-rich-quick mentality, where the values of productive land, clean air, and pure water were of no importance. So some of us went to work and succeeded in making the careless use of our natural resources a real issue, to the point of defeating the government that had been in power for over thirty years.

The Progressive Conservative Party, which succeeded the Social Credit Party, declared the Prime Plan was scrapped and made some very encouraging announcements concerning environmental issues. In due course a very comprehensive policy was drawn up and passed by the legislature, zoning and protecting the east-slope region to control logging and petroleum development. Sewage-treatment regulations were beefed up and environmental concerns in general were given so much better recognition that we sat back and breathed a sigh of relief. But not for long. Whenever people intervene to direct their representatives in government toward more sensible use of their mandate, they should be very aware that winning a battle does not necessarily mean the war is won. There had been two more elections, and the last one, in 1985, gave the government a victory with no effective opposition.

One day a large brown envelope came in the mail from an anonymous source within government. It contained a blueprint of a much-expanded version of the Prime Plan, which involved not only Alberta but Saskatchewan and Manitoba as well. It affected almost every river and watershed from Peace to the international border in southern Manitoba. It was unbelievably big. Yet it soon became very apparent that it was – and is – a serious and extremely dangerous plan, a nightmare of expense involving an enormous amount of land. And, of course, part of it was the Three Rivers Dam.

I had never really looked at any dams except in passing. Now that it was important to learn about them, there were two that I wanted to see: the Libby Dam on the Kootenay River just south of the border in Montana, and the Grand Coulee Dam on the Columbia in Washington State. The former was in trouble and had been out of operation almost from the time it was filled. The latter was one of the biggest in the world, and combined electrical-power generation with a massive irrigation project. So I stepped in my car to head west and south to Grand Coulee.

The highway led down below the face of the huge concrete dam to the spick-and-span town of Grand Coulee – a new town that had been built for the people who worked in this big installation. It was a pretty place, with wide streets lined on either side with houses, and adorned with evenly spaced fruit trees all in a mass of bloom. The town was set on a big natural bench below the face of the dam overlooking the river canyon.

About two or three blocks back from the edge of the drop-off above the river, I drove into one end of a wide street to see a curious sight. All along one side, drilling rigs were busy punching holes in the boulevard between the flowering cherry trees. Then I noticed a crack in the pavement running almost straight up the middle of the street. Parking the car, I walked out to look at it. It appeared to be a fresh crack, a small step about two to three inches high, with the low side toward the river. When I asked a man tending one of the drilling rigs what was causing it, he gave me a blank look and said he didn't know. A few houses farther along I saw a man in his garden, so I stopped and asked him. He straightened up with a worried frown and said, "We ain't exactly sure, but it looks like this whole place is about to take off and slide into the river." Later he told me, "I'm not supposed to talk about it, so if you want to find out more, you'll have to ask the engineers in charge."

The supervising staff at the dam treated me cordially and invited me to a good lunch, but nothing was forthcoming about the threatened slump on the far side of town. That was a problem they were investigating, and unwilling to discuss. From information received later, I gathered that they apparently were able to stabilize the slump by pumping wet concrete from the surface down onto the bedrock.

I headed back east to Libby, Montana, to find that the dam here is also of concrete, built at the top of a narrow gorge not far from the border. The lake was drawn down, but when full it flooded thousands of acres of prime ranching land north up the valley of the Kootenay for almost fifty miles into Canada. When I visited, a crew was working at the base of the dam with considerable heavy machinery. One of the repair crew summarized the situation neatly: "It ain't no secret. The damn fools that built this thing put it square on an active fault – mostly because it looked like the best place, I guess. Now we're rebuilding the footing under the dam, and it ain't an easy job. We've been busy at it for nearly two years and it ain't finished yet."

Dams can't be built just anywhere on a river, and really top-quality locations are not always available. Building one on a location that looks good but is not grounded on stable rock can be dangerous.

A concrete dam is normally of solid construction, but an earth-filled one has added risks. Consider the case of the Grand Teton Dam in Idaho. This dam had been built against the wishes of the residents of the area, which had been very plainly stated over a number of well-attended public hearings. Among the opponents was a retired geologist, who pointed out that the material to be used for the construction of the dam would not hold water. The bureaucrats and politicians, who (as is too often the case) were basing their proposal for the dam on political and what turned out to be questionable economic reasons, totally ignored him and everyone else in opposition, and the dam was built.

One day, when it was about two-thirds full, a tourist stopped on an overlook to take a picture of it. At that moment, squarely in the middle of the dam, water suddenly appeared and began to run down the face. The tourist ran to phone the police, while the breach rapidly widened and the whole structure began to collapse. The valley below the dam was rich farmland dotted with fine homes and buildings, and the area held ten small towns. Fortunately the county sheriff, who knew the geologist, had quietly set up a warning system by phone and this now became a lifeline. The whole valley was vacated with the utmost possible dispatch as the thundering flood bore down on it. Only eleven people lost their lives. If the break had occurred in the middle of the night, probably thousands would have died. The resulting damages cost the American government a billion dollars. Ironically enough, one of the major purposes of this $85-million project was flood control! It is a historic fact that "flood control" dams tend to increase the severity, while decreasing the frequency, of floods.

As I drove back home, there was plenty to think about, and I was busy mentally outlining and organizing a paper to be presented at the local public hearing. I had come to distrust these events as designed by officials to let people blow off steam, and likely to be ignored if the outcome of the hearing is unfavourable to government plans. But I wanted to give it my best shot.

This particular hearing was well attended, with overwhelming opposition to the Three Rivers Dam project on the Oldman. The fact that no Indians were present surprised me, and I wondered if they were aware of the proposal or had been invited. So I informed the Peigan band council of a meeting being held to discuss the dam at a hall in Lundbreck, a few miles down the Crowsnest River from the pass, and they sent a representative to speak for them. He was a powerful and dramatic speaker, well educated and very articulate, who made the government representative sound like a rank amateur on the platform, and he left no doubt of where the tribal council stood in respect to the proposed meddling with the river.

Subsequently the Peigans sent a representation to the premier's office in Edmonton, telling him that in reviewing their 1910 agreement for the building of the weir diverting water into the irrigation canal presently in use, they found that they had never been paid for the river bottom on which the weir stood, or the land under the service road attending the canal. In examining the original treaty, they had found that they owned the bottom of the river as well as water rights. They wanted to be paid now – or they would allow no more water to be taken out of the river.

The winter following the hearings wore on, with ominous silence on the part of the government. It was like waiting for a battle that somehow never came off. None of us heard of any decision, and the Peigans received no response to their request. Then came spring, and with the higher water following the break-up, the Peigans sent out a war party. A group of about forty men went down to the flat by the weir, where they camped in teepees and campers. When some irrigation personnel came along to close the weir to begin diverting water into the irrigation canal, they met armed Indians who refused to let them near the weir.

I was working at my desk a few days later with the radio playing in the kitchen when the program was interrupted by a special bulletin. A busload of about forty riot police had just arrived at the weir, plus two patrol cars full of officers; they had been sent by the attorney-general to disperse the Indians. It had to be one of the most callously stupid stunts ever pulled by a government in the entire history of the Royal Canadian Mounted Police. Anyone with an ounce of good sense knows the dangers of a confrontation between armed men over an issue where a case formally stated by the Indians had been ignored by government. All it would take to set off a local war was a shot fired by either side. I listened to the announcement in shock.

Chief Small Legs of the Peigans was at home a few miles from the weir, totally unaware of what was happening until the news bulletin came over the radio. He ran out to his pick-up and roared out of his yard, praying that he wasn't going to be too late. When he arrived, it was to find his men and the police facing each other tensely, their guns much in evidence. Jumping out of his vehicle, he strode purposefully between them, and, holding up a hand, said in a ringing voice, "The first shot fired here goes through my heart!"

Meanwhile a helicopter with a deputy minister aboard was circling overhead, and he was sensible enough to know that he was looking at potential murder and mayhem. At this point in the drama, far from his familiar office desk, he became so sick that the pilot brought the machine down to land not far away. The unfortunate civil servant almost staggered as he walked over to the chief and asked for a drink of water. Towering over the distressed official, the chief waved his hand grandly and intoned, "There's the river! Help yourself!"

Somebody chuckled. That broke the tension, and without another word the police got back in their vehicles and departed, no doubt feeling very relieved.

That night the victory drums were beating at the Peigan camp. If some of the old chiefs who signed the Treaty of 1877 were looking back from spirit land at this episode, they must have smiled. Meanwhile, the river flowed serenely through the weir unchecked on its journey to the sea. And very soon the Peigans learned that there is nothing like water, particularly no water, to make men move quickly – even politicians. The Peigans had waited more than half a century for satisfaction in this matter. Shortly after the confrontation, they got paid for their land, and the price was a great deal higher than it would have been in 1910.

Then came a government announcement through the news media that the Three Rivers Dam project had been shelved indefinitely. We wondered how long "indefinitely" might be, for government land-appropriation officials had informed the ranchers due to lose their property that it would be expropriated at a price based on the average price of land in the region. None of the threatened ranchers received notice that the deal was off.

Mountain Streams

T he song of wild mountain country is carried by tumbling waters running boisterous and free down rough wind- and ice-carved slopes on the first tumultuous bounds of their journey to the sea. The lyrics vary from full-throated roaring of river falls to the merry chuckling and tinkling of tiny rills, sometimes hidden and then revealed among the rocks. Springs bubble from secret reservoirs concealed in the sedimentary stone, leaping gaily, natural fountains playing in the sun among brilliant mountain flowers. Inevitably the small streams gather together to make creeks, and these follow the same pattern to form rivers winding like silver-blue ribbons down between cathedral groves of timber.

In the old days the Indians listened to the singing of the waters, and it was good. The streams were happy, they said, as they gathered across the face of the living earth; it was the marriage of the water, sun, and soil, making all life possible. Flowers and grass grew among the great trees beside them, joining with the wind to add their voices to the chorus. The Indians knew they were a part of

From *Andy Russell's Campfire Stories* (1998)

it along with the buffalo, antelope, wild sheep, and deer they hunted. The sun was the great spirit, the earth was the mother, and the water was the juice that flowed between. For was it not the sun that brought rain, warmed the earth, and caused the winter snow to melt? To the Indians it was very simple to understand. They drank of the waters, bathed in them to cleanse themselves, worshipped the sun, and thus were a part of the pattern of life on the face of the earth. Because of the abundance of other life on the plains in front of the mountains and in the great valleys between the ranges, they were hunters.

The first white men who came working their way upstream from the east were hunters too. They came by boat till the streams became too small and swift, then they went on horseback and on foot up along the creeks in search of beaver. The beaver were so thick in many places that they choked the creeks with dams, laying one above the other like steps woven of mud and sticks, with ponds between. There the trappers, with old moccasins covering their feet, and with their buckskin leggings shortened to the knee, waded as they set their traps, cursing the icy water, and the only part of them that got bathed, short of accident, was their feet and legs. But they kept up the relentless search for skins, piling up the pelts till the beaver had all but disappeared.

The trappers were a breed set apart by their chosen environment, and they looked with some contempt and a reluctant awareness on the change in their wild free ways that came as white settlers wound their way slowly west by ox team and covered wagon, across the folds of great plains lifting and falling under their wheels like swells in a sea of grass. Buffeted by storms, sometimes attacked by hostile Indians or held back by the distances, they forded rivers and smaller streams, cursing when their wagons and stock bogged in quicksand and wheels broke on the steep, rocky pitches of the banks. Sometimes men and animals drowned in the swift waters, but others fought their way on west, following their destiny towards a land of riches somewhere yonder beneath the setting sun.

When they came to deserts, they fought their way across them, too; no detours for them, no bending to the forces of nature; it was fight and fight some more – defeat the wilderness – every step of the way, while the pitiless sun shone down and the shining sand was like the floor of a red-hot oven. There were no waters singing here, and many died of thirst.

One group had come west to escape persecution in the eastern settlements. The Saints, they called themselves; their leader was Brigham Young and their guide the famed Jim Bridger, mountain man turned trader and guide for these wagon trains. He brought the Saints to a huge, wild, and inhospitable basin between the mountain ranges overlooking the glistening reaches of Great Salt Lake and stopped. He sat his horse, with the long fringes of his greasy buckskins stirring slightly in the hot wind. Taciturn for the moment, he silently contemplated these travel-worn, sun-scorched, but grimly determined people who had followed him to this place. Out of long ingrained habit, his eyes were on the move, making note of every detail near and far, reading things completely hidden to the others, signs as lightly written as the soft brush of owl feathers in the dust, where the bird had taken a desert mouse. His gaze swept out across the dry, parched earth past a lone cottonwood tree to the distant blue sheen of the lake so salty a fresh egg would float on it, then swung back up a watercourse along a river in a valley debouching from the mountains back of the wagons. Even the river lost itself in the sand and gravel beds before it reached the lake. It was tough, inhospitable country, where roving Indians did not tarry long.

Why would these people want to settle here? Brigham Young had answered that question by stating it was his instruction from God; they would settle in this spot because it was far enough away and hard enough to reach that nobody else would want it. How would they stay alive? They would use the streams coming down from the mountains to irrigate this land and bring it to life. The mountain man reputedly scoffed at that and offered the Mormon leader one thousand dollars for the first bushel of corn grown in this place. But Bridger had not reckoned with the know-how of these people or with their determination. For in due course they harvested their first crop of corn. History does not record if Brigham Young was ever paid, but the recollection of Jim Bridger's offer amused him and he was fond of telling about it in the years that followed.

Apart from the Spanish settlements in California, where irrigation had been used in the previous century, and some early efforts of farmers and ranchers in the plains of northeastern Colorado, this was perhaps the first time settlers utilized the streams in western North America on such a scale. But they and the horde of settlers to follow thought of water as something put there for man to use. They did not relate its presence to the life it supported in this great new land, for their fight to stay alive in the wilderness had become an ingrained thing, a characteristic still evident in our use of resources, and one that has proved to be shortsighted and very wasteful. Too many have looked on the great trees growing in the valleys and along the flanks of the mountains, their roots set deep in the water-moistened earth, as only something to be cut into planks and boards. They have not paused to see the beauty. If any of those early settlers loved the streams purely for their freshness and beauty, it was the children who played beside the crystal-clear cold water, fished for trout, and swam in them. They heard and began to understand the song.

Up along the foot of the Canadian Rockies, I grew up on a ranch on the edge of the frontier, exploring and fishing the creeks. One of them I came to think of as mine. It was the Drywood, and it nurtured me.

We lived in a comfortable home overlooking the forks where the creek swept down past the rugged flanks of Drywood Mountain, which stood with its great shoulders lifted in a never-ending shrug of patience with time, the elements, and the vagaries of men. The clear, icy water provided me with a playground – a place to fish for the softly coloured cutthroat and Dolly Varden trout and to swim in its deep pools. I left tracks on the sandbars with those of deer, bear, beaver, mink, and many other wild creatures, large and small, which shared their secrets with me, each of us adding a sentence to this story of the wilds. It was there on the edge of a beaver pond, by the gnarled feet of some giant cottonwoods, that I met my first grizzly face to face. The great bear towered at full height over me while I stood frozen in my tracks, scared, small, and very much impressed by this huge beast that chose to turn and leave without a hostile move.

It was there I heard and listened to the song telling me of the mysteries of life supported by this stream, life that ranged from the tiniest of larvae to great Dolly Varden trout as long as my leg, the one dependent on the other. For I caught the Dolly Varden and learned from looking in the stomachs of the smaller fish in its belly that my feeding on its delicious pink flesh had started with caddis larvae, fresh-water shrimp, and other bugs eaten by the trout's prey, all forming a part of the mysterious and intricately woven life pattern of the creek.

In winter the creek ran under ice frozen on its surface; then my tracks mingled with those of the things I hunted while the water murmured sleepily in its bed, shackled by the elements. Sometimes storms tore at the trees growing along its banks. In spring the ice thawed, and the creek roared with boisterous delight at being free and fed copiously on the run-off from melting snow. Then it was dangerous to fawns, cub bears, and small boys. Sometimes tragedy struck among the snags and rocks where the fierce waters flung manes of spray into the air and roared with utter savagery. In summer it was serene and lovely, harbouring hordes of tiny fish fresh-hatched from its colourful gravel beds, feeding them the minute things needed in their struggle to grow big enough for boys to catch. In the process, some of them in turn fed the great Dolly Vardens.

All life is wonderful and beautiful, said the song, and to the boy, watching sometimes in awe and listening to its music, wondering and waiting for what would happen next, a day seemed short. Time was something that began when the sun came up and ended when he fell asleep. To the stream and its foster parent, the mountain, time was as endless as its patience with all things – the fierce storms, the wind, heat, and cold. But there was no way of accounting for the ambitions of men who had never heard the song.

One day they came – men who had no feeling for what it means to live on the face of the land and be part of it, relating to the life patterns there. They knew only how to tear riches from it, leaving scars that could never heal – festering, scrofulous scars. They neither knew nor cared about the virtue and rewards of patience; otherwise they could have taken what they wanted without leaving hideous marks along their trails. They drilled holes down past millennia of rock, two miles or more towards the very heart of the earth, and there found residues of things long dead. They hurried, breathing hard in their excitement, for this was gold – black gold – poison gold laden with sulphur, the smell of Hades, gases and minerals to throw away or offer on the marketplaces of the world. In their tearing hurry to refine the valuables, they had not time for caution. They took what they wanted, released the stink to putrefy and poison the air, and poured deadly effluents into Drywood Creek. These killed every living thing within its waters for miles, even the old trees I had known along its banks. They transformed the stream from a thing of wondrous beauty into a twisted, tortured wreck as dead and lifeless as the body of a snake rotting in the sun. Even a dead snake supports some kinds of life, but the creek now supported nothing except a grey-green algae that turned the coloured rocks in its bed into featureless lumps of slime.

It is dead, this stream – as dead as anything can be and still have hope of being restored to life. As it stands, there is no way this can be done, for there is nothing in it for anything to eat; the once-pure waters stink.

Can the Drywood and others like it be revived? It is a question of how soon we learn to care and understand and how much we are willing to pay. The price of such carelessness is high. But there is really no choice. If we can claim the intelligence to create our technocracy, we must also find the way to manage it and repair the damage, thus returning the dead to the living, restoring the wasted waters so they again belong to nature – a place where trout swim and bright-hued dragonflies dip and dance on delicate wings as a prelude to laying their eggs.

Only then will the song resume.

Epilogue

When I scattered the ashes of my father and mother on a flower-strewn slope of a hill in southwestern Alberta facing the mountains, I knew what it meant to look back on some chapters of my life that were closed forever. There had been years when we shared bad times, but also many very happy periods, in a mixture much better than that experienced by most families on the frontier. We had not accumulated any great fortune in money, but we had acquired a deep appreciation of the wealth of the good earth and the creatures that occupied it with us. My brother and I knew what it meant to work hard, but we also had been given time to play. Neither one of us can look back wishing that it could have been much different, nor do we have many regrets.

My father was eighty-six years old when he died in Victoria, British Columbia. John and I visited him in the hospital there, and as usual we reminisced about various things. Dad's eyes lit up and I recall him laughing heartily even though it hurt him. When I left that evening, I took his hand in mine. He grinned at me and said, "I will be all right. Don't worry!" Two days later he was dead.

He and I had always been very close, with an uncanny ability

From *Memoirs of a Mountain Man* (1984)

to communicate even when we were many miles apart. We anticipated each other. One time when I was in California, lecturing, I woke up from a nap beside a friend's swimming pool and realized that I had distinctly heard him call me by name. A few hours later I got a message that he had suffered a heart attack. I left shortly after to visit him at his home in Victoria and found him a bit wan and shaken but otherwise cheerful. The attack had been very mild.

Another time, years before, I was involved in a car accident when my car was hit by a runaway vehicle coming from behind. Miraculously, although there were twelve people involved, nobody was hurt. I took a taxi home, and shortly after I arrived there, Father and Mother drove into the yard. He looked at me and inquired how I was feeling. I was amazed, because there was no way he could have found out so quick, since there was no phone at his ranch. He had been working in the garden at the time of the accident and knew to the minute when it happened. He went into the house and informed my mother that I had been in a smash-up, but that I was all right.

About a year after his death, I was unusually worried and concerned about a personal matter of some considerable importance. It is not often that I let such concerns interfere with my sleep, but I was awake this night, lying flat on my back in bed with both eyes wide open in the dark. Suddenly I saw a soft yet very distinct blue light shining in a corner of the room up near the ceiling. It hovered there for a few moments, then moved slowly until it was directly over me. I distinctly heard my father say, "Don't worry. Everything will be all right." Then the light disappeared. It was true that I had no need to worry. Since then, there has been no direct communication, but sometimes I feel that he is very close.

My mother spent her last years in a comfortable nursing lodge. I visited her whenever possible and she was bright and sharp, always full of animated talk, never failing to give me her opinions and advice. One night she just passed away in her sleep at the age of ninety-four – a gallant little lady whose tired heart quit beating.

My grandfather and grandmother lived to their late eighties. Their ashes are buried under a huge boulder on a bluff overlooking the St. Mary's River on the ranch that was founded by them in 1883, and that is still operated by a grandson, Frank Russell. It is a lovely spot and a grand place to rest.

Although I live in the evening of my life, I have some difficulty realizing that in the eyes of many people I am supposed to be an old man. The wisdom of the years tells me that getting old is a frame of mind, and the way to stay young is to listen to the dreams and learn to keep one's vision more ahead than behind. A neighbour asked me when I was going to retire. I replied, "Never! There is too much to do and enjoy." Perhaps it is the conclusion of a man who loves life, is not afraid of death, and has the good fortune to be doing things that he enjoys. The road of life has taken me a long way – far enough to know that material possessions are too often no advantage, and that so-called security is a mirage. How often I have seen rich men die without realizing their youthful dreams, or finding that their dreams of wealth are ashes in their mouths.

I still enjoy the feeling of a good horse between my knees. All this man really needs to be happy is some rich earth to grow food, a good gun or two, a fine fishing rod, a saddle, a collection of books, and what he stands up in. There is time to work and much to be done.

It is one hundred and two years ago, this year of 1984, since my grandfather stepped off a Red River cart not far from Fort Macleod. I have shared sixty-seven of those years with the country and have seen and experienced some great changes, some of them good and some of them bad. While there is joy and satisfaction in knowing that none of those years has been wasted, it is pleasant to look forward to the adventure and endeavour of sharing a few more by learning and working towards a goal. Each day is a bonus, every hour a boon, and the sky is the limit. If they nail the lid down on my coffin tomorrow, the world really doesn't owe me very much. My epitaph could read, "He passed by and knew happiness. He loved the earth and tried in his own time to make it a better place to live in for all things."

Henry David Thoreau summed up my philosophy of life in a letter to Harrison Blake on March 27, 1848, when he said:

> Pursue, keep up with, circle round and round your life, as a dog does his master's chaise. Do what you love. Know your own bone, gnaw at it, bury it, unearth it and gnaw it still. Do not be too moral. You may cheat yourself out of much of life, so aim above morality. Be not simply good; be good for something. All fables, indeed, have their morals, but the innocent enjoy the story. Let nothing come between you and the light. Respect men and brothers only. When you travel to the celestial city, carry no letter of introduction. When you knock, ask only to see God — none of the servants.

Bibliography

Alpine Canada. Photographs by J.A. Kraulis. Edmonton: Hurtig, 1979.

Andy Russell's Adventures With Wild Animals. New York: Knopf, 1978.

Andy Russell's Campfire Stories. Toronto: McClelland & Stewart, 1998.

The Canadian Cowboy: Stories of Cows, Cowboys, and Cayuses. Toronto: McClelland & Stewart, 1993.

Great Bear Adventures: True Tales from the Wild (editor). Toronto: Key Porter, 1987.

Grizzly Country. New York: Knopf, 1967.

The High West. Photographs by Les Blacklock. Toronto: Penguin, 1974.

Horns in the High Country. New York: Knopf, 1973.

The Life of a River. Toronto: McClelland & Stewart, 1987.

Memoirs of a Mountain Man. Toronto: Macmillan of Canada, 1984.

Men of the Saddle. Photographs by Ted Grant. New York: Van Nostrand Reinhold, 1978.

The Rockies. Edmonton: Hurtig, 1975.

Trails of a Wilderness Wanderer. New York: Knopf, 1970.